THE
BOOK OF
WHOLE MEALS

ALSO BY ANNEMARIE COLBIN

PUBLISHED BY BALLANTINE BOOKS

FOOD AND HEALING

THE
BOOK OF
WHOLE MEALS

A SEASONAL GUIDE
TO ASSEMBLING BALANCED
VEGETARIAN BREAKFASTS,
LUNCHES & DINNERS

Annemarie Colbin

Ballantine Books • New York

Library of Congress Catalog Card Number: 82-90850

ISBN 0-345-33274-1

Originally published by Autumn Press, Inc.

Illustrated by Richard Spencer
Book design and typography by Beverly Stiskin

Manufactured in the United States of America

First Ballantine Books Trade Edition: February 1983

20   19   18   17   16   15   14   13   12

Table of Contents

Special Situations

Part II: *The Practice*

Preparing Whole Meals

Acknowledgments

To my mother, my favorite guru and best friend, who taught me to ask questions and to reflect, and to Rod, Jodi, Shana, and Kaila Colbin, and all my friends and students who allowed me to learn by cooking for them.

It is impossible to list individually all the people to whom I am indebted for helping make this book happen; thus, I shall limit myself to thanking those most directly involved.

First, my gratitude to my teachers who in print or in person have helped to shape my thinking: Dr. Vander, Yogi Ramacharaka, Eduardo Kotliroff, Rainer Maria Rilke, The Preacher, Carl Jung, George Ohsawa, Irma Paule, Michio Kushi, Herman and Cornellia Aihara, Michel and Claude Abehsera, Jerry Canty, William Dufty, Shizuko Yamamoto, Brian Parker, Howard Parker, Rudolph Hauschka, and many others.

Thanks are due to my "karass"—Susan, Peggy, Diana, Rebecca, Alan, Elaine, Karen, Rowen, Ken, Marc, Margie, David, Stephen, Mort, Peter, and Bailey—the eclectic support group that saw me through the various stages of writing and rewriting, by encouraging me onward, reading parts of the manuscript, and helping point out the rough spots. A special mention must also go to Adelle Sardi, who, with Larry Conroy, tested and tasted most of the recipes, offering valuable, constructive, and enthusiastic criticism.

This book would never have come to be without the encouragement of my publisher, Nahum Stiskin. For their assistance I would also like to thank my editors Sandy McDonald and Lynda LeMole; Shirley Corvo, Deborah Balmuth, and Susan Willis, who checked and doubled checked every detail; and Sheila Datz who typed the manuscript. My thanks also to Richard Spencer for his elegant illustrations, and to Beverly Stiskin for her fine taste in designing this book.

Foreword

Dear Betty Crocker:
I've had varicose veins since I was sixteen. I had two bouts of phle-
bitis before I was twenty-five. I took diuretics regularly, had almost
constant pain and swelling in my legs. I couldn't do the things I
enjoyed—even going to museums or on long walks—without suffer-
ing. Almost immediately after eliminating sugar and white flour from
my diet and switching to whole foods, the pain stopped. No more
swelling, no more diuretics. No more allergies, colds, no illnesses in
two years since I set fire to your cookbook. I never knew I could feel so
good.

Does Betty Crocker ever get letters like that? I doubt it. But I do, every
day in several languages. Always the same story. Name the disorder and
I'll show you someone, somewhere, who got rid of it by switching to whole
foods and cooking from scratch.

After I first learned to cook in Paris fifteen years ago, I couldn't wait to
get back to Michigan to show off to my mother. While I demonstrated, she
watched silently before announcing, "You're cooking exactly like my
grandmother." When you're pushing 100, as she is, there's nothing new
except what's been forgotten.

While reading this book in manuscript one evening, I got a very dis-
tressed call from a pretty young actress, loaded with talent and drive. But
she'd burdened herself with unmentionable disorders, including one that
made auditions and casting calls an impossible ordeal. So I loaned her the
manuscript to see what might happen. As if I didn't know. In two weeks I
got a letter. She'd skipped the front of the book, copied out the grocery list,
started shopping and chopping and cooking and chewing.

"Now," she wrote, "I'm reading the first part to find out what
happened. You've changed my life." Not me, I told her. Not Annemarie
either. You undid it yourself.

Anybody can.

William Dufty
New York City

Preface

There is a change of consciousness spreading around the country as fast as a fire through dried brush. It seems to be a shift in mental focus, and one of its most striking aspects is that that the analytical, matter-oriented approach to reality is slowly moving over to make room for its opposite: a focus on energy, whole organisms, and the recognition that the latter cannot be reduced to their parts and be accurately described by them only.

This emerging world view is one of synthesis: all of creation is seen as one vast web of interrelated, living, complex systems. However, these interrelationships are not haphazard, but endowed with what George Leonard, in *The Silent Pulse* (New York: E.P. Dutton, 1978), calls "intentionality"—that is, a direction of movement, an unspoken agreement as to where to go. There seems to be an order to the universe, and we are not only part, but also co-creators of this order.

"Each being," says Leonard, "is the entire universe from a unique point of view, and it's possible for all these universes to work together harmoniously. . . . There are no chance events, since we are the architects of creation and all things are connected through us."

The new vision holds that, by virtue of being a co-creator of reality, each of us is also responsible for how his or her own reality unfolds. Thus, for example, the virus can no longer be blamed for being the cause of the disease; the sick person is equally responsible for it, having created an environment favorable to the development of the virus.

Once such responsiblity has been accepted, it's only a short step to the idea of self-determination: we can, if we wish, change ourselves and our circumstances so as to move in whatever direction we want to go. With this attitude comes inner freedom, and the possibility of well-being, positive cooperation with others, and joy.

Quite appropriately, this new world view has picked up the name of *holism*. To fulfill the demands created by its rapid emergence, colleges are now setting up courses in holistic studies. Holistic health centers are springing up everywhere, like mushrooms after the rain. Lawyers are working to develop holistic law. After the phenomenal impact of Fritjof Capra's *The Tao of Physics,* more and more physicists are interpreting their research into the nature of matter from a holistic viewpoint. Holistic education is being actively researched and implemented. In architecture, in business, in sports, the arts, and psychological therapies, the trend is now to consider the individual as a complex system inextricably related to its environment.

Although nutrition has been considered part of the holistic approach to health, there has been as yet no widespread consideration of a holistic approach to nutrition itself. This is precisely what I propose to explore in this book.

I encountered the concept that food is the cornerstone of health at the age of eleven, when I joined my family on a vegetable–broth fast. After that, I grew up mostly lacto-ovo-vegetarian, with occasional fish or chicken meals; although we were living in Argentina, our adoptive homeland, we only had meat once or twice a year. The eleven days I spent fasting changed my life: ever since then I've been fascinated by the effect that food can have on body, mind, and spirit. I also like to understand how and why things work: if a certain way of eating makes me feel better than another, I want to know the reason. Hence, to satisfy my own curiosity, I spent much time studying food.

In 1964, a few years after I came to America, I began exploring and applying some of the ideas of a philosophy and dietary approach known as macrobiotics, which helped me understand many things about diet that had remained obscure. I cooked for my family, adapting recipes from my Dutch-Hungarian-Argentine background, and studied various theories of food and nutrition; eventually I began to teach what I'd learned.

Through my cooking classes, I've met many people who want to make healthful changes in their diet; I've also met many who, intent upon developing a holistic view of life, are looking for a way to make that vision relevant to their daily living. For both types of seekers, the most pressing need seems to be a practical dietary approach (that is, something to *do*) coupled with a theory, based on understanding, that makes sense. For while ideas are useless unless they can be expressed in action, a technique lacks focus without a solid theoretical framework.

This theory/practice combination encourages our decision to accept responsibility for our lives, to support our self-determination, promote our well-being, and ultimately offers the possibility of a steadily joyful and positive outlook on life.

What you'll find in this book is my experience of a mutually supporting theory and practice that accomplish just that. The focus is on food, simply because there is nothing more basic; food maintains life, sometimes well, sometimes not so well. And at this point in time, I can think of few activities that can have a more profound effect on a person's life than a conscious change in diet.

Part I:
The Theory

Whether you and I and a few others will renew the world someday remains to be seen. But within ourselves we must renew it each day.

Hermann Hesse

A Kitchen Philosophy

Where We Are Now

Public concern over the quality of our national diet has been growing lately at an astonishing rate. Today most people are aware that serious doubts have been raised regarding the safety and healthfulness of our commercial food supply—even if they choose not to act upon that awareness. More and more, the historically recent practice of consuming industrially processed, chemically colored, flavored, freshened, preserved foods is being called into question, and the answers that have been coming in are far from reassuring.

Among the avalanche of material on the subject, scientific and otherwise, one carefully researched and far-reaching document stands out: the official report of the U.S. Senate Select Committee on Nutrition and Human Need, *Dietary Goals for the United States,* first published in February 1977. In essence, it states that "our diets have changed radically within the last 50 years, with great and often very harmful effects on our health. These dietary changes represent as great a threat to public health as smoking. Too much fat, too much sugar and salt, can be and are linked directly to heart disease, cancer, obesity, and stroke, among other killer diseases. In all, six of the ten leading causes of death in the United States have been linked to our diet."

To help reverse this situation, the report goes on to recommend a general increase in the consumption of complex carbohydrates such as whole grains, vegetables, and fruits; a decrease in the consumption of meat, and foods high in fat, sugar, and salt; an increase in the consumption of fish and poultry; and the substitution of polyunsaturated fats (vegetable oils) for saturated fats such as butter, lard, and shortening. It also urges reduced consumption of nonnutritive additives, colorings, flavors, and preservatives.

Looking beyond purely nutritional concerns, the report states that "the social, cultural, and psychological significance of food in our lives can scarcely be overestimated. Sharing of food is one of the prime social contacts; provision of food is one of the prime signs of caring . . . Nothing is more divisive than when people eat a different fare in different rooms. At a time when more and more meals are being taken away from the home, removed from the company of family members, perhaps more consideration should be given to the possibility that this trend is a factor that substantially contributes to the stresses found in modern family life . . . If you eat enough precooked, frozen, reheated, foil-and-plastic lunches out of machines, part of you will starve to death."

In statements such as these, the committee tacitly acknowledges that food is more than just the sum of its nutrients.

Of all the variables affecting our health, food is the easiest to handle, to alter, to tailor consciously to our needs; therefore, it can often be used to counterbalance other variables. Choosing our food can then become a balancing act through which we adjust to the total context in which we live.

To help us make informed choices in such a vital matter, let's take a look at some basic aspects of the quality of our nourishment.

"Natural" or "Artificial"?

The major difference among the foods available today comes down to quality. A long, thin carrot grown with chemical fertilizers and sprayed with pesticides is just not the same as a short, fat carrot grown with natural compost and unsprayed. The difference in quality may be a serious cause for concern: research has proven that pesticides and other petroleum-derived chemicals are dangerous; they have been implicated in the causation of cancer, liver and brain damage, high blood pressure, birth defects, and genetic mutations. Some are lethal: only one drop of the pesticide TEPP on the skin will kill a person.

Not all the dangers inherent in the thousands of chemicals now routinely used in food production have yet been proven; however, as Dr. Jacqueline Verret, a biochemist and researcher with the FDA for 15 years, writes in *Eating May Be Hazardous to Your Health* (New York: Simon and Schuster, 1974), "All of us are involved in a gigantic experiment of which we shall never know the outcome—at least in our lifetime." She goes on to state that "far more critical than acute poisoning is the subtle, long-term insidious poisoning of the body by certain chemicals that work slowly or cumulatively and whose ravages may not become evident for years. . . . We know that chemicals may leave their mark not only on the recipient but on future generations, through mutations which might not be detected for a hundred years or more—if at all."

The quality of today's food is changed not only by the elements added to it, but also by what is done to it: flaking, texturizing, pasteurizing, homogenizing, freezing, canning, condensing, spinning, juicing, et cetera. These processes alter and even destroy molecular structure; what effect this tampering has on us can only be intuited at this time.

We do know that the chemical treatment of food has been shown to be generally dangerous. Therefore, it seems safest to return to more traditional ways—growing our foods with natural methods and eating them fresh. If we look at the human body as part of the whole ecosystem, it becomes clear that we are built so as to digest foods as they grow in nature. Natural foods have been proven good over millennia. The new "improved," texturized, artificially colored and flavored foods, on the other hand, are the product of doodlers in the food technology departments of large corporations, and in the few decades that these foods have been around, their record for enhancing health is pretty dismal. I've never run across *anyone* who reported feeling better by switching to processed foods, but I've encountered many people whose health improved dramatically after a changeover to a more old-fashioned way of eating.

Nutrients: Quantity, Quality, and Proportion

Much has been written about our bodies' need for specific quantities of vitamins, minerals, protein, carbohydrates, fats. What is generally overlooked is the fact that, in whole foods, such elements appear in a certain *proportion* to one another. This is a crucial factor, for all natural foods contain the micronutrients required for their complete metabolism. Artificially induced changes in the structure of foodstuffs upset the relationship of these micronutrients to one another.

When refining, processing, and concentration alter the original proportion of nutrients, the food in question may then not be properly metabolized. This could be interpreted as a "nutritional deficiency." For example, it is well known that taking one of the B vitamins as a supplement increases the body's need for all the other B vitamins; thus, if you take a B_6 pill but neglect to take the rest of the B-complex, you are in effect creating a *deficiency* of B-complex. Paradoxically, you would become vitamin-deficient by taking vitamins.

Unfortunately, we do not know what is actually the correct proportion of nutrients for our optimum health. Nature, on the other hand, probably knows a bit more. We might consider the proportional relationships between the elements present in mother's milk, the human food *par excellence,* as a fairly trustworthy parameter.

Based on figures obtained from the *Nutrition Almanac,* it can be noted that *vitamins* comprise the smallest total amount of elements present; next in quantity come the *minerals*; then comes *protein,* then *fats,* next *carbohydrates,* and finally, *water.* In cooked grains, the same graduation occurs, except that fats and protein trade places. The same happens generally with fruits and vegetables, both cooked and raw. Meat, fish, and fowl, on the other hand, are totally devoid of carbohydrates, and their proportion of protein to water is only 1 to 4; in cooked brown rice this proportion is 1 to 27, in steamed greens it's 1 to 43, and even in a baked potato it's as high as 1 to 37. This may explain in part why high-animal protein diets require the addition of large amounts of additional water to the diet as well.

In mother's milk, there is four times as much fat as protein. In cooked oats, as well as in many fresh fruits, there's twice as much protein as fat; in wheat flour there's seven times as much, and in cooked beans and vegetables, the amount of protein can go as high as ten times the amount of fat. Hence, although adults probably need less fat than infants, we could assume that in a fully vegetarian regime a little extra oil or fat would be easily tolerated by the system. In raw food regimes, milk, nuts, and nut butters (which have 3 to 10 times more fat than protein), would provide the extra fat; a little vegetable oil in cooking would do the same.

However, if proportionately too much oil is used, there could be a metabolic call for a proportional rise in the other elements: for more minerals (salt), more protein (meat or other animal food), more carbohydrates (white flour or sugar). The vicious spiral can start at any point: for example, a high mineral (salt) intake may result in cravings for additional fats, protein, carbohydrates, and water—put them all together and you're "overeating."

It may be significant that in mother's milk there is only between 1 percent and 2 percent protein; on that proportion, a newborn baby doubles or triples its birth weight within six months. Yet, in the fractional approach of scientific nutrition, much has been made of our need for "adequate" protein. A "normal" diet may contain 12 percent protein. *High* protein (20%–30%) diets, recommended by orthodox and unorthodox nutritionists alike, became the fad of the last two or three decades. And while protein was being enhanced and extolled, carbohydrate became the fall guy, almost a synonym for "bad" and "fattening."

The latest research is beginning to show another picture. A high animal protein intake may cause arteriosclerosis, high cholesterol, hypertension, cancer of the colon, even faster aging. It overworks the kidneys, disturbs the body's calcium balance, and may even cause death by dehydration. A diet high in cow's milk protein (casein) may actually be quite harmful to infants, for it has been found to overtax the kidneys, "cause retention of urea, elevate blood ammonia levels, and cause the blood and other body fluids to be pathologically acidic," according to *Medical World News* editor Hara Marano ("The Problem With Protein," *New York* Magazine, March 5, 1979). "Protein is one element most oversupplied in our diets," reports Ms. Marano. "On the average, we consume twice as much as the recommended amount, which itself is figured with a plushy excess. . . . The obligatory daily need of the average 154-pound male is actually no more than 23.8 grams of protein—a peanut butter sandwich."

Although only animal-quality foods have been called "protein-foods," all plant products, including fruit, contain protein in varying proportions. In fact, most of the world's population has always obtained its principal protein supply from grains and other plant foods. The same was true of the United States until early in this century; interestingly enough, as plant protein consumption has given way over the years to the consumption of animal protein, there also has been a rise in the incidence of degenerative diseases, including cancer.

In our current food technology, carbohydrates are the elements subjected most assiduously to concentration and refining. As white sugar and white flour are presently the major source of carbohydrates for large segments of the population, it is only natural that carbohydrates are viewed with suspicion: stripped of most of their naturally attendant micronutrients, refined carbohydrates cannot be properly metabolized and do contribute to overweight.

In addition to removing micronutrients, the refining of carbohydrate-rich foods also removes the fiber, or roughage. This is the case not only with flour, but with sugar and juices as well. Dr. Dennis P. Burkitt, of the St. Thomas Hospital Medical School in London, has shown that low fiber diets are a major factor in incidences of constipation, diverticulitis, cancer of the colon, appendicitis, hemorrhoids, obesity, coronary heart disease, and diabetes. Dr. Burkitt found that the addition of fiber to the diet effectively reduced intestinal disorders, blood-lipid levels, cholesterol, and blood sugar; however, not all fiber had the same effect: cereal fiber worked far better than fiber from fruits and vegetables.

Unprocessed whole foods, such as whole grains, beans, vegetables, and fruit, are complex carbohydrates: they contain the complete amount of micronutrients and fiber necessary for their proper utilization by the body. Their consumption will not only maintain, but also restore health. Nathan Pritikin, author of *The Pritikin Program for Diet and Exercise* (New York: Grosset & Dunlap, 1979.), and director of the Longevity Center in Santa Monica, California, has obtained nearly miraculous results with a diet of 80% complex carbohydrates (grains, vegetables, fruit), 10% protein, and 10% fat, coupled with a walking exercise program: cardiac, diabetic, and hypertensive patients who could barely walk a few feet at the beginning of the program were walking six to ten miles after following it for six months.

It makes sense that eating whole foods will encourage our bodies to keep whole. After all, nature creates life with perfect sense and order: everything dovetails. If we heed the wisdom of this natural order, we'll most likely come closer to living peacefully, harmoniously, and in good health.

The Life Force in Foods

The currently accepted scientific viewpoint on food separates it into chemical components, such as vitamins, minerals, protein, carbohydrates, and fat. In order to determine the nutritional value, the only factor that is taken into account is the *quantity* of each element present. This view, although accurate, is only partial; it is the equivalent of counting trees when we wish to study the forest. To complete the picture, we need an understanding of *quality,* that is, of the essence and complexity of the forest as a living organism.

Consider the carrot. If we take it apart, we will find elements such as water, Vitamin A, carbohydrates, pigment, and the like. However, if we were to take all these separate elements, put them in a jar, and shake them up, we would not create a new carrot. Something would be missing: the life force that molds these elements into a definitive shape and texture. This "formative force," as Rudolf Hauschka calls it in *Nutrition* (London: Stuart & Watkins, 1967), is just as important to the event known as "carrot" as are all its physical attributes. In fact, this force could be called the *sine qua non* of the carrot's existence—without it there would be no carrot at all.

Cultures all over the world have long recognized the importance of this primordial formative force. The names given to it include the Hindu *prana*, the Chinese *ch'i*, the Japanese *ki*; in the West it has been described by the terms animal magnetism, bio-electrical energy, spirit, astral body, and so on. Dr. Harold Saxton Burr, professor emeritus at the Yale University School of Medicine, writes in *Blueprint for Immortality: The Electric Patterns of*

Life (London: Neville, Spearman, 1972) that not only human beings, but all forms of being "are ordered and controlled by electro-dynamic fields (L-fields) that are both invisible and intangible." Dr. Burr continues:

> Most people who have taken high-school science will remember that if iron-filings are scattered on a card held over a magnet, they will arrange themselves in the pattern of the "lines of force" of the magnet's field. And if the filings are thrown away and fresh ones scattered on the card, the new filings will assume the same pattern as the old.
>
> Something like this—though infinitely more complicated—happens in the human body. Its molecules and cells are constantly being torn apart and rebuilt with fresh material from the food we eat. But, thanks to the controlling L-field, the new molecules and cells are rebuilt as before and arrange themselves in the same pattern as the old ones.

When an organism dies, it disintegrates and reverts to its basic components—as if the matrix provided by the L-field had been removed. In order to stay alive, then, the organism must maintain its form, and the controlling L-field will provide it with identity throughout its life. However, a certain amount of change is necessary (such as growth), or is tolerated (such as tree pruning, hair cutting, or surgery). As Dr. Burr points out, in human beings such change also includes the continuous buildup and breakdown of tissue; as long as there is no excess of either, form is maintained in a most delicate balance between these two tendencies.

As an essential component of all living things, this formative, bio-electrical energy also suffuses the organisms that constitute our food supply. Invisible and immeasurable though it may be, it is very likely as important a "nutrient" as are vitamins, minerals, and the rest of the presently recognized elements.

Environment

We just took a few steps back from the "trees" of nutrition—vitamins and minerals—and considered the carrot as a *whole*. Now let's take another few steps back and look at the carrot itself as *part of a larger whole*. From that vantage point, we can observe that the carrot grows down toward the center of the earth; it thrives in temperate climates; it can be stored through the winter. A banana, on the other hand, grows on a tree, up toward the sky, in a tropical climate; when picked ripe, it begins to rot within a few days.

How do these characteristics affect us when we eat the carrot or the banana? If we view them from the angle of vitamins and minerals, then the above considerations don't matter at all; from that angle, all that matters is that we get our nutrients from somewhere, and whether the source is a carrot or a banana or a vitamin pill doesn't make much difference.

But if we look at the whole picture from further back, with us in it, a pattern of relationship begins to appear: when we consume food that grows in a particular climate, we will feel more "at home" in that environment, for by consuming part of that environment we have made it part of ourselves. Thus, generally speaking, if we eat carrots, we'll feel more comfortable, more attuned, in a temperate or cold climate; if we eat bananas, we'll feel most at ease under the hot tropical sun.

So far, so good. The problems arise when our food does not match our environment: then our bodies have to do a lot of adjusting. In informal surveys among my friends and students, I've found that the foregoing hypothesis is borne out: People who customarily eat large proportions of raw fruits and salads generally feel fine during the summer, but, come winter, they invariably report cold hands and feet. As soon as they switch to more "wintry" foods (such as root vegetables, beans, grains, cabbages, squashes, and dried fruit), their resistance to cold weather increases dramatically.

Time, Tradition, and Heredity

If we take yet *another* step back to get a wider panorama, the element of time enters into the picture. This can be very helpful, for the better our understanding of the traditions of the past, the more consciously we can lay the foundations for the future.

Since each region of the earth provides a different set of foods, over the centuries each society developed a traditional dietary pattern. In the mid-1930s, Dr. Weston Price, a dentist and member of the Research Commission of the American Dental Association, undertook a voyage around the world in order to study the effect of diet on people's teeth. He gathered an impressive amount of data and photographs as he made an in-depth study of isolated and modernized Swiss, Gaelics, Eskimos, North American Indians, Melanesians, Polynesians, Africans, Australian Aborigines, Torres Strait Islanders, New Zealand Maori, and Peruvian Indians. Invariably, Dr. Price found that those people who followed the traditional diet of their region (that of their ancestors) had uniformly good teeth with very few cavities, well-shaped dental arches (no protruding or crowded teeth), good bone formation, and great strength and endurance. Most interestingly, all the people in a tribe resembled each other, for their facial bone structure reproduced the tribal form.

On the other hand, those primitive people who had changed their diets upon contact with white settlers and began consuming sugar, jams, canned vegetables, and white flour products, within a very short time developed rampant caries; their children were born with bone deformities and changes in the dental arches which resulted in the improper alignment of teeth. As a result, they showed a different facial pattern, no longer resembling their parents. In essence, when the quality of the food changed, the people also changed, not only in health but also in appearance. If these "deformed" children reverted to the traditional diet based on natural, local foods, however, they again produced children with the classic tribal facial form.

"No phases of the problem of physical degeneration can be as important as knowledge of the forces that are at work and the methods by which they operate," wrote Dr. Price (*Nutrition and Physical Degeneration*, Los Angeles: The American Academy of Applied Nutrition, 1948). "It is clear from the data presented . . . that these forces can become operative with sufficient speed to make a difference in two generations, one succeeding the other. It is also clear from preceding data that these forces originate in the change of the nutrition of the parents."

In other words, deviation from a traditional diet of local, natural foods will very likely cause problems not only for the person eating the new foods, but also for that person's children. A return to a natural diet, on the other hand, can apparently correct most of the conditions caused by the first change. If we wish to regain our health, it does seem a good idea to pick up on some of the wisdom of primitive dietary systems, sensibly adjusted to harmonize with today's mobile and rapidly changing lifestyles.

In choosing a health-supportive diet, it is advisable to consider not only the local, traditional diet, but also the food traditionally eaten by one's ancestors. Each of us inherits a specific genetic makeup that causes us to respond more positively to some foods than to others.

A clear example is "lactose intolerance," a condition in which the individual cannot digest milk or milk products. Normally mammals stop producing milk-digestive enzymes shortly after they're weaned, and human beings are no exception to the rule. There are vast populations—particularly in Africa and the Orient—where children never touch milk after they are weaned, and therefore (as is normal among all mammals) cease producing the necessary enzymes for digesting it; if given milk or cheese as adults, up to 90 percent of the people are apt to react negatively. However, certain other ethnic groups—notably Northern Europeans, Hindus, Arabs, and the African Masai—have traditionally used the milk of animals as a necessary adjunct to their diet (often because other foods were scarce due to harsh geographic or climatic conditions); among them, "lactose intolerance" can be as low as 2 percent. This is one of the reasons why the foods that suit one person may sometimes not suit another.

Nutritional Individuality

"Every individual," wrote Hermann Hesse, "represents the unique, the very special and always significant and remarkable point at which all the world's phenomena intersect, only once in this way and never again."

In other words, we are all different. Nature is very inventive. Our genes, the intrauterine environment, and the general nutrition of our mother determine our basic *constitution* at birth; the subsequent interplay between our original constitution and the environment that we provide for it, especially our diet, determines the *condition* of our health at any given moment.

The distinction between constitution and condition is important in assessing our potential for attaining good health. I've found that people born with strong constitutions who have made themselves sick by improper food choices appear to respond most quickly to a healthful change of diet. On the other hand, those born with a weak, sickly constitution generally take longer to react and sometimes have more trouble. People with strong constitutions, however, may show no symptoms of illness for a long time, but when they're felled, it's often quite serious. Their counterparts, having been plagued with health problems all their lives, usually have been forced to take better care of their health; their illnesses may come on more gradually, and may be more easily treated.

Individuals also vary greatly in their reaction to different foods. I've heard, for example, of sugar causing not only depression, sleepiness, and anxiety, but also aggressiveness, nervous energy, even sexual arousal. Coffee awakens most people, but it puts others to sleep. Meat may make people tense or tired. Wheat can make one person happy, another a nervous wreck, and provoke sneezing fits in a third. Some people digest brown rice very well; others cannot, and do better with kasha, barley, or millet. Salt is another element which is greeted with a tremendous range of reactions: its use may make one person lean and gaunt, while it causes another to puff up from water retention.

This wide range of variability is no doubt the cause of the avalanche of books on food and health currently on the market. The variety of advice offered is as disparate as the variety of individuals offering it, and perhaps that's our clue: *all* the advice works—at different times, for different people. Each one of the books comes from a particular author's experience and represents the distillation of his or her understanding *up to that time*. Ten years later, the same author may—or may not—completely reverse his or her stand, after processing new information brought in by time and experience.

This book is no different: it's about what I've learned so far. Thus, I would like readers to consider it not as the last word on the subject, but simply as a guide to help them find their own way, for that is ultimately the goal. To get around the problem of our differences, each one of us must take on the responsibility to find out what is best for our individual condition at any given time. Although a doctor, a nutritionist, or others in the health field may help point us in the right direction when we're stuck, ultimately we fare best when we work out the details of our diet and health care for ourselves.

A Word of Caution

When one moves from a diet high in meat, dairy foods, sugar, and fats, to a whole grain and vegetable regime such as outlined in this book, some dramatic changes are apt to take place. Initially, there may be a profound feeling of well-being, but as the body begins to heal itself and discharge old, accumulated toxins, various physical symptoms (especially mucus discharges of some kind or another) may appear. An important distinction must be made here: some symptoms and illnesses are the result of continuing mistakes in eating and or living, and some are simply a temporary discharge of toxins. The former must be treated with changes in habits, adjustments in diet, or medicine; the latter, a result of the body returning to health, generally can be allowed to run their course and, if mild, usually require no treatment.

These two underlying causes of "dis-ease" often can be mistaken for one another. Therefore, after a major change in diet, if you encounter any physical or mental symptoms that you don't understand, if your weight drops more than 20% below normal standard, and especially, if you have some history of taking drugs or medicines—please consult a doctor, chiropractor, nutritionist, or other health practitioner that you trust.

Balance

Although we may have trouble describing the feeling of being "balanced," most of us know with fair certainty whether we've got it or not. We may be acutely aware of how hard it is to find this balance, and how easily we lose it; more often than not, we prefer the experience of feeling centered. But what exactly is this elusive "balance," and how do we go about achieving it?

One thing balance is not is immobility. Consider the tightrope walker: the downward pull of gravity is cancelled out by continuous small movements from side to side. Should the balancing movements stop, gravity would prevail: thus, the stability of balance can only be maintained by continuous motion.

The American Heritage Dictionary tells us that *balance* is "a stable state characterized by cancellation of all forces by equal opposing forces." In other words, it is the achievement of stability between opposites.

Everything in the universe has its relative opposite. The forces of expansion and contraction are present everywhere as continually alternating tendencies. Everything pulsates or vibrates; physicists report that even the hardest stone is made up of twirling particles! This pulsation extends first to one extreme, then the other, as on a seesaw or pendulum: waves rise and fall, night turns into day and day into night, winter becomes summer, flowers blossom and fade. Miraculously, amidst all this motion, patterns appear and hold, balance is achieved, and life manifests itself.

Our organism also is in continuous, fluid motion: the heart pumps, the breath travels in and out, blood rushes through the veins, cells grow and die. Within that movement we strive to keep stable, to maintain our form— thus, all forces affecting us must be more or less equalized.

When we speak of eating a "well-balanced meal," it is obviously not the meal we wish to make stable but ourselves. The "balanced" meal will actually be the stabilizer, the balancing factor. Yet how do we begin to relate the forces contained in food to those coming from our environment, or our climate or activity? What kind of food balances, say, the climatic effects of winter?

An understanding of the interplay of opposites formed the basis of ancient Oriental religions. In the West, concerned as we have been with identifying and analyzing individual parts that make up the whole, we have so far almost ignored the essential relationships between these parts and the corresponding whole. Now this worldview is changing: the holistic health movement has been spearheading an awareness of interconnectedness, and we are developing the language to express it.

In the Orient, such a language has existed for thousands of years, in what we have come to know informally as the Yin/Yang principle, or theory of opposites. I have found this principle to be extremely helpful as a general thinking aid. So did the Chinese: as the foundation of the five-thousand-year-old Chinese philosophy, the principle underlies most expressions of Oriental culture, from medicine and acupuncture to martial arts and flower arranging. It is even behind that extraordinary treatise on human relationships known as the *I Ching*.

With a basic understanding of this principle, we can discover how opposite forces interact; when we apply that understanding to the area of our diet, we learn which foods are the balancers for which conditions. By making informed choices, we can consciously maintain a continued state of healthful equilibrium.

Understanding Opposites

Essentially, the Yin/Yang principle is a value-free system of classifying universal phenomena into pairs of opposites. By understanding the laws that govern their interrelationships, we can work with, rather than against, natural forces and cycles.

In the original sense, the active, masculine cosmic aspect was designated as *yang*, and its complementary opposite, the passive, feminine cosmic aspect was called *yin*. Both spring from the "Undifferentiated One," or Infinity; together, interplaying in various directions, amplitudes, and speeds, they cause all visible and invisible phenomena. In a sense, *yin* and *yang* are like the positive and negative aspects of electricity and magnetism; fluid, dynamic, they do not remain still but continuously change from one into the other, attracting each other when they're most different, repelling each other when they are more alike.

Originally, *yang* has also been seen as light, motion, heat, and therefore expansion; *yin* connotes darkness, stillness, cold, and contraction. However, a slightly different version of *yin* and *yang* has become popular in the West during the past twenty years through the dietary philosophy known as macrobiotics. The macrobiotic concept still presents *yang* as the active, hot, light, male aspect—but also as contractive; *yin* is still passive, cold, dark, female—but it's also considered expansive. To avoid confusion, I will be using the terms "expansive" and "contractive" instead of "yin" and "yang."

The tendency to think of *yin* as bad and *yang* as good can be dangerous; this tendency is especially common among people who have studied macrobiotics, and it can cause many misunderstandings. Both the expansive and the contractive are necessary: too much expansion and we fly off into space, too much contraction and we become dried up dwarfs.

Fortunately, our body has an intelligence of its own, and will not let us go that far: a sugar binge will quickly balance a regime too high in contractive foods (meat, salt), while a yen for salt and protein often arises from following an expansive regime of raw fruits and juices. The meals in this book are designed to provide a comfortable range of expansive, contractive, heating, and cooling foods according to season.

Let's compare expansive and contractive qualities of foods:

MORE EXPANSIVE	MORE CONTRACTIVE
Vegetable quality	Animal quality
Sweet, sour, spicy flavor	Salty, bitter flavor
Of tropical origin	Of cold climate origin
Vegetables	Cereal grains
Fruit	Vegetables
Fish	Eggs
Raw foods	Cooked foods
Cooked for a short time	Cooked for a long time
Oil	Salt
Growing vertically up	Growing vertically down
Growing horizontally underground	Growing horizontally above ground
Fast growing	Slow growing
More variety	Less variety
More quantity	Less quantity

We can also classify foods on a graduated scale from the most expansive to the most contractive, (see Expansive/Contractive Meter below). You will notice that protein foods are on the contractive side and carbohydrate foods fall on the expansive side. Grains and beans are in the center as they're more contractive than vegetables, yet less contractive than meat; interestingly enough, they contain both protein and carbohydrates, thus their central position is earned on more than one level. The Expansive/Contractive Meter is a helpful concept because experience has shown that eating from one extreme to the other of this scale (meat, sugar) creates hyperactivity, tension, fatigue; while eating around the center (grains, beans, vegetables) can calm down our metabolic swings and help us become more centered.

When I speak of the expansive and contractive qualities of food, I'm referring to the subtle effects they have on our total energy system. Sugar may not be visibly expansive if we eat one candy bar, but it can create a feeling of spaciness—an expansion of the mind, in effect. Meat may not literally contract us, but it gives a feeling of compactness and tightness; in excess, it creates tension and hardness.

The concept of opposites is best applied to foods in a relative sense. That is, leaves are more "expansive" than roots; but they are less expansive than beer, for example. A detailed relative comparison of foods can be seen in the following table, based on Herman and Cornelia Aihara's *The Dō of Cooking*, Vol. 1 (San Francisco: The George Ohsawa Macrobiotic Foundation, 1972.)

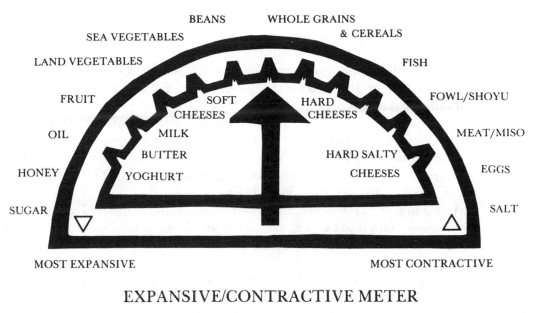

EXPANSIVE/CONTRACTIVE METER

Credit: Larry Conroy

Balancing the Opposites

Natural processes maintain balance through a pendulum swing, wide as the seasons or slight as that of the tightrope walker. Internal and external influences conspire to knock us off center, to disturb our balance regularly; then we call upon opposite influences that will bring us back to center, and thus we spend our lives. Naturally, the one particular event or influence will give rise to its opposite, in order to keep balance: summer turns into winter, night into day, love into hate. Similarly, a hot climate will produce expansive, cooling fruit such as pineapple and papaya, while a cold climate will grow contracted fruits that take well to cooking, such as apples and cranberries.

Eating primarily cooling foods (e.g., fruits, juices, raw salads, yoghurt) in cold weather creates, for many people, a lopsided condition; balance can be restored by warming influences such as motion (chattering teeth, exercise) or weight (heavy clothes). Balance *will* be made, one way or another, whether we like it or not, for that is the way the world works: the natural tendency is always to return to center, to keep the form. The question is, *how* will that balance be made? When we become aware of the pendulum swing, we can learn to anticipate the changeover point; then, before something drastic happens to force us to turn around, we can willingly choose to make a conscious and more gentle change of direction. As a result, we'll stop feeling that we are at the mercy of forces beyond our control, for we'll be able to choose the direction we want to take—whether it's lentil soup and warm feet, or fruit salad and three pairs of socks. And in that choice lies our freedom.

The Acid-Alkaline Balance

As with all opposites, the acids and bases (or alkaline substances) in our bodies must also strike a specific balance. To maintain a healthy condition, our blood needs to keep a pH of between 7.35 and 7.45; this is a narrow range, and we have many adjusting mechanisms to keep within it, including exercise, breathing, the secretion of various body fluids, and diet. If the pH drops to 6.9, death from acidosis, or diabetic coma, may result; if it rises to 7.9, death may occur from alkalosis, or tetany. The pH of water, 7, is taken as the neutral middle point; a lower pH means higher acidity, while a higher pH indicates the presence of alkalis, or bases. Thus stomach secretions, with a pH of 1.8, are highly acidic; blood on the other hand is slightly alkaline, while pancreatic juices, with a pH of 8.8, are strongly alkaline.

Regardless of their original quality of expansiveness or contractiveness, or taste, foods will be *acid forming* or *alkalizing* according to the mineral residue they leave in the body once they've been metabolized: phosphorus, sulfur, and chlorine form acids upon oxidation, while sodium, potassium, calcium, magnesium, and iron are alkalizing elements. Too much of either category will promote an uncontrollable craving for the opposite.

The following is a list of acid-forming and alkalizing foods arranged from the most expansive to the most contractive.

	ACID-FORMING	BUFFERS	ALKALIZING	
Most Expansive	Sugar/Honey	Milk	Coffee	Most Expansive
	Oil	Butter	Fruit	
	Nuts	Tofu	Potatoes	
	White flour	Soft cheeses	Raw vegetables	
	Whole grain flour	Salty cheeses	Cooked vegetables	
	Cereal grains/legumes	Shoyu	Sea vegetables	
	Fish	Miso	Kuzu	
	Fowl		Fresh beans	
Most Contractive	Eggs		Sea salt	Most Contractive
	Meat		Regular salt	

The buffers are in the middle because they'll take the edge off either category, alkalizing acid-forming foods and acidifying base-forming foods.

This chart may give you a clue as to why coffee is tempered by milk and/or sugar; why cookies taste best when washed down with milk, and why white bread needs butter; why cereal grains are balanced by miso and shoyu, while people who eat a mostly fruit and vegetable diet eschew salt. You may realize why meat and eggs, on the other hand, need salt, and why a high consumption of either animal protein or whole grains often calls for coffee. Finally, you may see why a diet high in fruit and vegetables and low in grains can develop one's sweet tooth to the point of embarrassment.

To keep our balance, then, both acid-forming and alkalizing foods need to be part of our diet, with a slight edge to the latter. All traditional diets follow this rule; on the other hand, those diets that concentrate on only one category ("high-protein," fruitarian, raw foods, only grain) are invariably unbalanced and will, sooner or later, cause a violent swing to the other side. In most cases, the initial change will feel good for a while, as balance is regained. In the long run, however, it is extremely difficult for most people to sustain a mostly acid-forming (protein—sugar—flour—grain) or a mostly alkalizing (fruit—salad—vegetables) diet for any length of time without deviations or health problems.

Intuition and Judgement

In order to make the right choices for our individual needs, our judgement must be sharp and accurate. For that we need not only facts and information, but also, even more importantly, a kind of inner *knowing*. This inner knowing, which flows out of a place deep within us, is called intuition: it emerges non-verbally, bypasses reason and logic, defies argument, and is usually on target. There are times when our intuition may be clouded or blocked; other times it may be functioning with finely tuned sensitivity. Some people's intuition operates on a regular basis; others have more trouble hearing the inner promptings, or may interpret them erroneously.

Invariably, when our judgement is functioning well, it is of great help in day-to-day living: if our choices are appropriate, our life flows smoothly and joyfully. Strengthening our intuition will improve our judgement, and for this there are various techniques available ranging from meditation to both physical and mental-spiritual exercises. The easiest and most important one is simply *paying attention*.

Not surprisingly, a change to a healthful diet has a noticeable effect on the quality of our understanding: as toxins are cleared out and energies flow more smoothly, the nervous system begins to function better and mental clarity improves. Many people have also found that as they began to eat whole foods, and especially whole cereal grains, they developed a more holistic outlook—the basis of all true intuition.

We *can* know, deep inside, whether the food we're eating will make us better or worse. In following dietary advice, I think it is crucial that we first filter it through our own understanding. We sometimes tend to follow the advice of experts even if our own signals are contradictory; if the advice doesn't work, we then blame the expert. Most of the time, when our intuition sends out affirmative signals, it's safe to proceed; when the signals are negative, then it is time to make changes, reverse direction, take a new tack.

Occasionally we may have some trouble translating our intuitive knowledge into action for lack of facts or information. Thus, studying and conscious learning will also help strengthen our judgement. Ultimately, we may reach the point where we can eat whatever we want—for we'll want only the foods that are exactly right for us at any given time. But until we get to that level of understanding, we have plenty of work to do.

Menu Planning

In light of all the foregoing considerations, I keep the following guidelines in mind when choosing my food:

1. I try to use foods as close to their natural, whole state as possible: unhulled, unpolished, unpeeled if the skin is edible, with roots and tops of vegetables together when feasible. Thus, I'll prefer whole wheat to wheat germ or bran, dried fruit to concentrated sweeteners, carrot tops in the same dish as carrots, and so on. (The only partial foods that I do use regularly are oil, salt, shoyu (soy sauce), tofu, *kuzu* powder, and maple syrup—my compromise with our need for variety in tastes and textures).

2. Whenever possible, I try to serve foods grown without chemical fertilizers or pesticides. Not just for health reasons, but because time and again I have found that organic foods—grains, vegetables, fruit, nuts, seeds, eggs—do consistently taste better.

3. I completely avoid frozen, canned, chemically treated, freeze-dried, or otherwise processed foods (including such things as sulphured dried fruit and canned or frozen "health" foods).

4. On the whole, I prefer locally grown produce, or at least those that grow in a similar climate zone (this means that, in New York City, I'll seldom have tropical fruit or hot spices).

5. Following a traditional approach, I use whole grains as my main protein source, supplemented by dried legumes, fresh vegetables, fruit, nuts, and seeds. On special occasions I may have some eggs or fish.

6. Regarding expansion and contraction, eating from extreme to extreme of the food scale (meat and sugar, for example) may cause disruption and imbalance. Eating those foods that are placed in the middle of the scale tends to create centeredness and harmony. This again brings us to whole grains and vegetables as a principal source of nourishment.

7. To get a balanced energy flow, as well as to provide a wide array of nutrients, I try to serve several varieties of foods in each meal. Thus, I'll choose among roots and leaves, stalks and bulbs, grains and seeds, tubers and pods, fruits and nuts, and vegetables and sea vegetables.

8. For aesthetic as well as nutritional reasons, I include foods of different colors in each meal. For example, a plate with brown rice, lentils, and carrots is only brown-red, and thus too lopsided; I would add bright green broccoli or salad, and maybe chopped parsley on the carrots, thereby bringing both lightness and balancing nutrients into the picture. I also avoid having several mixed dishes together—as a contrast

to a casserole, I would serve plain baked squash rather than stir-fried vegetables.

9. Rather than worrying about the size of servings, that is, the quantity of foods, I pay attention to their proportion. After some experimenting, I found that I, as well as a sizeable number of adults of my acquaintance, fare very well with the following proportions: Of the total daily volume of food, 40 percent to 50 percent whole grains (depending on season and other factors), 30 percent to 40 percent cooked and raw vegetables, 5 percent beans or peas, and the rest, fruit, sea vegetables, desserts, et cetera.

10. Children need different proportions; when they eat too much grain they often become congested and sluggish. In my experience, between 25 percent and 40 percent whole grains (including bread and pasta) appears to be enough for them, and parents must be careful to keep within the quota. (It fills up fast, what with a piece of bread here and a cracker there, oatmeal for breakfast, and brown rice or noodles for dinner.) The remainder of the children's diet might consist of 40 percent to 50 percent vegetables and salads, plus beans, sea vegetables, fruit, nuts, seeds, and some fish or eggs if desired. The children I know who have been raised this way seem exceptionally strong and healthy.

Food Categories

When planning a meal, I first choose the main focus, that is, the protein base, consisting of some form of whole grain cereal. Most of the time—though not necessarily always—I will supplement it by dried beans or peas, or soy products such as miso or tofu.

Next I pick complementary foods from among the fresh vegetables that are in season, keeping in mind color combinations and contrasts in texture and shape, as well as taste. In this category I also include dried mushrooms and sea vegetables. Fruits, nuts, and seeds are additional complementary foods which I generally use in lesser amounts. On the whole, I try not to use the same vegetable in more than one dish in the same meal.

I keep seasonings mild, and use only unrefined or cold-pressed vegetable oils in cooking.

Rarely do I eat animal foods, preferring to leave the occasional egg or piece of fish for special outings, or when entertaining. I also use very few sweeteners, and avoid sugar and honey entirely. I consider most milk and milk products harmful, so I almost never eat them.

Let's get down to specifics.

Whole Grain Cereals and Flours

Whole, unpolished cereal grains have been the staple food for civilizations since time immemorial; they are often associated with religious ritual.

Christians pray to receive their "daily bread." The Roman goddess of agriculture was Ceres, who presided over the festival of Cercalia. In the East, rice has long been revered as the staff of life. The Japanese deity who symbolizes food and prosperity is the "Great Grain Spirit."

"No civilization worthy of the name has ever been founded on any agricultural basis other than the cereals," wrote Professor Paul C. Mangelsdorf, agronomist and director of the Harvard Botanical Museum, in *Scientific American,* July 1963. "The grain of cereal grasses, a nutlike structure with a thin shell covering the seed," he noted, "contains not only the embryo of a new plant, but also a food supply to nourish it. Cereal grains, like eggs and milk, are foodstuffs designed by nature for the nutrition of the young of the species. They represent a five-in-one food supply which contains carbohydrate, proteins, fats, minerals, and vitamins. A whole grain cereal, if its food values are not destroyed by the over-refinement of modern processing methods, comes closer than any other plant product to providing an adequate diet."

After learning to cook with most of the grains, I settled on short-grain brown rice as my favorite for cooking versatility and taste. Freshly ground whole wheat flour is the major ingredient in my homemade bread, which warms the house and comforts the spirit with its delicious aroma. I find barley is a wonderful addition to soups, or mixed in different proportions with rice as a grain dish. Oats, whole or rolled, often grace our breakfast table and form the base of cookies.

Kasha, the staple seed-grain of snow-bound Russia, is certainly the most warming and invigorating of the cereals; on days when the snow and wind are out there playing tag, kasha-cream in the morning, with shoyu and sunflower seeds, keeps us warm and energized until noon. In addition, millet, rye, corn, and the ground version of these grains, all find a place on our table in an almost limitless array of recipes.

Beans and Other Legumes

Beans have always been a traditional protein complement to whole grains: lentils and barley, rice and beans, couscous and chickpeas, and similar combinations are consumed in tandem in many areas of the world. Modern nutritionists validated this tradition when they discovered that the amino acids in beans dovetail perfectly with those in grains, providing complete proteins equivalent to—and often *superior* to—those found in animal products.

Among my own favorite dried legumes are the Japanese aduki (or adzuki) beans, which make an excellent complement for brown rice. (Oriental folklore has it that they are an effective remedy for all kinds of kidney problems.) Next on my list are lentils, split peas, chickpeas, and kidney, pinto, and lima beans.

Some people have trouble digesting beans, finding that they produce intestinal gas. There are several ways to deal with that problem: 1) Cover beans with three times the volume of water, soak 6 to 8 hours, then drain, and cover again; cook, unsalted, until done (about 1-1½ hours), then season to taste. This method is said to get rid of some of the water-soluble elements that cause gas; 2) Cook the beans with a 3-inch piece of kombu seaweed, no salt; 3) Eat something with miso in it at the same time; as miso, a fermented product, contains enzymes and bacteria beneficial to the intestines, its presence will aid in the proper digestion and assimilation of the beans; 4) Put up with the gas; 5) Don't eat beans.

Vegetables

Vegetable foods (including grains and beans) are really our only sustenance, for even when we eat animals, the animals themselves originally consumed vegetables; we're just getting them once removed.

My first choice in vegetables is whatever is traditionally local and in season. Since I live in New York City, the choice is not always easy: there isn't much that's really local unless you count weeds and the shrubbery of Central Park. Fortunately, however, we do have many excellent food stores with staggering arrays of vegetables and fruits from every climate. The sheer abundance makes choosing difficult, and I often find it necessary to exercise my judgement and curb my greed.

In winter I choose the type of vegetables that would normally keep well, without refrigeration, if they are stored in cold cellars or barns: onions, carrots, squashes, cabbage, turnips, rutabagas, parsnips, and sometimes exotic roots such as celeriac, burdock, black radish, daikon (a Japanese white radish) and parsley root. These vegetables are all considered relatively warming, and therefore are appropriate to balance a cold season.

However, in our modern society, the situation is complicated somewhat by the fact that our home environment generally bears little resemblance to the weather outside, unless it happens to be in the 69°–75°F. range. When it's 15°F. outside and snowing, but it's a comfortable spring temperature inside, we have to compromise to maintain balance. I've found that warm weather produce, rather than tropical fruits, offer the best balance to central heating. Thus, I prefer additional vegetables such as watercress, broccoli, string beans, escarole, chicory, parsley, scallions, celery, and beets, with occasional salad greens and radishes.

In the summer I reverse the proportions: larger amounts of greens, cooling vegetables such as cucumbers, sprouts, and mushrooms, and hardly any roots, except for carrots and onions. If I lived in another part of the country, I'd simply pick from what is available in local markets, keeping in mind the basic guidelines relating food to climate. Anyone whose environment is substantially different from mine, of course, will want to adapt the recipes in this book accordingly, by substituting, adding, or omitting ingredients.

Sea Vegetables

A novel item, and an acquired taste for most westerners, sea vegetables have been used as a staple food in Japan for millennia. In the western hemisphere seaweeds have been consumed in small measure in the form of dulse and Irish moss; agar-agar is used widely as a jelling and thickening agent.

Rich in trace minerals, especially calcium, iron, and iodine, sea vegetables are also an important vegetarian source of Vitamin B_{12}, a substance often lacking in vegetarian diets; thus they are an important addition to any diet that is low in or devoid of animal products.

Since their flavors vary, I like to keep on hand most of the varieties currently available in health food stores and Oriental food markets: namely, kombu, hiziki, nori, arame, dulse, and kanten or agar. Dried sea vegetables keep indefinitely, without refrigeration.

Fruit

Fruits are cooling and refreshing; they're a natural adjunct to sunshine and warmth. In the summertime, I buy strawberries, cherries, peaches, pears, apricots, and watermelon, and occasionally some oranges; I'll buy bananas for my children or myself if we're in the mood for some creamy, natural sweetness. In the winter in my part of the country, I prefer apples and perhaps cranberries at Christmastime; once in a while I serve pears. If the weather is really cold, I prefer cooked dried fruit, or baked apples.

I usually serve fresh fruits as a snack by themselves, rather than as dessert after a meal centered on whole grains. Some nutritionists claim—and I tend to agree, on the basis of plain "feeling"—that the combination of cereals and fruits in the same meal can be hard on the digestion. If I do use fruits for dessert, I prefer them cooked.

Nuts and Seeds

Like grains and beans, nuts and seeds are also both the beginning and the end of a plant. But, because they contain 40–60% fat, they are best used sparingly: a handful of nuts contains about half a handful of oil! Since people who are prone to skin problems may excrete this excess fat in the form of blemishes and pimples, they would do best to avoid nuts and seeds entirely.

On the positive side, nuts and seeds are high in essential polyunsaturated fatty acids, vitamins A and E, calcium, iron, magnesium, potassium, fiber, lecithin, and protein that complements cereal protein. Used in moderation, they make excellent accents for almost any dish. Sesame seeds (the smallest and most yang of seeds) are very high in calcium, containing almost ten times the amount of this mineral as in an equal weight of milk. Sunflower seeds are a good source of vitamin E and a delightful addition to grains, salads, and steamed greens. Pumpkin seeds—whether store bought or harvested at home—are great for snacking, especially when roasted.

Almonds, cashews, and walnuts are my own favorites among the nuts; I find that if I have a good supply of them in the house, along with sesame and sunflower seeds, I can handle everything from last-minute desserts to quick snacks to plain dishes that need fancying up.

Condiments

SALT: Salt, (sodium chloride or NaCl) is the only inorganic mineral compound that human beings have been consuming regularly for thousands of years (inorganic minerals in the form of petroleum-derived food additives have been consumed for only the past 30 years or so). Wars have been fought over salt, long treks made to gather it, and trade routes developed to exchange it; in the Roman Empire, it was even used as currency (the word *salt* is the etymological root of the word *salary.*)

Current opinion on our real need for salt varies. The Senate Committee on Nutrition points out that Americans generally consume too much table salt. Many people would benefit from a drastic reduction of salt, and some—particularly those who regularly consume mostly meat, fats, and dairy foods, and few vegetables—would be better off going totally salt-free if they switch to a grain-and-vegetable regime.

Most of us, however, react well to a moderate amount of salt in our diet. Because it tends toward crystallization, densification, and tightening, salt has a contractive effect, thus it can help to balance overly expanded people who tend to be expanded, loose, "all over the place," and unable to concentrate. By adding a little more salt to their diet, these people often manage to "get their heads together."

Since I prefer unrefined and untreated foods, I use a naturally produced sea salt which has been sun-dried, washed, and again sun-dried. Sea salt has a slightly higher mineral content than commercial salt with traces of copper, magnesium, silicon, calcium, and nickel; it also tastes milder.

Commercial white salt is generally extracted from inland salt mines, heat-treated at extremely high temperatures, then "iodized" with potassium iodide. Dextrose (a sugar) is added to stabilize the latter, together with sodium bicarbonate, which keeps the color white, and sodium silico-aluminate as an anticaking agent. Besides the excessive sodium concentration here, it seems to me quite ridiculous to have sugar in my salt.

I keep my seasalt in a small covered jar and always sprinkle it by the pinch, rather than shake it from a shaker or measure it by the teaspoonful; that way I can feel in my fingers how much salt I'm actually using, and automatically I'll use no more than I need. I find it preferable to under-salt, as it's easier to add more than to fix a dish that's too salty. And, most importantly, I only use salt in cooking, never at the table, for that makes too sharp a taste and creates excessive thirst. At the table I prefer to season foods with shoyu or sesame salt.

MISO (soybean paste) and SHOYU (natural soy sauce): These flavorful fermented soy products, important ingredients in traditional Japanese cookery, are now widely available in this country. Both contain all the essential amino acids, and thus are excellent protein boosters. They also contain enzymes, lactic acid, and microorganisms that benefit the intestines, much as yoghurt does; for this reason they are helpful in the assimilation of complex carbohydrates such as grains and beans.

Salty, aromatic, and hearty, miso is a paste made from soybeans, water, salt, fermenting bacteria, and sometimes a grain such as rice, wheat, or barley. It is fermented in wooden barrels for 12 to 36 months, much like cheese. Generally used as a soup base and flavoring agent, miso is also delicious in sauces, spreads, and dressings.

Shoyu, or natural soy sauce, (sold in this country for many years as "tamari"), is a liquid flavored by the fermentation of equal parts soybeans and cracked, roasted wheat, plus sea salt. It is a wonderful flavoring for soups, vegetables, grain dishes, spreads—almost anything. I usually keep it in a small bottle with a perforated top so that I can sprinkle it over food as I cook. "Genuine tamari" is a soy sauce made without the wheat, for a darker and deeper flavor.

SESAME SALT (GOMASIO): A delicious condiment, gomasio is prepared by grinding together roasted sesame seeds and sea salt. By varying the proportions, one can adjust the taste: a ratio of 14 to 1 is my favorite—not too salty, yet with spirit. Sprinkled on rice, noodles, or vegetables, it adds salt, protein, calcium, and flavor simultaneously.

KUZU POWDER (KUDZU): Extracted from the root of the kuzu vine, this white, lumpy starch has a high iron content, plus fair amounts of calcium and phosphorus, and a little sodium. It is used mostly to jell liquids: 1 tablespoon will thicken a cup of liquid to the consistency of sauce or gravy; 2½ tablespoons will thicken it to a firm, jello-like mass that can be sliced when cool. Kuzu has no taste of its own but will take on any flavor added to it. I find it an invaluable element in my kitchen.

UMEBOSHI PLUMS (plums pickled in brine): These salty-sour little plums, which have been pickled in salt for 12 to 24 months, can be found in many health food stores or oriental markets either whole or in paste form. Because of their sour taste, they make a delicious addition to salad dressings and spreads; the pits can be cooked with vegetables or stews for extra tanginess.

OTHER SEASONINGS AND FLAVORINGS: Aromas sometimes have an uncanny effect on our emotions: one whiff and we're back into childhood, reliving a romance, feeling warm and cozy, or perhaps uneasy and depressed. Bland food dulls the spirit, even though at times it may be good for the body; I've found that one of the quickest cures for the "blahs" is a meal with plenty of strong taste and rich aroma to it.

For desserts, I rely on cinnamon in both stick and powder form, grated lemon peel, nutmeg, mace, allspice, ground ginger, and vanilla. I use green herbs, sparingly, to season many dishes; among the dried ones, my favorites are oregano, basil, bay leaves, thyme, and tarragon, and among the fresh ones, scallions, parsley, and dill. Once in a while I'll use a tiny amount of stronger spices such as ground cumin seed, curry, and coriander—just enough to make the food smell delicious.

For sharp flavors, I don't really like black pepper, for it doesn't combine well with grain and vegetable dishes (it seems more suited to meat-based meals). However, fresh grated ginger or horseradish can provide plenty of sharp flavor in both cooked and raw dishes; I also like a Japanese horseradish powder called *wasabi*.

In dishes that need no cooking, such as salad dressings, dips, and spreads, I find that pressed garlic and raw grated onion or daikon are all fine spirit lifters.

Lemon juice is a classic sour flavoring. I also like to sprinkle brown rice vinegar lightly over stir-fried vegetables, or add a dash to lighten a dense soup or stew. Umeboshi paste can also be used to impart a sour flavor, but it comes with a fair amount of salt in it, which may be appropriate in some dishes but not in others.

The most interesting aspect of seasonings and condiments is the way they can change the intrinsic quality of a dish. A light soup with clear broth and mild vegetables becomes heartier, more dense, with the addition of miso. A pot of contractive rice and beans will be lightened by freshly chopped parsley or scallions. Plain boring vegetables can be lifted by a dash of oregano or curry. And cooking errors can be amended by calling in opposites: too much salt, for example, can be neutralized by either a sour flavor, more water, something oily (tahini), or something bland (potato), depending on the nature of the dish.

Oil

Oil is comparable to salt in that a small amount is necessary, but a lot can be damaging to our health.

"Essential fatty acids" are the basis for a smooth metabolism; they also provide protection against the cold, both as an insulating layer under the skin and through the energy liberated during their assimilation. In *Nutrition and Your Mind: The Psychochemical Response* (New York: Harper and Row, 1972), Professor George Watson writes: "High-fat diets have been found to be superior in helping maintain normal body temperatures in cold climates. Neither high-protein nor high-carbohydrate intakes can effectively do this."

On the other hand, the U.S. Senate report *Dietary Goals for the United States,* notes that "Incidence of cancer seems to be related as much to unsaturated as saturated fats." Moreover, Dr. Julian Whitaker reported in *Runner's World* magazine (May 1978) that tests with volunteers showed that "both cream and vegetable oil (an unsaturated fat) inhibited blood flow in the capillaries . . . The vegetable oils clogged the system nine hours longer than the cream."

The wisest course is always moderation and careful judgment. One person may need little or no extra oil, whereas someone else may need— and can function well on—quite a bit more. Since at times the national average of fat intake has gone as high as 40 percent of the total diet, most people could afford to reduce the amount of fat and oils in their diet. However, in doing so they might encounter a slight problem: given the typical fat-filled national diet, our clogged and overworked livers, which handle fat metabolism, *expect* to encounter plenty of fats in each meal. A sudden drop of these elements in the diet may cause a feeling of dissatisfaction and unfulfillment for a while, even though there may be no hunger.

With a change towards less fatty foods, the body will begin to cleanse itself, and eventually the liver will stop wanting all that heaviness. However, it may take several years to get over a case of "fat tooth." To reduce oil intake, it may help to cut down on salt.

I do cook with oil but keep it minimal: mostly I use it in sautéed vegetables and in salad dressings. Occasionally I'll make a deep-fried dish as a treat. On the whole, in a diet in which there is no dairy food, nor any other animal fats, the total amount of fat is automatically lower than average.

As long as one is going to use oil, it makes sense to buy oil of the best quality. This means oil of vegetable rather than animal origin, so as to avoid the cholesterol and saturated fatty acids associated with animal fats. It also means *unrefined* oils. Commercial oils are solvent-extracted at high heat, bleached, and chemically treated to ensure a pale, bland, odorless oil with an extremely long shelf life and practically no nutritional value. Unrefined oils, on the other hand, are mechanically pressed, unheated, and filtered once (to remove impurities); they retain chlorophyll, lecithin, vitamin E, carotenoids, and trace minerals such as magnesium, copper, calcium, and iron. And each oil retains its original distinctive color, aroma, and taste. "Cold-pressed" oils have been filtered more thoroughly; they are lighter than the unrefined oils, and have neither taste nor aroma.

For sautéing, I like unrefined light sesame, corn, safflower, and dark sesame oil; each adds its own distinctive bouquet to a dish. For salad dressings I like olive or corn oil, or any of the "cold-pressed" oils with no taste; for an occasional deep-fried dish, I'll use "cold-pressed" safflower or soy.

Sweeteners

Most people are aware by now that sugar is one of the worst of the modern "foods." Research has implicated it as a causative agent in heart disease, obesity, rheumatism, gout, nearsightedness, hypoglycemia, diabetes, acne, indigestion, mental illness, and perhaps even criminality.

People who stop eating sugar usually report that they feel much better (once they've gotten over the "withdrawal symptoms" of tiredness, anxiety, and depression). They attest to benefits ranging from higher spirits, a more relaxed feeling, and restful sleep, to fewer colds and dental problems, and improved health in general.

Unfortunately, giving up sugar can be much harder than it might at first seem. Sugar is everywhere—not only in such obvious foods as desserts and soft drinks, but in soups, cured meats, salad dressings, commercial breads and cereals, and thousands of other manufactured foods. Those determined to avoid sugar completely have little choice but to prepare all their foods at home from scratch, or to start frequenting natural food stores and restaurants—and make a habit of reading labels. They are then apt to run across countless foods prepared with honey, which—except for a few trace minerals—has little to recommend it over sugar. In fact, honey is almost twice as sweet as sugar, and just as capable of causing cavities.

Still, most of us occasionally feel the desire—and sometimes the need—to add a little sweetness to our diet. Whenever possible, I sweeten desserts with fruit—fresh or dried—or fruit juices. (It's amazing the sweetness cooked fruits have all by themselves!) In the few cases where a concentrated sweetener is essential, I prefer to use rice syrup, barley malt, or maple syrup. Both rice syrup and barley malt are prepared by fermentation: the fermenting bacteria convert the grain's starches into simple sugars; the resulting mash is then boiled down into a syrup and strained. Since this process removes less water and fewer nutrients from the carbohydrate than the process whereby cane and beet sugar are crystallized, rice syrup and barley malt are less disruptive of the body's mineral balance.

Maple syrup is much too concentrated a sweetener for regular use, but as an occasional indulgence, poured sparingly over pancakes or blended into cakes or pies, it is hard to beat for delicate, delicious flavor.

Animal Foods

More and more people are turning toward vegetarianism these days for a variety of reasons, whether ecological, ethical, or health-related. They quickly find that a substantial reduction in the intake of animal protein and a total avoidance of meat can bring a number of benefits, including less fatigue, increased energy and alertness, and a generally "lighter" feeling. In my experience, a mostly vegetarian regime, with some fish or eggs once or twice a week, is highly satisfactory.

It is possible, of course, to be a meat-eater and stay quite healthy; but eating meat isn't necessary. It is also possible to be a complete vegetarian and enjoy full health; then again, vegetarianism isn't necessary. It's all a matter of personal choice. I've seen children, born into meat-eating families, who are natural vegetarians much to the distress of their relatives. I've also seen the reverse—children of vegetarian parents who respond well to eating meat.

There are times and places where eating some meat can help to balance the individual and the environment—in the winter if one is outdoors a lot or in arctic climates. However, it's virtually impossible these days to buy good-quality meat at anything less than astronomical prices. Traditionally, people hunted wild animals which had fed on a natural diet and were healthy enough to have survived the hardships of their environment. The meat thus obtained was of a vastly better quality than that of the animals raised for slaughter today in crowded conditions, artificially fed, and forcibly fattened. Many of the chemicals added to their feed have been shown to be carcinogens, and these elements remain in their tissue to be assimilated by the consumer. No wonder more and more people "just don't like" eating meat any more!

Of all the other types of animal protein available, fresh fish seems the most easily digested, as well as the lowest in fat and the highest in NPU (protein that can be fully utilized by the body). Fish caught locally is generally best; when available, fresh ocean fish is preferable to river fish, because the oceans are not yet as polluted as the rivers, and because ocean water has more trace minerals, which remain in the fish. Freshness is of utmost importance because old or spoiled fish can cause serious gastrointestinal trouble (old fish have soft flesh that breaks easily, eyes that are dull and filmed, and a fishy odor; fresh fish have a scarcely noticeable smell).

Inland, or in places where it's hard to get fresh fish, I would substitute fowl, preferably free-ranging and raised without antibiotics or hormones in the feed, that is, "organic." (If this type of poultry is not available, the next best choice would be Kosher chicken.) I've found also that the eggs produced by naturally-fed chickens are superior to ordinary eggs in taste, appearance, and freshness.

Dairy Foods

From a holistic viewpoint, milk appears to be a food designed by nature exclusively for babies—no adult animal nurses from its mother, or from anyone else's, for that matter.

Research is, in fact, turning up evidence that the consumption of milk and its derivatives may be actually quite harmful to most people's health. In *Don't Drink Your Milk* (New York: Wyden, 1977), Dr. Frank Oski, M.D., blames cow's milk for symptoms ranging from allergies and nasal congestion to anxiety, hyper-activity, irritability, and fatigue. (It is ironic that this country, while turning away from meat in the quest for better health, at the same time should come to embrace yoghurt as a "health food.")

You *do* outgrow your need for milk. As Dr. Oski points out, "It is natural to lose the lactase activity in the gastro-intestinal tract. It is a biological accompaniment of growing up. Most people do it. All animals do it. It reflects the fact that nature never intended lactose-containing food, such as milk, to be consumed after the normal weaning period."

Why do we persist? One reason may be the belief in the myth that the only adequate source of calcium are dairy foods. But, as Dr. Oski notes, people in other countries who shun milk "are neither toothless nor lying about immobilized because of repeated bone fractures."

Having eaten and not eaten milk products at various times in my life, I've decided I'm much better off without them. My skin inevitably breaks out if I eat butter or cheese; and if I have any appreciable amount, my face actually looks different—puffy and pasty. From my own and my family's experience, as well as that of many people I know, I can verify the fact that it's possible to get along perfectly well without milk or milk products. To their absence I attribute the fact that we find ourselves getting practically no infections, no allergies, few colds, no cavities, and remaining in generally excellent health. Hence, you'll find no cheese, butter, or yoghurt in this cookbook—but as you will see, there's still enough calcium, protein, and other nutrients to satisfy your needs.

Beverages

Probably the most important aspect of eating, apart from swallowing, is chewing. And the greatest enemy of chewing is drinking liquids with a meal: they "wash down" the food thus sparing our jaws, but not our stomach and intestines. Vegetables and fruits are high in water content, as are grains and beans cooked in water. With a diet based on these foods, therefore, the body gets a large amount of fluid directly from the food itself, so ideally, we shouldn't be thirsty after a meal. The only element in this style of eating that might induce thirst is salt: a high salt intake demands a correspondingly high intake of fluids, or else there's bound to be kidney trouble. To be safe, it's best to keep one's salt intake low. I find the best thirst-quencher to be plain, unflavored, room temperature spring water. There are other choices as well, each with its own special properties, some beneficial, some dubious.

Water

I don't like city water primarily because it is full of pollutants and chemicals (such as chlorine and fluorides) required by law. Therefore, I use spring or well water exclusively for both drinking and cooking. Many people prefer to drink distilled water, but this water, in the process of being vaporized and condensed, has been stripped of all its naturally occurring minerals. Since its osmotic pressure (density) is much lower than that of the fluids within our body, it could, as all refined products do, leach minerals from the body, weakening and demineralizing the organism, perhaps eventually creating symptoms of deficiency.

Tea

A cup of tea fifteen minutes or so after a meal can be most enjoyable. A word of caution, however: steeping dried leaves, flowers, twigs, roots, or bark in hot water releases not only flavor, but also medicinal substances. It seems wise, therefore, to be cautious with herb teas; to drink them indiscriminately, with no concern for their properties, is tantamount to going to the medicine cabinet and just helping yourself.

To find the tea that's best for you, ask your friends what their experience has been, read some herb books, and try out, cautiously, what appeals to you. One of the safest and best all-purpose teas on the market today is *bancha*, a Japanese green tea that should be roasted to a medium brown for optimal flavor; it is sold, roasted, under the name of *kukicha*. These teas aren't overly aromatic, so they make a very pleasant, subtle finishing touch after any meal. They're also quite "neutral," insofar as they don't do anything: they don't stimulate, medicate, or sedate you in any way, so they can be drunk at any time, hot or cold. I sometimes like to add other herbs to a base of bancha or kukicha, such as mint or lemon grass.

Regular black tea is a mild stimulant; it contains an alkaloid, theine, which is similar to caffeine, but only one-twentieth as concentrated. I may occasionally drink a cup of black tea with lemon, but find it too sharp for regular use. Whenever I find myself in a coffee shop not wanting either tea or coffee, I ask for some hot water (or "tea with the teabag on the side") and use my own herb tea bag, which I carry with me.

Coffee

Coffee is a crutch for the mind. In many people, it stimulates the logical, reasoning, thinking powers, the flow of words, the analytical, cause-and-effect-grasping mentality. Most of our western society runs on coffee: there would be many empty offices, and countless unwritten books and newspapers if coffee were to disappear from this world.

Coffee can wake you up and crank your motor, so to speak, but in my experience, the coffee I drink today makes me sleepy tomorrow. Then I need another cup to lift that fog, and the vicious circle is in full swing.

Drinking coffee or taking any other stimulant is morally no more wrong than riding in a car: they both get you where you want to go, fast. Like everything else in this world, whatever we do has a pro and a con: the con is that neither car nor coffee is conducive to developing your own strength. Those who are trying to regain their health, who wish to be fit and trim, already know that they're better off walking than driving. Because what happens when the car is taken away, or the coffee, is that you find yourself flabby. The momentum doesn't hold: the clear thought goes muddy, becomes unreal. Soon you find that you cannot function without coffee, and there you are, bound. Once again, you must make a choice. "Those who want to make logic their own personal possession," wrote Rudolph Hauschka in *Nutrition*, "must avoid taking coffee and letting it do their thinking for them."

Because it's a bean that grows on the cool side of the mountains, gets roasted darkly, and has a bitter flavor, coffee has contractive elements that balance its expansive effect. It is also alkalizing (caffeine is an alkaloid), so it's attractive to people who acidify their systems through a high intake of animal protein, sugar, flour products, and even whole grain cereals. It stimulates the body by whipping up the adrenal glands, so it is very taxing on the kidneys.

Once having decided to give up coffee, some people have no trouble; others may go through withdrawal for a few days, experiencing tiredness, fogginess, even some piercing headaches. In that case, the only way out is through. Often, sleeping a lot will help. When the "withdrawal" is over, the payoff is a clearer head and more sustained energy.

There are some coffee substitutes on the market, made of grains and chicory, which are quite pleasant. Although they don't deliver the caffeine punch, their appearance and aroma are reminiscent of the real thing. They come in both instant and non-instant varieties; I usually prefer those that contain no molasses or other sweeteners. I also like to make my own "un-coffee;" you'll find it in the Basic Beverages section.

Juices

Whether bottled or fresh from a juicer, juice is not a "whole food": the juice is extracted, and the pulp discarded. Thus, by virtue of their concentration of elements, fruit or vegetable juices may provoke a relative "deficiency" of fiber and minerals. (This can translate as a craving for crunchy foods or snacks, a case of the "munchies.") Therefore, I would always prefer eating the whole fruit or vegetable rather than throwing off the body's balance by consuming just the juices. Drinking juices also gives you considerably more food elements than you would naturally consume if you ate the whole vegetable. For example, you might eat one, maybe two raw carrots at a sitting; a glass of carrot juice, which you could consume in the time it takes you to chew two bites of the first carrot, contains seven or eight carrots. This may be a larger load than the body is used to handling and could strain the system.

If you would like to have the benefit of the whole vegetable or fruit, but for whatever reason prefer to consume it in liquid form, you could liquify it in a blender with an equal volume of water, straining it if you wish. Some marvelous combinations are possible: try carrot-celery-parsley, or apple-banana-peach. However, I would consider a juice like this a food, rather than a drink, and would not accompany it with any other kind of food.

Sometimes I do use bottled fruit juices to sweeten desserts since they are the least concentrated sweeteners available. On the few occasions when I do use extracted juices, I view them more as medicine than as food. They can be an invaluable aid in correcting imbalances quickly. For example, an excess of tightness and contraction caused by too much salt, animal protein, or a lack of greens, responds very well to apple juice. Excess acidity, which may stem from the overconsumption of animal protein, flour products, fats, or sweets, can be quickly corrected with a glass or two of carrot-celery-beet juice. Once the imbalance has been corrected, however, no more need be consumed; in fact, any more would create a further imbalance.

Alcohol

Alcoholic beverages have been popular for thousands of years in most cultures. They are generally used for social occasions, feasts, in celebrations, in religious rituals, and sometimes as mind alterers.

Alcohol appears to balance the intake of animal proteins; it seems to "cut" the heaviness of meat, fish, fowl, and cheese. The expansiveness of alcohol will also dissolve tension; inhibitions are loosened and jolliness ensues. Yet, since all things become their opposite when they reach their extreme, so the lack of inhibition may turn into aggressiveness, jolliness into depression and gloom. Alcohol, therefore, is a substance best approached with caution and consumed in moderation. For an occasional drink, perhaps to accompany some fish, your best choices are beer, preferably brewed without sugar (this means mostly the imported kind, although some domestic brands are now "naturally brewed"); *sake*, or rice wine, drunk from thimble-sized cups; and, in wine country, the local vintage, when prepared under natural methods.

In the Kitchen

Cooking: Why, and How

Several nutritional schools of thought recommend raw foods as the best kind of nutrient for human beings; they consider such foods "alive" and believe that the application of heat is detrimental and destructive. In theory this argument sounds quite reasonable—but in practice, it doesn't work very well. As any city dweller who has ever tried to follow a regime of raw vegetables and fruit can attest, it is difficult to maintain such a diet: the average seems to be two years. Inevitably, dissatisfaction and cold feet set in.

By nature, humans can survive comfortably in temperatures of 80°F. to 90°F.; at cooler temperatures we need clothes and shelter in order to stay warm. Naturally unsuited for anything but balmy, tropical climes, we have nevertheless spread to all corners of the globe, braving all sorts of inhospitable conditions. We enjoy an adaptability unknown to the rest of the animal kingdom, and the secret of that adaptability lies in the art of cooking. Hot food helps us incorporate warmth so we can better face the chill winds.

Cooking is also an invaluable aid to digestion. There are similar elements in both activities: a mechanical breaking up, chopping, or grinding of the food, as well as warmth, moisture, darkness, and time. In fact cooking is a kind of pre-digestion, for it serves to break up or soften the cell walls, starches, and cellulose fibers of our food, thereby making its nutrients more easily available for assimilation. (It has been shown that more vitamin A can be absorbed from a cooked carrot than from a raw one.) As do all other activities, digestion takes time and energy—and sometimes a considerable amount of both. (For example, vegetarian animals must eat all day long, but carnivorous animals need only one big meal every day or two, after which they must spend time lying around digesting it.) If our food is cooked, and thereby takes less energy to be digested and assimilated, we are bound to have more time and energy at our disposal for other activities such as building bridges and writing books. I know I've found that, with properly prepared food, not only do I need to eat less, I also do have a lot more energy.

Cooking also serves to change the intrinsic qualities of food by altering temperature, flavor, consistency, shape, and liquid content. Thus, by using different cooking techniques, we are able to transform our food and render it more appropriate to our specific needs of the moment.

The following factors make foods relatively more cooling or warming:

MORE COOLING	MORE WARMING
cold	heat
sweet, sour, spicy flavor	salt
open cooking	pressure cooking
short cooking	long cooking
more water	less water

Different methods of applying heat result in different degrees of expansion and contraction:

BOILING: The most expansive, it adds water and removes minerals.

STEAMING: Expands the food by adding water (steam).

BROILING: Heat applied from above makes the juices run out, creating a slightly more contracted condition.

SAUTÉING: By virtue of medium heat, and sealing in the nutrients by a thin film of oil, this is a contractive method.

BAKING: Surrounding the food with dry high heat causes it to become more contracted.

DEEP-FRYING: Oil and high heat create a crisp coating that seals in all nutritive elements by quick, strong contraction. However, if improperly done, this extreme can turn into its opposite and produce soggy, oily, expanded food. As with all extremes, moderation is advisable.

PICKING: Through the action of salt and time, expansive vegetables are contracted and made more stable. In a sense, pickling is the opposite of boiling: it removes water and adds minerals (salt).

In addition, meals are made more expansive by elaborateness and variety, and more contractive by simplicity and less variety.

Setting Up the Kitchen

Kitchens are not what they used to be. In the past forty or fifty years, they have become smaller and smaller, especially in apartments. In extreme cases they have shrunk to a two-burner hotplate, a small sink, and an under-the-counter refrigerator, all hidden in a closet—a far cry from the cozy kitchen of yore that served as a gathering place and focus of family life.

Environment is important for any concentrated activity and will make a noticeable difference in what you produce. Therefore, if you have any control over the matter, look for the following elements in choosing or creating a kitchen:

• GAS HEAT: It is easier to control than electric and is a more yang and focused form of heat.

• BRIGHT DAYLIGHT: If this is not possible, incandescent bulbs are preferable to fluorescent, as the latter reportedly can cause adverse reactions. (See *Health and Light,* John Ott [Old Greenwich, Conn.: The Devin-Adair Co., 1973].)

• A WOODEN WORKING AREA: For chopping, kneading, and general sorting out of foods—try a good-sized (24-by-36 inch) butcher block cutting board.

• PROXIMITY OF WORK AREA, STOVE, AND SINK: One of the best layouts is to have the work area in front of, rather than next to, both stove and sink.

• WORKING SURFACES AT A COMFORTABLE HEIGHT: If you are 5'7" or less, this probably will mean "dining height;" if you are taller, "counter height."

• TOOLS AND STAPLES WITHIN EASY REACH: Knives, pots, wooden spoons, and other gadgets should be stored near work area; the most used staples—salt, oil, herbs, shoyu, miso, et cetera—within arm's reach of the stove.

Tools

Tools are extensions of your hands and therefore should feel as though they are a part of you. First of all, find a good knife for chopping and peeling vegetables. One is all you will need, but it may take several purchases to find "your" knife. The weight should be comfortably distributed; the tang, or extension of the blade, should be at least half the length of the handle, and firmly secured with rivets. Make sure, also, that the blade is thin so that it cuts easily; thick blades always sound like they are breaking the vegetable (and often they are), whereas a thin one noiselessly divides.

My own favorite knife is a Japanese model with a tapered, 7-inch molybdenum blade which has the advantage of being easily sharpened on the unglazed bottom rim of a cup. Since the sharpness of a knife is crucial to its effectiveness, this is no mean consideration. I also have a rectangular, 7-inch long, 1½-inch wide, Japanese stainless steel vegetable knife that I like; the shape is very handy for it allows one to chop straight down without the knuckles hitting the board.

You will need also at least a half dozen wooden stirring spoons of various sizes, a two-cup measuring cup, a set of measuring spoons, a grater with both coarse and very fine grating surfaces, one wooden or metal spatula as well as one that is rubber (not plastic), a hard brush for scrubbing vegetables, and a potato peeler (good for shredding carrots). Large cooking chopsticks also are very handy for stirring. Eventually, you might want to add some paring knives, flame tamer, a wire whisk, a garlic press, and an apple corer which you may not use very often, but which has practically no substitute.

Cooking Utensils

It is very important that you have a set of pots and pans that you're comfortable with. When you buy a pot, pick it up and hold it. Is the weight pleasant in your hand? Does the handle suit your grip? Don't purchase anything that's too heavy for easy handling or so light as to seem insubstantial. Also, check to see that the handles are solidly attached and made of a durable material. (Note: plastic handles can burn if they're screwed flush with the body, and if you habitually allow the flame to come up around the sides.)

The materials that I like are, in order of preference, porcelain enamel, cast iron, Corningware, glass, stainless steel, and stoneware. (Because aluminum has an unpleasant smell to me and discolors certain foods, I feel it isn't stable and could get into the food. Some people do claim that aluminum cooking utensils are a major cause of digestive upsets. Teflon is also on my "non grata" list for being plastic and easily scratched off the surface of the pan and into the food.)

If you buy porcelain, be careful when you are cooking so as not to scratch it with metal utensils; do not bump it (the porcelain may chip) and do not allow it to heat up while dry or it may crack. To clean porcelain, soak the pot with a mild soap; this will remove most foods, even when caked on. Do not use steel scouring pads which leave unsightly, and unfixable, scratches. To get rid of discolorations and restore a bright surface, rub lightly with either baking soda or one of the non-scouring stainless steel cleaning powders now available (such as Cameo), which you can use on both steel and enamel.

The size, kind, and number of pots and pans you'll need will depend on how many people you'll be cooking for. The following basic collection should take care of from one to twelve people:

    one 1-quart saucepan
    one 1½-quart saucepan
    one 2-quart saucepan
    two 3-quart saucepans
    one 9-inch cast iron skillet
    one 6-quart soup pot or Dutch oven
    one 4-quart stainless steel pressure cooker
    one 3- or 4-quart covered ovenproof baking dish
    two shallow, lasagna-style baking dishes
    one 9-inch loaf pan
    two glass 8- or 9-inch pie plates
    two cookie sheets or black steel "bundt pans"

You might also want to invest in a set or two of ovenproof glass containers for leftovers. Pyrex makes an attractive, graduated set of four, with covers that can be inverted to accommodate stacking.

There are only two electrical appliances that I find essential (or at least difficult to do without): a blender and a toaster oven. The former can't be beat for creating creamy drinks, soups, sauces, and dips. The latter is great for toasting bread, baking a small dish, quick broiling, or heating without waiting around for a large oven to heat up.

For grinding nuts, seeds, or mashing beans for spreads, I find a Japanese mortar and pestle set called a *suribachi* almost irreplaceable. The inner surface of the mortar, instead of being smooth, is scored by straight lines, and the texture makes the grinding action of the pestle so much more effective. Suribachis come in various sizes and can be found in most Oriental food markets and some health food stores, or they can be purchased by mail from natural food companies.

You may also want to buy a grinder for grain. Here you have several choices. For occasional coarse grinding, your blender will be sufficient or, if you want to grind a small amount at a time. one of the electric coffee grinders now on the market would probably do. The best utensil for self-reliance and energy saving is a handmill with stone grinding surfaces; it can do double duty by supplying you with exercise and freshly ground breakfast cereal every morning. However, if you do a lot of baking, it probably would be worth your while to buy an electric flour mill which can deliver 5 to 10 pounds within a half hour.

Buying, Storing, and Preserving Food

A Shopping List for the Beginner

Let's suppose you have never bought anything in a natural food store, and your cupboard is empty. You're willing to try some of the recipes in this book, but you don't want to go into hock for it, nor be saddled with a lot of things you won't use. As a beginner's kit, then, you might want to purchase the following staples:

1 pound organic short-grain brown rice
1 package whole wheat or buckwheat noodles ("Japanese pasta")
1 pint shoyu (natural soy sauce) or tamari
1 pint unrefined sesame oil
1 pound sea salt
1 pound brown-rice or barley miso
1 pound jar tahini
1 4-ounce package of kuzu
1 pound lentils, kidney, or aduki beans
1 package kukicha or bancha tea, or cereal coffee
1 package brown rice cakes
1 jar unsweetened apple butter
1 package nori sea vegetable

These items probably will cost no more than dinner for two in a good restaurant, and you can get several meals out of them. If you decide you like the cuisine and want to continue, besides refilling the rice, beans, and noodle stock, you might buy some of the following ingredients.

GRAINS: Millet, bulghur, kasha, rolled oats, couscous

FLOUR: Whole wheat flour, whole wheat pastry flour, soy flour, fresh cornmeal, rye flour

BEANS: Chickpeas, split peas, black beans, pinto beans

DRIED FRUITS AND NUTS: Raisins, prunes, unsulphured apricots, dried apples, almonds, walnuts, cashews, sunflower seeds, unhulled sesame seeds

SWEETENERS: Rice syrup ("Yinnie"), barley malt, maple syrup

SPREADABLES: Natural peanut butter, salted sesame butter, fresh tofu

DRIED VEGETABLES: Hiziki, wakame, kombu, agar-agar (kanten), shiitake mushrooms

OILS: Unrefined corn oil, dark sesame oil, unrefined olive oil, cold-pressed soy or safflower oil (for deep-frying)

CONDIMENTS: Brown rice vinegar, umeboshi plums or paste, arrowroot flour, carob flour, natural mustard

BEVERAGES: Mu tea, mild herb teas, spring water (in five-gallon jugs)

With these items in your cupboard, and once you've obtained the necessary fresh produce, you can make almost all the recipes in this cookbook.

Storing Food

Glass jars are best for keeping dried staples such as whole grains, beans, dried fruits, nuts, tea, et cetera; glass cleans more easily than plastic and adds no flavor or odor to food. You can save jars or look for reasonably priced ones in "5 & 10" stores and supermarkets. (Pyrex has a nice line of stackable glass containers with plastic covers in various sizes; there are other pretty decorator-style containers as well.) Another idea is to befriend a cook at a local restaurant and collect the empty mayonnaise gallon-jars—they look great on kitchen shelves when filled with beans and grains.

Flour is best when fresh; if you can't grind your own, buy just enough for a week or so. If you must keep it longer, refrigerate it.

Of all the other staples listed, only maple syrup, apple butter, and definitely tofu need to be refrigerated. I don't find it necessary to refrigerate unrefined oils even though many people insist that it is; in the fifteen years that I've used them, none has ever gone rancid on me. Unrefined oils still contain the anti-oxidant Vitamin E that is a natural preservative, and I do use them up in six to eight weeks. Refrigerate your oils if you prefer, and if you have room in your refrigerator.

Miso should be stored in glass, and needs refrigeration if the enzymes are very active and begin to grow a white mold; if this happens, stir the mold back in (it's harmless) and refrigerate. Umeboshi plums, shoyu and tahini need no refrigeration.

The best techniques for fresh vegetables depends on your living quarters. If you live in a house that has a cellar or a cold porch, you could set space aside there to store all winter vegetables as well as grains, beans, and flours. In an apartment, you can keep onions in a bin and squash on shelves (making sure they don't touch one another and that they are eaten within three to four weeks). Keep parsley refrigerated in a glass jar with a little water; ginger root loose in the refrigerator door egg holder, garlic also, because it's such a handy spot, even though garlic doesn't need to be refrigerated. To keep carrots and leafy vegetables from wilting, store them in open plastic bags in the refrigerator. Leave cabbage unwrapped, but daikon and other radishes should be wrapped loosely in plastic. I like to keep fruit ready to eat at room temperature—that's when the flavor is at its fullest.

Preserving Food

Foods can be kept from spoiling by either expansive or contractive techniques. For thousands of years, societies all over the world have used the contractive methods of drying, salting, and pickling. These methods are simple and require only sun, air, wind, and salt (which can be found in mines or made by evaporating seawater under the sun). No special technology is required, yet foods preserved in this manner remain edible indefinitely and can travel very well at any temperature. In some cases, their nutritional value is actually enhanced: most pickling and fermenting processes, for example, add beneficial bacteria and lactic acids to foods and increase their vitamin B content.

During the past two hundred years, other food-preserving techniques have emerged such as canning (in water or oil) and preserving with sugar, with cold (refrigerating and freezing), and with petroleum-derived chemical preservatives. These methods need more and more complicated technology as the list progresses (even home canning is technological, for you need cans or jars, made in factories).

Although perhaps applicable to a larger variety of foodstuffs, canning, freezing and use of preservatives has a lot of drawbacks. For example, food in cans may spoil and turn poisonous, and the consumer has no foolproof way of knowing whether this is the case. And as we noted earlier, the addition of chemical preservatives, or of any other chemical substances, changes the quality of our food supply in a rather drastic manner. Their noxious effects, ranging from birth defects to cancer, are becoming increasingly obvious.

The only new preserving technique that I use is simple refigeration which is basically no different than putting foods in a cool porch or cellar. Among the older techniques, I prefer dried foods first, then pickled ones. These naturally preserved foods also taste quite delicious—and quite distinct from the original. Isn't a raisin an entirely different experience from a grape?

Cutting Vegetables

In the process of preparing and cooking food we are, on a subtle level, rearranging the energy pathways of foodstuffs. Thus, cutting vegetables becomes an interaction between the cook and the food, rather than a mechanical action that could just as well be relegated to devices or machines. Eventually, through practice, you will become one with your vegetables, so that you can cut or chop with your eyes closed—your hands will know exactly where to go. At that stage of expertise, it becomes really fun to handle foods.

Anyone who has ever seen a Japanese chef at work knows what artistry with a kitchen knife can accomplish: carrots are deftly turned into sheets, cucumbers into fans, radishes into flowers. I'm not suggesting that you repeat those feats every day for the entertainment of your family, (although I'm sure they'd love it if you did). What I am suggesting is that your cutting technique is an integral part of your meal and deserves your most earnest attention.

First, make sure you stand directly in front of the table, with your back as straight as possible without being stiff, your arms loose at the shoulders, and holding the knife comfortably but not tight. Secure the vegetable to be cut with one hand, tucking fingertips under knuckles for safety's sake. Hold the knife with the other hand, keeping your elbows slightly away from your body. To slice, bring the knife down, the tip a bit lower than the heel, and hit the vegetable with the blade about one-to-two inches from the tip of the knife; then slice forward, and down, and bring the knife back up, so your hand makes a circular movement. Think of the wheels of a steam engine going backwards, and put your consciousness at the back of your elbow in the depression between the two bones: make your movement stem from there, rather than your shoulder or wrist.

The reduction in size brought about by cutting makes a difference in cooking: the smaller or thinner the pieces, the shorter the cooking time. For aesthetic reasons, it's preferable to cut all the vegetables to be cooked together into pieces of roughly the same size; then you can place the vegetable that takes longest to cook in the pot first, adding others in order.

Each vegetable has its special cutting technique; these are my favorite ways to treat specific vegetables, but you may want to invent techniques of your own.

ONIONS AND OTHER ROUND VEGETABLES WITH "POLES" (such as turnips and acorn squash): Cut lengthwise "north-south," then place each half cut side down and cut again "north-south," in thick or thin slices according to the dish. (With squash you may quarter this way, scoop out the seeds, then cut lengthwise one more time into eighths.)

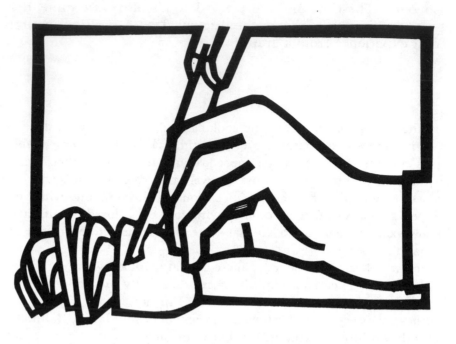

For dicing, keep all the lengthwise slices together, and cut them cross-wise "east-west" the same width.

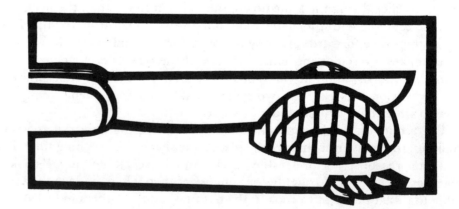

CARROTS AND OTHER LONG VEGETABLES (such as parsnips): The classic way is to slice them thinly on the diagonal, which seems to make them taste sweeter. Another way is to cut irregular chunks by rotating the carrot ¼ to ⅛ turn with each cut. For julienne strips, you can follow either one of two techniques: make small piles of diagonally cut slices and cut these lengthwise into strips, or cut the whole carrot into two-inch chunks, each chunk lengthwise into slabs, then turn these over 90 degrees and cut them into strips. (The first method works best with very thick carrots, the second with thin ones.)

DAIKON (Japanese radish): Cut into crosswise slices, then pile these up and slice into strips, or dice them. Large chunks can be made by cutting slices ½-to-one inch thick, and quartering these.

BURDOCK: Sliver it as if you were sharpening a pencil with a knife, or cut it into slices, straight across or on the diagonal.

ZUCCHINI: Cut in half lengthwise, and each piece lengthwise once again; then slice crosswise into chunks. Or simply slice crosswise into thin rounds. Another method is to slice the zucchini in half lengthwise, then the two halves into two-inch pieces, face down, and each piece into very thin lengthwise slices (this way is particularly tasty if you're serving the zucchini raw, as with a dip).

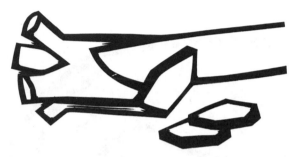

CABBAGE: First slice in half lengthwise, then place the cut side down and slice again lengthwise into quarters: cut out the core at this point. To shred, cut each quarter crosswise into very thin strips. (With salads that are to be served immediately, I also like to cut round lettuce heads this way; the result is crisp and crunchy.)

BUTTERNUT SQUASH: Cut the "neck" off, then cut this across into round slices, which then can be put in piles and quartered. Cut the rounded section in half lengthwise, scoop out the seeds, and quarter or slice thinly or cut into chunks, according to the dish.

BROCCOLI: Cut a slice off the bottom, where it's usually a bit dirty and irregular, and discard. To remove the thicker part of the skin, make a tiny cut into the stem at the bottom, hold the peel between your thumb and the blade, and pull: this way you remove only the toughest part. Then separate the flowerettes from the stems and use them whole. The stems you can cut thinly on the diagonal, or first in half lengthwise, then each half into two-inch pieces; place each piece cut side down and slice lengthwise very thin.

CUCUMBER: If waxed, peel; if not, either score with a fork or cut away strips of the peel so there is a striped effect. Slice thinly into rounds, or follow the same technique as for the zucchini.

Special Situations

Eating Away from Home

Whether you brown-bag it to the office every day, have hungry off-spring with refillable lunch boxes, or indulge in an occasional picnic or out-of-town trip, you may be looking for some practical ideas on how to make your good food portable. Let me then give you a few suggestions which have worked very well for me.

First of all, get a wide-mouth thermos (if you have children, one for each). Thermoses come in one-to-four-cup sizes: the first is perfect for lunchboxes, the last for picnics. Once you have that, plus some wax paper or small plastic bags, you can prepare any of the following, and more, according to your imagination.

- Fried rice and vegetables in a thermos, raw celery or a pickle wrapped in wax paper, a small bag with mixed nuts and raisins
- Thick lentil or vegetable soup in the thermos, tofu-spread sandwich with sprouts, fresh apple
- Salad with dressing in the thermos, rice balls in a wax paper bag, a cookie or two
- Vegetable stew with chopped parsley in the thermos, rice-cake peanut butter sandwich in a wax paper bag, fresh pear
- Rice and beans in thermos, raw cucumber sticks or dill pickles in a plastic bag

The idea is always to include some form of whole grain, as well as something raw or pickled, to lighten up the meal and provide some good quality expansion. Leftovers from dinner will give you the basis from which to create new recipes in a few minutes, plus a number of dishes found in the recipe section lend themselves well to packing in wax paper, traveling, and being eaten out of hand—or sandwich. (Try Croquettes, Empanadas (turnovers), Norimaki, Spinach Fritters, Rice-Lentil Loaf, Hummus on Pita Bread.)

Of course, if you're traveling, it's not always so easy to cook. If I go on a trip where I may be eating out often, I usually take along a small kit containing: 1) a small bottle of shoyu for seasoning; 2) a small jar with miso to make soup in the morning instead of coffee or tea; 3) herb teabags; 4) enough puffed rice cakes to last the trip (about a pack per day, replenishable at health food stores); and 5) umeboshi plums as an antidote for indigestion (and hangovers among my friends).

When traveling abroad, or through different climates, I try to keep in mind the maxim "When in Rome, do as the Romans do." Thus, I usually concentrate on local traditional foods, freshly prepared. Depending on my condition and the quality of the food available, I may eat only vegetables, or I may try also the local breads, pasta, and a small amount of animal protein.

In the typical American coffee shop or roadside restaurant, my children and I manage with such items as tunafish on rye, poached eggs, omelettes, English muffins, assorted vegetables, plain salads (with a lemon wedge and oil for dressing), boiled or baked potatoes, rye toast, soup (split pea, lentil, or bean) and fresh fish fillets (without the tartar sauce).

In more formal restaurants, my favorite combination is broiled fish, potato, vegetable, and salad. If I want a vegetarian meal, I ask for a combination of vegetables, a potato, and again a small salad. (In either case, I might omit the potato and eat some rice cakes either before, during, or after the meal.) In Italian restaurants, I am partial to the escarole soup, pasta with white clam sauce, or oil and garlic (on the side, since they always give you too much), or pesto, a terrific fresh basil sauce (even though it does have some Parmesan).

There's one instance of "eating out" where you might not always be able to order food to your liking: dining in the homes of friends or family. Family reunions, especially, pose a problem if you have changed to a diet radically different from the one you were raised on. You don't want to insult the cook, and after all, the person who provides the food does so with the intention (conscious or subconscious) of drawing everyone together into one loving, interconnected group. If you refuse the food and disdain it, you will disturb the harmony and put everyone on the defensive. Yet if you eat it, you may perhaps feel that you are jeopardizing your health.

How to solve the dilemma? In situations like these, a loving attitude and a little tact can go a long way. For example, one of my students has continued to attend all her family's get-togethers since she became a vegetarian. In five years she has never broken her diet—and no one has ever noticed. Her secret? She doesn't make an issue of her vegetarianism (since she's sure no one would go along with her anyway). Instead, she just eats what she wants, never drawing attention to her choice of food, and never playing the game of "I'm eating better than you."

Whatever choices you make, "wise" or "unwise," diplomatic or direct, I would urge you to relax, go with it, enjoy, be grateful. Please don't subject yourself to any guilt-trips over "eating badly"—you'll probably pay anyway, so why suffer guilt on top of that? Try to accept the consequences of your choices gracefully and gratefully, as interesting lessons. After all, most mistakes can be either fixed, healed, or forgotten.

If You Live Alone

If you live by yourself, cooking has a totally different dimension—mostly smaller. Still it is possible to cook balanced, nutritious meals for one, simply and efficiently, without hours of work. In fact, it's easy.

Once or twice a week, cook up a pot of brown rice and a pot of beans. Now you have the basics. Stir-frying vegetables takes about five minutes; making a salad is equally fast. Then you can heat up a portion of the rice and beans, separately or mixed together. And there's your dinner, ready in about fifteen to twenty minutes—nutritious, balanced, and satisfying.

For variety's sake, with basically the same ingredients, you can prepare the following combinations:

• Mix vegetables and rice, serve the beans and salad on the side
• Make miso soup with the vegetables, heat the rice and beans together, and serve with the salad
• In hot weather, mix rice, beans, salad, and toss the whole thing together with dressing. Sauté an apple for dessert
• Make soup out of the beans and vegetables, eat the rice topped with sesame seeds, and try a salad with miso-dill dressing
• Make soup out of the rice and vegetables; refry the beans and use as topping for the salad

And so on. Try varying your grain: noodles sometimes, or kasha. Only your imagination is your limit in preparing good, wholesome, delicious meals every day, just for yourself. And do occasionally invite a friend to share the bounty with you.

Entertaining

I do not choose my friends on the basis of their food preferences; therefore, I often have dinner parties for people whose ideas about what is right to eat are quite different from mine. Initially, I agonized—what to serve in good conscience? Then, with time, I developed some basic guidelines.

First of all, I won't serve my guests anything that would go against my principles. (Whenever I've ignored this instinct, the food either didn't come out right, or people didn't eat it, or, if they did, the reaction was ho-hum.) And—perhaps most importantly—I serve my kind of food with the same straightforward, unapologetic attitude everybody else seems to adopt when serving—that is, "Here's the best I've got; I hope you enjoy it."

The last meal in each seasonal section of this book was designed for dinner party entertaining; these are my "company meals," and I have served them many times to all kinds of people, always with great success. Everybody will find something in these meals to suit their preference; the difference will come in the proportions they choose. I've found that the best policy is to let everybody help themselves. Some may omit the fish and eat everything else; others may eat a small amount of fish and a larger proportion of the grain; a third group may help themselves to a large amount of fish and proportionately smaller amounts of grain and vegetables. For large parties, you can try raw vegetables with dips, crackers with various spreads, hearty soups (such as Russian Soup), and substantial salads. Some of the desserts in the recipe section (such as apple delight and fruit compotes) are easy to make in quantity.

Sharing food with guests is an age-old means of profound communication, and as such it merits your closest attention and personal concern. A healthful meal served in that spirit will nourish the soul as well as the body, and help create a harmonious feeling of togetherness between you and your guests.

> You must chew your drinks, and drink your foods.
>
> —*Mahatma Gandhi*

After all this preparation, you would do yourself—and the food—a great disservice if you just gulped your meal and ran. Be sure to allow enough time to chew well and eat consciously.

Your teeth exist for a specific purpose: to grind your food to a pulp so that your stomach and intestines can further proceed to break down and assimilate it efficiently. (Neither your stomach nor your intestines are equipped with teeth themselves, and if they are confronted daily with chunks of bread and pieces of carrot, digestive distress is certain to ensue.) Chewing well will thoroughly mix the food with saliva which contains ptyalin, the enzyme necessary to begin the breakdown of starches and other carbohydrates. If the ptyalin doesn't get them, no other digestive juice will either, and you'll end up with a very uncomfortable, bloated feeling. Chewing also enhances circulation to the brain: exercising the masseter and temporal muscles stimulates the temple area—thus chewing well might even help us think better.

If at any time you find yourself partaking of food that you think isn't good for you, don't swallow it quickly without chewing; most likely, such an approach will cause indigestion. You'll be better off chewing slowly, enjoying the food, and accepting it gratefully.

The role that spirit plays in the assimilation of food is recognized in the worldwide custom of saying grace (which is "thank you," from the Latin *gratia.*) Saying or even thinking grace makes us pause, so that we approach our meal with no hurry. It may help us reflect on the miracle that, once again, we have been given sustenance. Food is a blessing, and, if we eat carefully and consciously, we can transmute that input into an output of positive action, honest living, clear thinking, and love.

Part II:

The Practice

Recipes & Menus for the Four Seasons

"It is good and comely for one to eat and drink, and to enjoy the good of all his labour which he taketh under the sun all the days of his life . . . for it is his portion."

Ecclesiastes

Preparing Whole Meals

The recipes in this book are organized in menu sets—six sets for each season: dinner for one evening, and breakfast and lunch for the following day. Lunch, and sometimes breakfast as well, will incorporate foods left over from the previous evening's meal.

In many of the sets, however, you'll find that breakfast has nothing to do with either dinner or lunch. This is done to avoid monotony. At other times, you may be surprised that I suggest "couscous and chickpeas" or "Oden soup and toast" for breakfast since these are not your usual morning fast-breakers. But if people eat steak and eggs for breakfast, why not soup and rice? Besides, a hearty meal in the morning gives the body fuel for the day that can be fortified with a light lunch. For example, if my children have vegetable soup and rice for breakfast, I can pack them a sandwich for lunch in good conscience; if they have toast or cereal in the morning, soup and rice are packed for their noon meal.

In the recipes that make up the menus, I have attempted to cover all the cooking techniques and as many variations in form and texture as possible. My hope is that, in addition to the recipes, you will also learn a technique and find it easy to make a certain recipe even though the ingredients you have on hand are quite different. For example, soups, salads, stews, and stir-fried vegetables can be made with practically any vegetable, not just the ones called for in a recipe; tougher vegetables only require longer cooking. If you want to use red beans instead of white beans, don't agonize over whether it's permissible or not — just *do* it! The fun of cooking with natural foods is that they are all basic foods and, therefore, no limit need be set on your creativity. By experimenting and combining elements in new and interesting ways, you will develop a personal cuisine that will keep you and your family consistently happy and healthy.

If natural food cookery is new to you, follow several sets of menus to the letter for awhile — especially the first two of each season, which provide the most basic information in terms of *what* and *how*. Subsequent meals are more elaborate.

In using this book, therefore, feel free to do what you like: either follow the menus exactly, substitute one dish with another, use individual recipes as in any other cookbook, or follow the various cooking techniques and ideas for meal arrangement, but change the ingredients.

The recipes and menu sets also feature the following guidelines:

Comments: This section will contain whatever explanations are necessary about each meal and whether it requires a simple or complicated preparation, as well as offering an occasional comment on the expansive/contractive balance of the meal.

Nutritional Values: This section identifies the foods from which the major nutrients are obtained in each set of meals. I only have focused on those elements most often asked about, namely, protein, vitamins A, B-complex, and C, calcium, and iron. There are of course many more nutrients present. All meals in this book are excellent sources of unrefined, complex carbohydrates and fiber, and, except for the eight or ten recipes that call for eggs or fish, all the meals in this book are cholesterol-free.

Utensils: This section provides a quick rundown of the pots, pans, and special utensils used for each meal so that you can see at a glance whether you have the necessary baking pan or garlic press or whatever. Knives, wooden spoons, measuring cups and spoons, and rubber spatulas will not be mentioned since these utensils are normally on hand.

Order of Preparation: One of the trickiest aspects of preparing a meal is to have everything ready at the same time, especially if you're cooking with ingredients which are relatively new to you. When you decide to make one of the complete meals outlined in the following pages, you may need some help to get a feel for organizing your cooking time. If so, follow the "order of preparation" numbers along the margins that are a guide to dovetailing the preparation of all the dishes in the meal. Begin with the number "1" and simply follow in sequence the instuctions next to each number. The suggested order of preparation is based on the premise that food which must be cooled is prepared first and food which takes the longest to cook is prepared next. Vegetables are washed and sliced as close to cooking time as possible to avoid drying and the loss of nutrients and energy by oxidation. Dishes that don't hold up well over time are made last, as are those that take a short cooking time and lose sparkle when reheated.

Most of the dinners are designed to be prepared in 1½ hours or less; lunches may take from 15 to 30 minutes. (Allow more time if you are a novice in the kitchen.) Preparation of breakfasts will vary from 10 to 40 minutes. A meal usually will take as long to prepare as the longest-cooking dish plus ten minutes. There are exceptions: for example, sauerkraut and pickles are prepared ahead and it will take ten to fourteen days before they are ready for use; and cold soups or aspic need 4 to 6 hours of chilling. The "Comments" section of the menu will warn you if the meal you're considering has a dish that is prepared ahead of time.

Preparation Time: Found at the start of each recipe, the first time interval indicates how long to work at the food with your hands. The second interval indicates free time (while the dish soaks, cooks, cools, pickles, or rests) that can be spent doing something else.

Yield: All recipes are designed for four or five people, that is, four big servings, or five medium ones, although this may vary according to appetites. Please adjust quantities according to your needs. If there are too many dishes for you in one meal, please do not hesitate to cut. The menus lean toward abundance and variety to show you the many foods that are available for putting together vegetarian meals.

Measuring: Certainly the introduction of standard measuring cups and spoons was a vast improvement over the old "Take a piece of butter the size of an egg" system, especially for people who didn't see a lot of cooking done at home. If you want to ensure that a dish comes out pretty much the same each time you make it, or if you want to try something you've never made or perhaps have never eaten before, you will need reliable measuring tools. Quantities for all the recipes are given in the standardized form of cups, tablespoons, or ounces. However, once you really get in touch with the essence of cooking, you'll realize that there are dishes in which exact quantities of ingredients are not essential. For instance, you may decide to sauté vegetables in a pot, adding water as well as a sprinkle of this and a pinch of that until it looks like soup, and simply cooking it until it smells good and the color is right.

No beverages are mentioned in the menus since it is assumed that you will finish each meal with a beverage of your choice. For suggestions, however, please see the chapter on Beverages.

And now, let's cook.

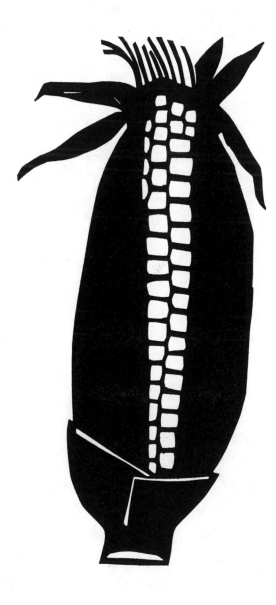

Fall Meals

Fall Menus

	Dinner	Breakfast	Lunch
Menu No. 1 PAGE 67	Miso Soup Brown Rice Aduki Beans Sautéed Carrots, Onions, 　Squash Cabbage Salad	Soft Rice with Sesame 　Salt	Aduki Bean Soup Fried Rice with Vegetables Pressed Salad with 　Pignoli Nuts
Menu No. 2 PAGE 73	Soba (Buckwheat Noodles) 　with Sauce Istanbul Squash and Onions Steamed Garlic Broccoli Hiziki with Mushrooms 　and Tofu Peanut-Apple Mousse	Rice Cream with Prunes	Squash Cream Soup Sautéed Vegetable-Soba Boston Salad with 　Istanbul Dressing
Menu No. 3 PAGE 79	Leek Pie Kasha String Beans Tahini Watercress-Radish Salad 　with Umeboshi Dressing Apple Delight	Waffles with Apple- 　Peanut Butter	Kasha Croquettes Steamed Collard Greens
Menu No. 4 PAGE 85	Split Pea Soup Whole Wheat Spaghetti Root Vegetables in 　Kuzu Sauce Steamed Kale with Seeds Oatmeal Cookies	Cereal Puffs with 　Nut Milk	Spaghetti and Vegetables 　au Gratin Coleslaw with Sesame- 　Vinegar Dressing
Menu No. 5 PAGE 91	Millet Croquettes Baked Squash Green Salad with Tofu- 　Ginger Dressing Tahini-Apple Custard	Crêpes with Miso-Tahini 　or Tahini-Maple 　Spread	Clear Consommé Millet with Fried Onions Steamed Carrots
Menu No. 6 PAGE 97	Carrot Cream Soup Couscous Chickpeas Ginger-broiled Fish Red Cabbage Salad with 　Princess Dressing Apple Pie	Couscous with Chickpeas Stir-fried Vegetables	Fish Salad in Pita Bread 　with Tahini-Lemon 　Dressing

Dinner	*Breakfast*	*Lunch*
Miso soup	*Soft Rice with Sesame Salt*	*Aduki Bean Soup*
Brown Rice		*Fried Rice with*
Aduki Beans		*Vegetables*
Sautéed Carrots,		*Pressed Salad with*
Onions, Squash		*Pignoli Nuts*
Cabbage Salad		

Comments

Since the dinner menu calls for miso soup, a two or three day supply can be made by preparing only the soup base. However, do not add the miso to the whole pot; add it only to individual servings.

To measure salt for the rice or any other grain, use one three-finger pinch (with thumb, index, and middle finger) per cup of water. Generally the amount of your pinch will be the right amount of salt for your body. When the rice has cooked, you can keep it in a covered bowl or pot near a window at room temperature for a day or two, making sure that air circulates in the container so the rice will not mold. In the summer, rice should not be stored at room temperature for more than 24 hours.

The leftover rice from dinner is used for both breakfast and lunch; leftover aduki beans and vegetables are used for lunch. The sesame salt for breakfast should be made ahead of time. It can be used as a delightful seasoning over many grain and vegetable dishes; in addition to flavor it offers a complementary protein boost. In many instances, sesame salt helps to ameliorate mild headaches, stomach distress, or nausea. Also, try miso soup with rice for breakfast instead of tea or coffee; many people find it a highly energizing combination.

Nutritional Values

Complementary proteins are obtained from the rice, beans, and sesame seeds, and additional protein from the miso, tofu, and pignoli in the lunch salad; vitamin A from the carrots, carrot greens, and squash; the B-complex vitamins from the rice, miso, beans, and vegetables; and vitamin C from the scallions, carrots, onions, squash, cabbage, lettuce, and celery. Calcium is supplied by the tofu, beans, miso, carrot tops, sesame seeds, sea vegetables (nori, kombu), and pignoli nuts; and iron by the miso, rice, beans, carrot greens, sesame seeds, and sea vegetables.

Utensils

Dinner: Two 2- or 3-quart covered pots, small bowl, 4-quart pressure cooker or 3-quart covered pot, skillet or saucepan, salad bowl, small cup or bowl.

Breakfast: 2-quart saucepan, suribachi or serrated mortar.

Lunch: Covered soup pot, skillet, blender or suribachi, salad press (obtained from an oriental food/utensil store). An improvised salad press can be made from a bowl, plate, and stones or similar weights.

Dinner

Aduki Beans

Serves: 4
Time: 3 minutes, 1½ hours

2 cups aduki beans
8 cups water
1 2-inch piece kombu seaweed
3 tablespoons shoyu (natural soy sauce) or to taste

1. Start the beans; move on to rice.

Wash the beans in more than enough tap water to cover; drain well. Place the beans, water, and kombu in a 2- or 3-quart pot and bring to a boil; then reduce heat and simmer covered for about 1½ hours or until soft. Season with shoyu to taste.

Brown Rice

Serves: 4
Time: 2 minutes; 1 hour

3 cups short grain brown rice
5 cups water
½ teaspoon sea salt or to taste

2. Cook the rice; move on to salad.

Place the rice in a 3-quart pot and add more than enough tap water to cover. Swirl the rice thoroughly, then drain well. Repeat two or three times if necessary until the rice rinses clean. Add the water and salt; bring to a boil, reduce heat to minimum, cover, and simmer for 1 hour. (If possible use an asbestos pad or flame tamer.)
NOTE: If a pressure cooker is used, raise pressure to 15 pounds and cook over minimum heat for 40 minutes. When rice is cooked, turn off heat and allow pressure to return to normal before opening.

Cabbage Salad

Serves: 4
Time: 10 minutes; 30 minutes

½ small head green cabbage
1 teaspoon sea salt
1 tablespoon lemon juice
1 teaspoon olive oil

3. Prepare the salad; go on to soup.

6. Finish the salad; return to soup.

Shred the cabbage very fine into a salad bowl; sprinkle with salt, mix well, then allow to stand for ½ hour or longer. (The salt removes water and acids from the leaves, making the cabbage easier to digest.)
When the cabbage is ready, squeeze gently between your palms to express any remaining water; if desired, rinse the cabbage lightly to remove most of the salt, then drain and squeeze well. Combine the lemon juice and oil. Pour over the cabbage and toss.

Miso Soup

Serves: 4
Time: 15 minutes

2 or 3 dried Shiitake mushrooms
5 cups water
2 sheets nori seaweed
1 8-ounce cake tofu
2 tablespoons barley or brown rice miso
Chopped scallions

Soak the mushrooms in 1 cup water for 10 minutes. Bring the remaining 5 cups water to a boil in a 2- or 3-quart soup pot. Wave the nori sheets over medium heat until the sheets shrink and turn green; crumble the nori and add to the boiling water.

Remove refreshed mushrooms from the soaking water; add the soaking water to the soup. Cut off and discard the mushroom stems and slice the mushrooms into thin strips; add to the soup, then reduce heat and simmer for 5 minutes. Now dice the tofu and add to the soup; cover the pot and simmer for 5 minutes more.

Dissolve the miso in a small amount of soup stock. Stir the miso into the soup, then immediately remove the pot from heat. Serve garnished with chopped scallions.

NOTE: Double or triple the recipe and make enough soup base to last two or three days, but do not add the miso to the whole pot. Since boiling or reheating will destroy vital microorganisms, add the miso only to individual servings—approximately 2/3 teaspoon each or to taste.

4. Make the soup;
   move on to vegetables.

7. Finish the soup;
   go back to vegetables.

Sautéed Carrots-Onions-Squash

Serves: 4
Time: 10 minutes; 15 minutes

4 medium yellow onions
1 tablespoon corn oil
6 carrots
1 teaspoon shoyu (natural soy sauce)
3 small yellow squash (each 6 inches long)
2 or 3 tablespoons finely chopped carrot tops or parsley

Peel the onions and cut into ½-inch pieces. Heat the oil in a covered skillet or saucepan; add the onions and cook over medium heat stirring once or twice. While the onions cook, cut the carrots in thick diagonal slices; add to the onions and stir. Cut the squash lengthwise once, then across in thin slices and add to the mixture. Sauté for a minute longer then sprinkle with shoyu. Now cover the pan and reduce heat to minimum, allowing the vegetables to steam in their own moisture for 10 minutes. Without removing the cover, gently shake the pan occasionally to prevent burning.

Chop the tops of 2 carrots as fine as you would parsley; add to the vegetables, mixing well. Remove from heat and serve.

5. Slice and cook the
   vegetables;
   return to salad.

8. Finish the vegetables.

Soft Rice

Serves: 4
Time: 15 minutes

3 cups cooked brown rice
2 cups water

Combine the rice and water in a 2-quart saucepan, breaking up lumps with a wooden spatula. Bring to a boil, then reduce heat and simmer very slowly uncovered for 15 minutes or until creamy; stir often. Serve sprinkled with sesame salt (gomasio).

Sesame Salt (Gomasio)

Time: 25 minutes

14 tablespoons sesame seeds
1 tablespoon sea salt

Wash the seeds by swirling them in 2 cups of water; drain well in a fine-mesh strainer. Place the seeds in a small steel or cast iron pot* (the high temperatures used for dry-roasting will crack material other than metal). Roast the seeds over high heat, stirring constantly for 10 to 15 minutes. When the seeds turn light brown and are fragrant, pour them into a suribachi and grind for 5 minutes; add the salt and continue to grind for 10 minutes longer. Store the seeds in an airtight container and use as a condiment.
NOTE: A ¾-quart pan is ideal if the layer of seeds is thick enough (1 inch); a thick layer prevents the seeds from popping out of the pan.

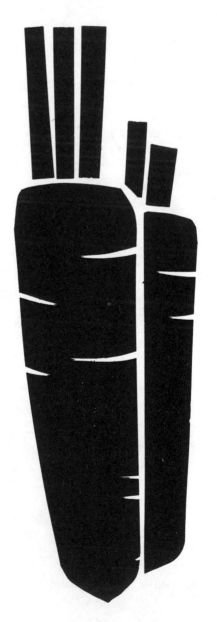

Pressed Salad with Pignoli Nuts

Serves: 4
Time: 10 minutes; 25 minutes

1 head romaine lettuce
1 carrot
2 stalks celery
1 tablespoon sea salt
½ cup pignoli nuts (pine nuts)

Wash the lettuce, pat dry, and shred the leaves into a bowl. Scrub the carrot and shred with a potato peeler and add to the lettuce; then chop the celery into small pieces and add to the mixture. Sprinkle the salad with salt, toss, then pack into a salad press or place a plate directly on top of the vegetables and an 8 to 10 pound weight on top of the plate. Allow to stand for 25 to 30 minutes.

Now pour off the water from the salad and lightly rinse away the salt if desired. Add the pignoli nuts and serve.

1. Prepare the salad; go on to soup.

4. Finish the salad.

Aduki Bean Soup

Serves: 4
Time: 3 minutes; 25 minutes

2 cups cooked aduki beans
½ cup rolled oats
4 cups water
Shoyu (natural soy sauce) to taste
Chopped parsley

Place the beans, oats, and water in a blender or suribachi and purée until creamy. Transfer to a soup pot and simmer for 15 to 20 minutes, then season with shoyu. Serve garnished with chopped parsley.

2. Make the soup; move on to rice.

Fried Rice with Vegetables

Serves: 4
Time: 10 minutes; 15 minutes

1 teaspoon unrefined sesame oil
1 clove garlic, minced
½ teaspoon oregano
1 cup leftover sautéed carrots-onions-squash
2 cups cooked rice
1 teaspoon shoyu (natural soy sauce)
1 tablespoon water
¼ teaspoon brown rice vinegar

Heat the oil in a skillet over medium heat; add the minced garlic, browning it slightly for 10 seconds. Stir in the oregano, then the leftover vegetables and rice. Reduce heat to medium-low, and cook for 10 minutes or until thoroughly heated. Combine the shoyu, water, and brown wine vinegar and add to the rice mixture; cover and cook for 5 minutes longer.

3. Prepare the rice; return to salad.

Dinner	*Breakfast*	*Lunch*
Soba (Buckwheat Noodles) with Sauce Istanbul Squash and Onions Steamed Garlic Broccoli Hiziki with Mushrooms and Tofu Peanut-Apple Mousse	Rice Cream with Prunes	Squash Cream Soup Sautéed Vegetable-Soba Boston Salad with Istanbul Dressing

Comments

For a quick dinner that will be ready in 30 minutes, make only the soba and sauce, the broccoli, and a salad. Serve the mousse hot for dessert. The breakfast prunes require overnight soaking. You might want to retain the salted cooking water from the noodles for soup stock and/or keep the vegetable trimmings, including the skins of onions, and periodically cook them up in a pot of water to make a stock. Refrigerate the stock until ready to use in soups, dressings, and sauces or use as a cooking liquid for grains.

Nutritional Values

Complementary proteins are obtained from the whole grain pasta and sesame sauce, and additional protein from the tofu, peanut butter, rice cream, squash, and broccoli; vitamin A from the squash, broccoli, and carrots; the B-complex vitamin from the pasta, rice cream, broccoli, squash, hiziki, and sesame sauce; and vitamin C from the onions, broccoli, apple juice, parsley, and salad. Calcium is provided by the sesame sauce, hiziki, tofu, and kuzu; and iron by the pasta, sauce, hiziki, and prunes.

Utensils

Dinner: 6-quart pot, large colander or strainer, two 2- or 3-quart covered saucepans, two 1½-quart saucepans, medium bowl, individual custard cups.
Breakfast: Medium bowl or saucepan with cover, 2-quart saucepan.
Lunch: Covered soup pot, 3-quart covered saucepan or wok, small mixing bowl, blender or suribachi, salad bowl.

Dinner

Peanut-Apple Mousse

Serves: 4
Time: 15 minutes; 1 hour

1 cup water
4 tablespoons crunchy peanut butter
2 tablespoons apple butter
5 tablespoons kuzu
1½ cups apple juice
¼ teaspoon vanilla
Roasted peanuts

1. Prepare dessert and chill; go to hiziki.

Place the peanut butter and water in a 1½-quart saucepan over low heat until the peanut butter dissolves. In a small bowl combine the apple butter, kuzu, and apple juice, mixing well; add to the peanut butter. Continue to cook over very low heat, stirring constantly, until the mixture has a thick and creamy consistency, then simmer for 5 minutes more, stirring gently. Quickly spoon into individual custard cups and chill. Serve garnished with roasted peanuts.

Hiziki with Mushrooms and Tofu

Serves: 4
Time: 10 minutes; 30 minutes

4 Shiitake mushrooms
2 cups water
½ cup hiziki seaweed
1 teaspoon sesame oil
4 ounces tofu, cubed
2 tablespoons shoyu (natural soy sauce) or to taste

2. Soak hiziki; move on to noodles.

5. Cook the hiziki; return to noodles.

9. Add the tofu and shoyu; return to broccoli.

Soak the mushrooms in ½ cup of the water; soak hiziki in remaining water for 10 minutes.
Remove hiziki from the water; retain soaking water allowing it to settle. Heat the oil in a 2-quart saucepan; add the hiziki, and sauté briefly. Chop the mushrooms, discarding the stems; add to the hiziki. Carefully pour the soaking water into the hiziki making sure the gritty residue is not included; bring to a boil, reduce heat, cover, and simmer for 15 minutes.
Add the tofu and shoyu and simmer for 15 minutes longer.

Soba (Buckwheat Noodles)

Serves: 4
Time: 5 minutes; 15 minutes

1 pound buckwheat noodles or Japanese pasta
4 quarts water
1 teaspoon sea salt

3. Heat water for noodles; move on to squash.
6. Add soba to boiling water; move on to sauce.

In a 6-quart pot, bring water to a rolling boil; add salt if the noodles are unsalted.
Break pasta in half, add to the boiling water and stir once with a wooden spoon, then reduce heat, and simmer uncovered for 10 to 15 minutes or until thoroughly cooked.

Pour the noodles into a colander and drain well; rinse lightly under cold running water to avoid stickiness. Return the noodles to the pot and cover to retain moisture. Serve topped with Sauce Istanbul.

NOTE: To reheat, add ½ inch water to the pot, cover, and steam briefly.

11. Drain and rinse the noodles.

Squash and Onions

Serves: 4
Time: 10 minutes; 25 minutes

1 butternut squash (2 pounds)
3 medium yellow onions
1 tablespoon corn oil
½ teaspoon oregano
½ cup water
¼ teaspoon sea salt (optional)

Wash and scrub the squash; cut into 2-inch pieces (see *Cutting Vegetables*). Peel the onions, cut in half lengthwise, then slice into ½-inch-wide strips. Heat the oil in a 2-quart saucepan, add the onions, and sauté until transparent; add the squash and oregano and sauté for another 2 or 3 minutes. Now add the water and if desired, the salt; reduce heat, cover, and cook for 25 minutes.

4. Prepare the squash; go back to hiziki.

Sauce Istanbul

Serves: 4
Time: 5 minutes

10 tablespoons sesame tahini (about ¼ cup)
2 tablespoons shoyu (natural soy sauce)
10 tablespoons water

Place the tahini in a bowl and slowly stir in the shoyu until the mixture stiffens and begins to form a ball. Slowly add 3 tablespoons of the water and continue adding water, one tablespoon at a time, until the mixture has reached a light, creamy consistency. If the sauce begins to curdle at any point, add more water and blend. Serve cold over hot soba.

7. Prepare the sauce; go on to broccoli.

Steamed Garlic Broccoli

Serves: 4
Time: 5 minutes; 10 minutes

1 bunch broccoli
1 clove garlic
½ cup water

Wash and chop the broccoli, separating the stems and flowerettes; mince the garlic.

Place the broccoli stems in a 1½-quart saucepan with the water and garlic; cover and steam for 4 minutes. Uncover and stir the stems; arrange the flowerettes on top, then cover and steam for another 4 minutes. Serve with a sprinkling of roasted sesame seeds, or Sesame Salt (gomasio).

8. Prepare the broccoli; return to hiziki.
10. Finish the broccoli; return to noodles.

Rice Cream with Prunes

Serves: 4
Time: Overnight; 10 minutes, 40 minutes

1 cup prunes
3 cups water
1 cup rice cream
5 cups water
½ teaspoon sea salt or to taste

Soak the prunes in the water, covered, overnight. Use prepackaged rice cream or make your own as follows: Wash and drain 2 cups brown rice; spread the rice in a shallow baking pan and roast at 350°F. for 15 to 20 minutes or until medium brown. Store in an airtight container and grind as needed in an electric coffee grinder or hand mill.

Pit and chop the prunes. In a 2-quart pot, dissolve the rice cream in water (use soaking water from the prunes as well); add the salt and bring to a boil over medium heat, stirring until the rice cream starts to thicken. Reduce heat and continue stirring for 2 to 3 minutes; then cover and simmer over minimum heat (use an asbestos pad or flame tamer) for 25 minutes, stirring occasionally. Add the chopped prunes and continue to cook for at least 15 minutes more. (Rice cream will improve with longer cooking.)

Squash Cream Soup

Serves: 4
Time: 10 minutes

3 cups leftover squash and onions
3 cups water
Sea salt to taste
Chopped parsley

Purée vegetables and water in a blender or suribachi until creamy, or strain through a sieve or food mill. Transfer to a soup pot and add the salt; heat thoroughly but do not boil. Garnish with chopped parsley.

1. Make soup;
   go on to salad.

Boston Salad

Serves: 4
Time: 8 minutes

1 or 2 heads Boston lettuce
2 carrots

Wash the lettuce well, separating the leaves and removing any dirt; gently tear the lettuce leaves into small pieces and place in a salad bowl. Shred carrots with a potato peeler; add to the lettuce, tossing lightly. Spoon Istanbul Dressing over individual servings.

2. Prepare salad;
   move on to sautéed vegetables.

Istanbul Dressing

Time: 2 minutes

½ cup Sauce Istanbul
2 tablespoons lemon juice

Combine the ingredients, mixing well.

Sautéed Vegetable-Soba

Serves: 4
Time: 15 minutes

1 cup mushrooms
1 teaspoon corn oil
½ cup bean sprouts
Shoyu (natural soy sauce)
1 cup sautéed broccoli
2 cups soba noodles cooked

Trim the dark end of the stem from the mushrooms and discard; slice mushrooms thinly lengthwise. Heat the oil in a 2- or 3-quart pot over medium heat; sauté the mushrooms with a few drops of shoyu. Add the bean sprouts and cook for 2 minutes, then add the broccoli and soba noodles. Stir gently until thoroughly heated, adding a few drops of shoyu after every one or two turns of the spoon. Serve immediately.

3. Prepare the vegetable-soba.

Dinner	*Breakfast*	*Lunch*
Leek Pie	*Waffles with Apple-*	*Kasha Croquettes*
Kasha	*Peanut Butter*	*Steamed Collard Greens*
String Beans Tahini		
Watercress-Radish Salad		
with Umeboshi Dressing		
Apple Delight		

Comments

The fluffy kasha as well as the salad and dessert balance the oil in the leek pie and string beans and lighten the richness of the dinner meal. For the same reason, the collard greens for lunch are steamed and served plain with the fried croquettes.

For a different kind of breakfast, serve the leek pie cold with either hot soup or cereal coffee.

Nutritional Values

Complementary protein is obtained from the kasha, string beans, tahini sauce, whole wheat waffles, and peanut butter; abundant vitamin A from the watercress and collards; the B-complex vitamin from the kasha, whole wheat, leeks, string beans, tahini, and collards; and vitamin C from the string beans, watercress, radishes, apples, and collard greens. Calcium is supplied by the kasha, tahini, kuzu, watercress, peanut butter, and collards; and iron by the kasha, tahini, raisins, watercress, and collard greens.

Utensils

Dinner: Large mixing bowl, 9-inch pie plate, rolling pin, wax paper, three 2- or 3-quart covered saucepans, 4-quart covered pot, salad bowl, small saucepan, blender or suribachi.

Breakfast: Waffle iron (preferably without teflon lining), blender or large mixing bowl, small mixing bowl.

Lunch: 3-quart covered pot, large bowl, medium skillet.

Leek Pie

Serves: 4
Time: 30 minutes; 45 minutes

CRUST: 9″ pie shell

2 cups whole wheat pastry flour
¼ cup sesame or corn oil
¼ teaspoon sea salt
½ cup water

1. Make the pie crust;
   while it rests, go to dessert.

Place the flour in a large mixing bowl; pour oil over the flour, then cut in with 2 knives, one in each hand, crisscrossing and stirring until most lumps are broken up. Now rub the mixture quickly between your hands, until it resembles wet sand; the mixture is ready if a handful retains its shape when squeezed. Dissolve the salt in the water and add to the flour, mixing quickly and well; gently squeeze (do not knead) until the dough is firm and moist. Allow the dough to rest in the bowl for 20 to 30 minutes. Do not cover if the dough is very moist so it can dry a bit; otherwise , cover the dough. Preheat oven to 375°F.

4. Roll out crust and bake;
   move on to filling.

Roll the dough thinly between two sheets of wax paper and lightly oil a pie plate. Peel off the top sheet of paper and invert the plate over the dough; slip one hand under the papered side of the dough and gently turn over dough and pie plate. Peel off the remaining paper; fit dough into plate and trim off any excess. Decorate the edge by fluting with a fork and pinching between the thumb and two fingers. Poke the bottom of the shell a few times with a fork and pre-bake for 16 minutes.

6. Remove pie shell from oven;
   return to filling.

Remove pie shell from oven, but do not turn off the heat.
NOTE: Leftover dough can be made into crackers. Roll the dough in a ball, pinch off small pieces, and flatten between the palms of the hands. Bake at 375°F. for 15 to 20 minutes or until lightly browned.

FILLING:

Time: 10 minutes; 23 minutes

5 or 6 leeks
1 tablespoon sesame oil
1½ cups water
2 tablespoons kuzu
1 or 2 tablespoons shoyu (natural soy sauce) or to taste

5. Prepare leek filling;
   return to crust.

7. Finish the filling, fill pie,
   and bake;
   go on to kasha.

13. Check pie, and if done,
    remove from oven;
    return to string beans.

Slit the leeks in half lengthwise and wash carefully. Chop each leek very fine crosswise, discarding only the roots and the last inch of green top. Heat the oil in a 2- or 3-quart saucepan and sauté the leeks for 5 minutes; add ½ cup of the water, then cover and simmer for 8 minutes.
In a small bowl, dissolve the kuzu in remaining cup of water; add to the leeks, stirring until the mixture thickens. Stir in the shoyu, mixing well, then pour immediately into prebaked pie shell. Bake for 15 minutes.
Remove pie from oven. Serve hot, cold, or at room temperature.

Apple Delight

Serves: 4
Time: 10 minutes; 6 minutes

2 pounds McIntosh apples
½ cup raisins
1 cinnamon stick
Water

Wash, quarter, and core the apples; cut each quarter into three pieces. Place the raisins and cinnamon stick in a 4-quart pot; add just enough water to cover the raisins, then add the apples (but do not mix). Cover and cook over medium heat for 5 minutes; allow to cool.
Invert the pan with the apples and raisins in a bowl so that the raisins are on top. Discard the cinnamon stick before serving.

2. Prepare dessert;
go to string beans.

15. Transfer apples to serving bowl.

String Beans Tahini

Serves: 4
Time: 25 minutes

1½ pounds string beans
2/3 cup water
2 tablespoons shoyu (natural soy sauce) or to taste
4 tablespoons tahini

Snap the ends off the beans, break them in half; and wash. Place the beans in a 2- or 3-quart saucepan with water; cover and simmer for 10 minutes. Add shoyu and cook for 10 minutes more.
Remove beans from heat and carefully blend in the tahini. (Do not boil the tahini or it will curdle.) Spoon over individual servings of kasha and serve immediately.

3. Prepare string beans; return to pie. Remove apples from heat.

12. Add shoyu to string beans; return to pie.

14. Finish the string beans; return to dessert.

Kasha

Serves: 4
Time: 5 minutes; 15 minutes

2 cups whole brown kasha (buckwheat groats)
3¾ cups water
½ teaspoon sea salt

Bring water to a boil in a 2- or 3-quart pot.
Add the salt and kasha; reduce heat to minimum. Cover, and cook for 15 minutes or until fluffy.

8. Boil water;
go on to salad.

10. Add salt and kasha to water; return to salad.

Watercress-Radish Salad

Serves: 4
Time: 10 minutes

1 bunch watercress
6 medium radishes

9. Prepare the salad; return to kasha.

Hold the bunch of cress firmly in one hand, and with the other break in two with a wringing motion; wash well, and drain. Slice the radishes crosswise into thin rounds, discarding tips. Place the radishes and watercress in a salad bowl and toss. Serve individual portions topped with Umeboshi Dressing.

Umeboshi Dressing

Time: 3 minutes; 8 minutes

4 pitted umeboshi plums
1 cup water
¼ cup olive oil
Handful of parsley

11. Prepare the dressing; return to the string beans.

Combine the pitted plums and water in a small saucepan and simmer for 8 minutes; allow to cool. Place the cooled plum mixture, oil, and parsley in a blender or suribachi, blending well. Spoon over individual salad portions.

Breakfast

Waffles

Serves: 4
Time: 30 minutes

2 cups water
1 tablespoon corn oil
2 eggs
½ teaspoon salt
2 cups whole wheat pastry flour

In the following order, place water, oil, eggs, salt, and flour in a blender and blend at low speed for 2 minutes. Pour or spoon portions of the mixture into a hot waffle iron. Since whole wheat waffles take longer to cook than those made with white flour, cook until crisp, medium brown in color, and hollow sounding when tapped. Serve topped with Apple-Peanut Butter.

Apple-Peanut Butter

Serves: 4
Time: 3 minutes

½ cup apple butter
¼ cup peanut butter

In a small mixing bowl, combine the two butters thoroughly, adding a few drops of water for a smoother consistency. Spread lightly over waffles.

Kasha Croquettes

2 cups cooked kasha
½ cup whole wheat flour
3 scallions
½ bunch parsley
½ teaspoon sea salt or 1 tablespoon shoyu (natural soy sauce)
Oil for frying

Place the kasha and flour in a large bowl and with wet hands, squeeze the mixture continuously through your fingers for 8 to 10 minutes or until it holds a shape. Chop scallions and parsley into fine pieces and add to the mixture; sprinkle in the salt or shoyu and work the mixture with the hands another 1 or 2 minutes. Form the dough into flat, 2-inch diameter patties, smoothing over any cracks in the edges.
Heat ½ inch oil in a medium skillet and fry patties over medium heat until lightly browned on each side; drain on brown paper. To keep warm, place in a 150°F. oven until ready to serve.

1. Prepare the croquettes; move on to greens.

3. Fry the croquettes, and 10 minutes before they're done, return to greens.

Steamed Collard Greens

Serves: 4
Time: 4 minutes; 10 minutes

1 bunch collard greens
Water
Sea salt to taste
1 bay leaf
Several drops of rice vinegar or lemon juice

Trim 2 to 3 inches from the collard stems and wash the leaves well; slice twice lengthwise then chop crosswise in thin pieces.
Place the collard pieces, salt, and bay leaf in a 2- or 3-quart pot with ½ inch water; steam over low heat for 8 to 10 minutes. Add the vinegar or lemon juice during the last 2 minutes of cooking.

2. Prepare the greens; return to croquettes.
4. Steam the greens.

Dinner	*Breakfast*	*Lunch*

Split Pea Soup
Whole Wheat Spaghetti
Root Vegetables in
  Kuzu Sauce
Steamed Kale with Seeds
Oatmeal Cookies
	Cereal Puffs with
	  Nut Milk
		Spaghetti and Vegetables
		  au Gratin
		Coleslaw with Sesame-
		  Vinegar Dressing

Comments

The split pea soup for dinner is one of the easiest soups to prepare; split pea and lentil are the only dried legumes that do not require soaking and that will cook in approximately one hour.

Whole milk with dry cereal is a widely-used combination for breakfast. The nut milk on the breakfast menu is a non-dairy variation but is equally as satisfying. Like whole milk, nut milk is rich in protein, calcium, and fats. Try it as a replacement in recipes whenever water, juice, or regular milk is called for.

Nutritional Values

Complementary proteins are obtained from the split peas, whole wheat spaghetti, oats, kale, sunflower seeds, cereal, and nut milk; vitamin A from the kale, cabbage, and carrots; the B-complex vitamins from the grain products as well as the seeds, nut milk, split peas, kale, and daikon; and vitamin C from the daikon, kale, parsnips, and cabbage. Calcium is supplied by the daikon, burdock, kale, parsnips, cabbage, nut milk, and sunflower seeds; and iron by the split peas, kale, nut milk, raisins, and shoyu.

Utensils

Dinner: 3-quart covered soup pot, two 2-quart covered saucepans, 4-quart pot, 1-quart saucepan, 2 large and 1 small mixing bowl, egg beater or wire whisk, blender, 1 or 2 baking sheets, two soup spoons.

Breakfast: Blender and cereal bowls.

Lunch: 1½-quart saucepan, shallow baking dish, wire whisk, small mixing bowl or jar, large mixing bowl, salad bowl.

Dinner

Split Pea Soup

Serves: 4
Time: 5 minutes; 1 hour

1 cup green split peas
6 cups water
1 large carrot
1 medium onion
¼ teaspoon sea salt or to taste
1 tablespoon miso
1 cup croutons, fried or baked

1. Prepare the soup;
   go to dessert.

Wash and drain the peas and place in a 3-quart pot with the water. Bring to a boil, reduce heat, cover, and simmer. Scrub and cut the carrot into chunks and peel the onion and cut into quarters; add both to the peas. Simmer for 1 hour or until the carrot is soft.

9. Finish the soup.

Mash the carrot pieces with a fork against the sides of the pot until the green soup is orange-flecked; add the salt and simmer for 5 minutes longer. Dissolve the miso in 2 tablespoons water, add to the soup and stir. Serve garnished with croutons.

CROUTONS: Time: 10 to 20 minutes

Cube 4 slices of whole grain bread. Fry in 1 inch safflower oil until crisp; or bake at 375°F. for 15 to 20 minutes.

Oatmeal Cookies

Yield: 4 dozen
Time: 10 minutes; 25 minutes

1 cup water
1 cup raisins
1 cinnamon stick
4 cups rolled oats
1 cup whole wheat pastry flour
2/3 cup sunflower seeds
1/2 cup dried coconut (optional)
1/4 teaspoon salt
1/3 cup corn oil
1/3 cup barley malt or honey
1 teaspoon vanilla
Juice and grated rind of one lemon
2 eggs

2. Make the cookies;
   move on to spaghetti.

Preheat oven to 375°F. Bring the water to a boil in a small pan; add the raisins and cinnamon stick and simmer covered while the rest of the ingredients are put together. In one bowl, mix the oats, pastry flour, seeds, coconut, and salt; in another bowl, mix the remaining ingredients beating well with a wire whisk until thoroughly blended. Remove the cinnamon stick from raisins, then purée the raisins and cooking water in a blender. (If raisins are still hot, loosen the blender top to allow air into the container.)

Blend the raisins into the oats mixture; allow to stand while you oil two baking sheets. Add the oil mixture to the oats and raisins; mix well. Place flattened tablespoonfuls of batter on cookie sheets. Bake for 15 minutes, then turn cookies over and bake another 10 minutes or until lightly browned.

Whole Wheat Spaghetti

Serves: 4
Time: 2 minutes; 25 minutes

3 quarts water
1 pound whole wheat spaghetti
1 teaspoon sea salt

Bring water to a boil in a 4-quart pot.
Add salt to the boiling water; break the spaghetti in half and drop into water. Cook uncovered over medium heat for 25 minutes, stirring occasionally with a chopstick.
Drain the spaghetti, reserving the water; rinse the spaghetti quickly in cold water. Return to the pot and cover to retain moisture.

3. Heat the water;
   go on to root vegetables.
5. Add the pasta to boiling water;
   check the cookies: turn over if ready;
   go on to kale.
8. Drain and rinse pasta;
   go back to soup.

Root Vegetables in Kuzu Sauce

Serves: 4
Time: 10 minutes; 25 minutes

1 medium daikon (7 to 8 inches)
1 tablespoon dark sesame oil
1 parsnip
2 burdock roots, washed and slivered
½ cup water
3 dried mushrooms (Shiitake)
1 cup water
1 tablespoon kuzu
2 tablespoons shoyu (natural soy sauce) or to taste
1 scallion, chopped

Scrub and dice the daikon. Heat oil in a 2-quart saucepan and sauté daikon over medium heat. Wash and dice the parsnip and add to daikon; scrub the burdock, shaving it as you would a pencil, and add to the vegetable mixture. Stir for 2 to 3 minutes, then reduce heat. Add ½ cup water, cover, and simmer for 20 minutes.
Discard the stems of the mushrooms and soak the caps in 1 cup water for 10 minutes (retain the soaking water). Slice the mushrooms caps into thin pieces and add to the simmering vegetables.
Dissolve the kuzu in the mushroom soaking water. When the vegetables are tender, stir in the kuzu, then raise heat to medium, and continue stirring until the sauce thickens. Add the shoyu and continue stirring for 2 to 3 minutes more. Ladle the sauce over spaghetti and serve garnished with chopped scallion.

4. Prepare root vegetables;
   return to pasta.

7. Add kuzu and finish vegetables;
   check cookies;
   go back to pasta.

Steamed Kale with Seeds

Serves: 4
Time: 5 minutes; 5 minutes

1 bunch kale
Water
Pinch of salt
¼ cup sunflower seeds, raw or roasted

6. Prepare the kale: return to root vegetables.

Wash and chop the kale; place the wet kale in a 2-quart saucepan with ½ inch water over medium heat. Sprinkle with salt and cover; when the kale starts to hiss, reduce heat, and steam for 2 minutes; then mix in the sunflower seeds, cover, and steam for 3 minutes more. If not served immediately, tilt the cover of the pan to allow steam to escape.

Breakfast

Cereal Puffs with Nut Milk

Serves: 4
Time: 5 minutes

½ cup almonds
½ cup cashews
4 cups water
5 cups puffed whole grain cereal (corn, millet, wheat, or rice)
Sweetener to taste

Place almonds, cashews, and 2 cups water in a blender at medium to high speed. Stop occasionally to allow the nuts to sink to the bottom; continue until mixture is thick and creamy. Add the remaining water (and sweetener if desired), blending well. Pour 2/3 cup over each serving of cereal or to taste.

Lunch

Bechamel Sauce

Serves: 4
Time: 10 minutes; 15 minutes

3 tablespoons corn oil
5 tablespoons whole wheat pastry flour
1½ cups boiling water
½ teaspoon sea salt or to taste

1. Make the bechamel sauce; go on to spaghetti.

Heat oil in a 1½-quart saucepan; in a larger pot, bring water to a boil. Add the flour to the heated oil and cook until it has a nut-like fragrance. Remove the flour from heat and slowly add boiling water while briskly beating the mixture with a wire whisk until thick and smooth; add the salt. Return the mixture to the heat, cover, and simmer for 15 minutes, stirring often. This method almost always produces a sauce without lumps.

Spaghetti and Vegetables au Gratin

Serves: 4
Time: 10 minutes; 20 minutes

3 cups cooked whole wheat spaghetti
Leftover root vegetables in kuzu sauce
Leftover kale
1 large grated onion
1½ cups bechamel sauce
½ cup brown bread crumbs

Preheat oven to 375°F. Combine the spaghetti, vegetables, and grated onion in a large mixing bowl, then transfer to a shallow, oiled baking dish. Cover with Bechamel Sauce and sprinkle with breadcrumbs. Bake for 20 minutes or until the crumbs are browned.

2. Prepare the spaghetti casserole and bake; move on to salad.

Coleslaw

Serves: 4
Time: 10 minutes

¼ head cabbage
1 teaspoon sea salt
½ cup carrot, coarsely grated

Shred the cabbage and sprinkle with salt; allow to stand for 10 minutes; grate the carrots. Squeeze the cabbage gently to express remaining water and, if desired, rinse lightly to remove most of the salt. Combine the cabbage and grated carrot in a salad bowl. Add Sesame Vinegar Dressing and toss lightly.

3. Prepare the coleslaw.

Sesame-Vinegar Dressing

Serves: 4
Time: 1 minute

1 tablespoon sesame oil
1 tablespoon rice vinegar

In a small bowl or jar, blend the ingredients well, then add to the salad. Since this is a strong-tasting dressing, use only enough to lightly moisten the salad.

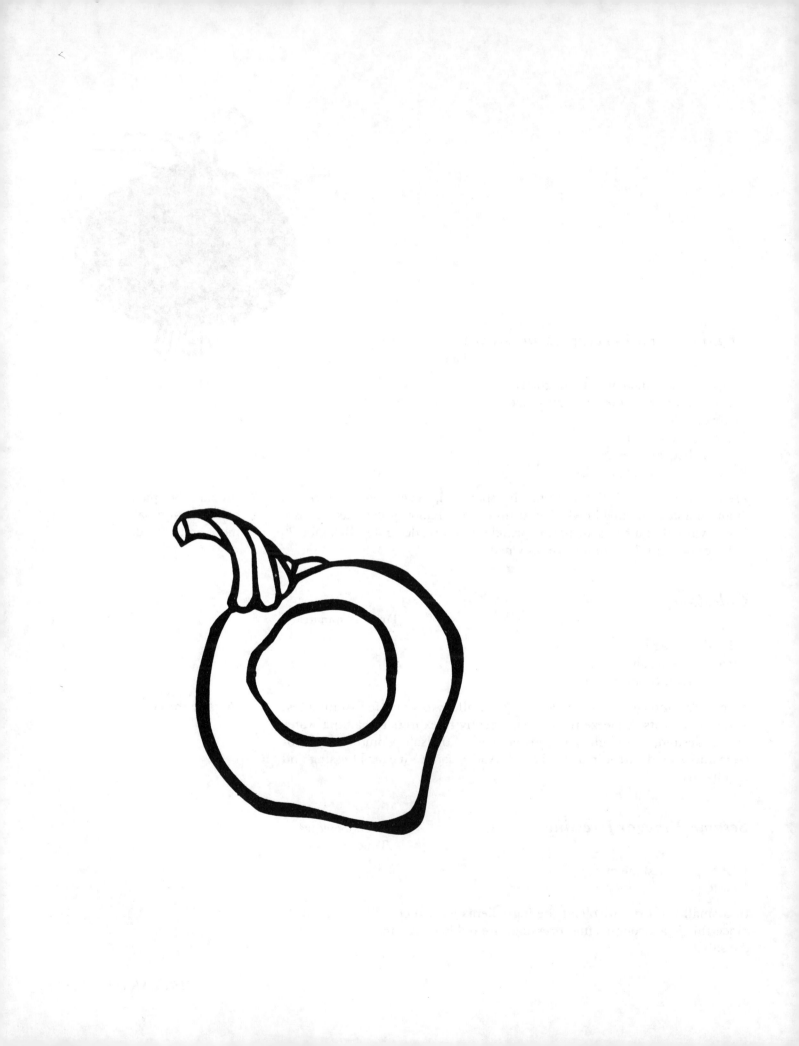

Dinner	*Breakfast*	*Lunch*
Millet Croquettes	Crêpes with Miso-Tahini	Clear Consommé
Baked Squash	or Tahini-Maple Spread	Millet with Fried
Green Salad with		Onions
Tofu-Ginger Dressing		Steamed Carrots
Tahini-Apple Custard		

Comments

You may want to make enough croquettes at dinnertime to use for lunch the following day, serving them either cold or reheated in a 375°F. oven for 10 minutes. Or you can switch menus and serve the millet with onions for dinner and the croquettes for lunch, thereby shortening the preparation time of dinner.

Almost everyone enjoys crêpes. Since they will take some time to prepare, make crêpes on weekends or whenever you don't have to leave the house early. Those on the breakfast menu can be filled with all kinds of sweet or salty fillings, or you can create a filling of your own. For a great brunch, set out a pile of crêpes along with a variety of fillings and allow everyone to roll their own.

Nutritional Values

Protein is obtained from the millet, whole wheat crust, and crêpes and is complemented by protein in the tofu, tahini, and miso. Vitamin A is obtained from the squash and carrots; the B-complex vitamin from the whole grains, squash, tahini, tofu, and carrots; and vitamin C from the salad, scallions, onions, and carrots. Calcium is provided by the squash, tofu, tahini, onions, and carrots; iron is found in the millet, greens, tofu, miso, tahini, and carrots.

Utensils

Dinner: Pressure cooker or 4-quart covered pot, skillet or heavy metal pan, wok for deep frying, baking dish or baking sheet, salad bowl, blender, fine grater, 2-quart saucepan, shallow baking pan, one large and one small bowl.

Breakfast: Blender or large mixing bowl, ladle, two 8- or 9-inch skillets, two small mixing bowls.

Lunch: Covered soup pot, skillet, 1½-quart covered saucepan, steamer basket (optional).

Dinner

Millet Croquettes

Serves: 4
Time: ½ hour; 40 minutes

3 cups millet
5 cups boiling water
1 teaspoon sea salt
1 large carrot, grated
1 large yellow onion, grated
Sesame or safflower oil for frying

1. Prepare millet and cook;
   go on to dessert.

Wash and drain the millet; dry-roast in a metal pan or skillet, stirring constantly until it begins to turn color and has a nut-like aroma. Place the millet, water, and salt in a pressure cooker and cook for 20 minutes. Or use a 4-quart pot with a cover and cook over low heat for 40 minutes.

4. Uncover millet and cool;
   go on to salad.

When the millet has finished cooking, spread it in a large, shallow baking pan and allow to cool.

6. Knead millet and shape
   croquettes;
   return to custard.

Place 3 cups of the cooked millet in a large bowl (reserve the rest for lunch); add grated carrot and onion. Squeeze and knead the mixture through your fingers for 5 minutes to make it sticky and mushy. Form into flat, 2-inch diameter patties, packing firmly and shaping well so the edges won't crack and allow oil to seep into the croquettes.

8. Fry the croquettes;
   while they fry, check
   squash.

Heat 2 inches of oil in a wok and deep-fry the croquettes for 8 to 10 minutes or until a crisp, light brown crust is formed. Drain on brown paper and warm in a 150°F. oven until ready to serve.

Tahini-Apple Custard

Serves: 4
Time: 15 minutes; 2 hours

1½ cups apple juice
½ cup water
4 tablespoons agar-agar flakes
1 teaspoon vanilla
1 tablespoon tahini
Roasted almonds

2. Prepare the custard and
   chill;
   move on to squash.

Combine the apple juice and water in a 2-quart saucepan; bring to a boil; stir in the agar-agar, then reduce heat and simmer for 5 minutes. Remove from heat and add the vanilla. Pour into a shallow pan and chill until set (1 hour in the freezer or two in the refrigerator).

7. Check custard (if set,
   finish preparing, otherwise continue chilling and
   check again while frying
   the croquettes);
   return to croquettes.

Remove from refrigerator and break up the agar-agar with a spatula. Place the pieces in a blender; purée at low speed until creamy, continually pushing contents of the blender down with a rubber spatula. Blend in the tahini and pour into individual custard cups. Serve garnished with almonds.

Baked Squash

Serves: 4
Time: 5 minutes; 1 hour

1 medium acorn squash
Sea salt
Corn oil

Preheat oven to 450°F. Cut the squash in half, scoop out the seeds, then cut into eighths. Place the pieces in a baking dish and sprinkle with salt and a few drops of oil. Bake face up for 1 hour or until the tips begin to char. Remove squash from oven and serve immediately.
NOTE: If desired, the seeds can be dried, then roasted and used as a condiment.

3. Bake the squash; return to millet.

9. Remove squash from oven when done.

Green Salad

Serves: 4
Time: 10 minutes

½ head leaf lettuce
1 bunch watercress
2 stalks celery

Wash the lettuce, pat dry, and cut into thin slices. Wash the watercress and cut the thick stems into small pieces. Wash the celery, and cut into thin slices on the diagonal. Combine the vegetables together in a salad bowl; toss lightly. Place in individual bowls and top with Tofu-Ginger Dressing.

5. Prepare the salad and dressing; return to millet.

Tofu-Ginger Dressing

Serves: 4
Time: 5 minutes

½ teaspoon fresh ginger, grated
1 8-ounce cake soft tofu
1 teaspoon sea salt
¼ cup water
2 tablespoons sesame oil
2 tablespoons brown rice vinegar

Grate the fresh ginger very fine. Combine the ingredients in a blender and purée until creamy.

Crêpes

Serves: 4
Time: 45 minutes; 15 minutes

2 cups water
1 egg
¼ teaspoon sea salt
2 cups whole wheat pastry flour
Oil

1. Prepare the batter; while it rests, go on to fillings.
3. Make the crêpes.

In the following order, place the water, egg, salt, and flour in a blender and blend at low speed for 2 to 3 minutes. Allow the mixture to stand for 15 minutes.

To hasten the cooking process, use two 8- or 9-inch skillets. Oil one of the skillets and place over medium heat; ladle ¼ cup batter into the center, tilting the skillet quickly in all directions so the batter spreads easily; repeat with the other skillet. Pour only enough batter to cover the bottom of each skillet so the crêpes will be light and thin. Cook for 4 minutes or until the edges begin to shrink, then lift the edge with a spatula and make sure the bottom is lightly browned. Flip the crêpe over, press down lightly with the spatula, and cook for 2 minutes more. Place crêpes on individual serving dishes. Spread filling over each crêpe, then roll and serve.

Miso-Tahini Spread I

Time: 10 minutes

¼ cup tahini
1 tablespoon brown rice miso
¼ cup water
Peel of 1 orange, grated

2. Prepare the fillings; return to crêpes.

In a small bowl, combine the tahini, miso, and water, mixing until creamy. Stir in the grated orange peel and serve.

Tahini-Maple Spread

Time: 5 minutes

¼ cup tahini
3 tablespoons maple syrup or to taste
¼ cup water

In a small bowl, blend the tahini and maple syrup until it thickens. Add water a little at a time until the mixture reaches the desired consistency.

Steamed Carrots

Serves: 4
Time: 15 minutes

1 pound carrots
½ cup water

Cut the carrots diagonally into thin slices. Combine the carrots and water in a 1-quart pot; cover, and steam over minimum heat for 10 to 12 minutes or until tender. A steamer basket may be used, but it is not essential.

1. Prepare the carrots; move on to millet.

Millet with Fried Onions

Serves: 4
Time: 10 minutes

¼ cup water
1 tablespoon shoyu (natural soy sauce)
2 medium yellow onions, chopped
1 tablespoon oil
2½ to 3 cups cooked millet
3 tablespoons fresh parsley

Combine the water and shoyu; chop the onions. Heat the oil in a skillet; add the chopped onions and sauté until light brown. Add the millet to the onions, then stir in the shoyu mixture, and heat thoroughly. Stir with a wooden spoon to break up any lumps.
Chop the parsley. Turn off heat under the onions and millet, and add the parsley, mixing well.

2. Fry the onions and add millet;
go on to soup.

4. Chop parsley and add to millet;
go back to soup.

Clear Consommé

Serves: 4
Time: 15 minutes

4 cups water
3-inch piece kombu seaweed
2 tablespoons shoyu (natural soy sauce) or to taste
Sea salt to taste
½ cake soft tofu (4 ounces)
1 handful watercress leaves

Combine the water and kombu in a soup pot and bring to a boil; reduce heat, cover, and simmer for 5 minutes. Add the shoyu and salt; discard the kombu. Cut the tofu into small cubes; add to the simmering stock, and cook for 5 minutes more.
Turn off heat under the soup; add the watercress. Allow the soup to stand for 1 minute before serving.

3. Prepare the soup; check carrots, then return to millet.

5. Turn off heat and add watercress.

Dinner	*Breakfast*	*Lunch*

Carrot Cream Soup
Couscous
Chickpeas
Ginger-Broiled Fish
Red Cabbage Salad with
  Princess Dressing
Apple Pie
	Couscous with Chickpeas
	Stir-fried Vegetables
		Fish Salad in Pita Bread
		  with Tahini-Lemon
		  Dressing

Comments

This dinner is an ideal one to serve guests no matter what their food preferences. Not only does it have something for everyone, but everything can be prepared in advance except the couscous and fish, each of which takes only 10 minutes to prepare. For a completely vegetarian meal, omit the fish; the meal will remain a balanced one. If you also omit the fish salad for lunch, prepare oatmeal for breakfast and use the breakfast menu for lunch.

Couscous is a wheat product also known as *semolina*. It is not a whole grain, therefore, it should be used as a complement or special occasion dish, and not as a major protein source. Couscous traditionally is served with chickpeas to provide complementary protein.

Nutritional Values

Complete protein is obtained from the fish and complementary proteins from the couscous and chickpeas; abundant vitamin A from the carrots, parsley, and chicory; the B-complex vitamin from the fish, chickpeas, carrots, pie crust, bread, and couscous; and vitamin C from the parsley, red cabbage, chicory, apples, lemon juice, and sprouts. Calcium is supplied by the chickpeas, chicory, parsley, kuzu, and tahini; and iron by the chickpeas, fish, chicory, raisins, and tahini.

Utensils

Dinner: Two 3-quart covered pots, pressure cooker, shallow baking pan, salad bowl, jar or cruet, fine grater, large bowl, rolling pin, wax paper, 9-inch pie plate, blender, 1½-quart saucepan.

Breakfast: 2-quart saucepan, covered skillet or wok.

Lunch: One large and one small mixing bowl.

Dinner

Chickpeas

Serves: 4
Time: Soaking time plus 1 hour

2 cups dried chickpeas
6 cups water
½ teaspoon sea salt (optional)

1. Soak the chickpeas 2 to 6 hours, depending on process used. Start the chickpeas 1½ hours before serving;
go on to pie.

Wash chickpeas and pick out any stones. Soak for 8 hours in cold water; or bring the beans and water to a boil, cook for 2 minutes, turn off heat, and soak for 2 hours. After the beans have swelled, add enough water to cover; cook in a pressure cooker for 50 minutes or simmer on the stove for 1½ to 2 hours. Add the salt 10 minutes before the beans have finished cooking. Pour off excess water before serving. (If desired, reserve the water for making soups.)

Apple Pie

Serves: 4
Time: 20 minutes; 40 minutes

CRUST:

3 cups whole wheat pastry flour
1 cup rolled oats
¼ teaspoon sea salt
½ cup corn oil
½ to ¾ cup apple juice

2. Prepare the pie crust;
move on to soup.

Combine the flour, oats, salt, and oil in a large bowl. Stir with chopsticks or a fork, then rub the mixture between your hands until it looks like wet sand. Add the apple juice and mix quickly without kneading to form a wettish ball. Allow the dough to rest uncovered for 15 minutes; it will dry and become firm.

5. Roll out and bake crust;
go on to apple filling.

Preheat oven to 375°. Divide the dough in half and roll one of the halves between 2 sheets of wax paper. Peel off the top paper and invert an oiled pie plate over the dough; slip one hand under the papered side of the dough and gently turn over dough and pie plate. Peel off the paper and fit the dough into the pie plate, trimming off any excess. Decorate the edge by fluting with a fork or pinching the dough between the thumb and two fingers; prick the bottom of the crust with a fork. Bake for 10 minutes.

8. Roll out top crust, fill pie, and bake;
go on to salad.

Roll out the top crust for the pie. Fill the pie shell with the apples. Pour in the raisin sauce and cover with the top crust, fluting the edges with a fork. Poke several small holes in the top to allow steam to escape. Bake at 350°F. for 35 to 40 minutes. Allow to cool before serving.

FILLING:

3 pounds apples, Golden Delicious or McIntosh
1 tablespoon lemon juice
1 cup raisins
1 cup apple juice

1 teaspoon vanilla
1 teaspoon cinnamon
1½ tablespoon kuzu dissolved in ½ cup water

Wash, quarter, and core the apples; slice the quarters into twelfths and sprinkle with lemon juice to keep the apples from turning brown. Combine the raisins, apple juice, vanilla, and cinnamon in a small saucepan and simmer for 5 minutes or until the raisins swell.
Add the dissolved kuzu to the raisin mixture, stirring constantly over medium heat until it thickens.

6. Start the apple filling: check crust, if cooked, remove from oven.

7. Continue with filling; move on to top crust.

Carrot Cream Soup

Serves: 4
Time: 10 minutes; 20 minutes

1 pound carrots
1 medium onion
2 tablespoons corn oil
6 cups water
½ teaspoon sea salt
1 handful of fresh parsley, chopped

Chop carrots and onion into chunks. Heat the oil in a 3-quart pot and sauté the onions for 2 to 3 minutes or until just wilted; stir in the carrots. Add the water and salt* and bring to a boil; reduce heat, cover, and simmer for 20 minutes or until carrots are soft.
Pour the soup into a blender and purée, then transfer back to the pan and reheat.
Chop the parsley. Pour the soup into individual serving bowls and garnish with ½ teaspoon of parsley.
*NOTE: The soup should not be salty, or it will lose its delicate flavor.

3. Prepare the soup; go on to fish.

11. Purée the soup; check the pie.

15. Chop parsley for soup; remove fish when done.

Ginger-Broiled Fish

Serves: 4
Time: 10 minutes; 40 minutes

3 pounds fresh fillets (scrod, bluefish, et cetera)
2 tablespoons shoyu (natural soy sauce)
2 tablespoons water
2 tablespoons sesame oil
1 teaspoon freshly grated ginger
Parsley sprigs

Wash and dry the fillets and place in a shallow baking dish. Combine the rest of the ingredients except the parsley, mixing well. Pour over the fish and marinate for 30 minutes or longer.
Ten minutes before serving time, preheat the broiler and broil the marinated fish until done. If the fillet is very thick, it may need to be turned over one time. Serve medium-sized portions (3 to 4 ounces) garnished with parsley.

4. Marinate fish; return to pie.

13. Broil fish; go on to salad.

Red Cabbage Salad

Serves: 4
Time: 10 minutes; 30 minutes

½ head red cabbage
1½ teaspoons sea salt
¼ head chicory, chopped
2 stalks celery, chopped

9. Prepare salad and
   dressing;
   move on to couscous.

14. Toss the salad with
    dressing;
    return to soup.

Shred cabbage very fine; sprinkle with salt, mixing well, and allow to stand ½ hour. Chop the chicory and celery. When the cabbage is ready, squeeze gently to express any remaining water, and, if desired, rinse lightly with water to remove the salt; drain well. Place the cabbage in a salad bowl; add the chicory and celery.
Toss the salad with Princess Dressing and serve.

Princess Dressing

Time: 3 minutes

Juice of 1 lemon (4 tablespoons)
2 tablespoons shoyu (natural soy sauce)
2 tablespoons unrefined corn oil

Combine the ingredients in a cruet or jar and shake vigorously.

Couscous

Serves: 4
Time: 5 minutes; 15 minutes

3 cups couscous
1 tablespoon olive oil
2-inch piece kombu seaweed
5 small dried fish* (optional)
4¾ cups water
1 tablespoon shoyu (natural soy sauce)
½ teaspoon sea salt or to taste

10. Prepare the couscous and
    stock;
    return to soup.

12. Ten minutes before serv-
    ing, pour boiling stock
    over couscous and cover;
    go back to fish.

Place the couscous in a large bowl, sprinkle with the oil, then rub the mixture quickly between your hands to coat all the grains with oil. Transfer the couscous to a serving dish and set aside. Combine the kombu, fish, and water in a 2-quart pot; bring to a boil, reduce heat, and simmer for 5 minutes. Season the stock with the shoyu and salt, then strain, and pour back into the cooking pot. Since the couscous will absorb most of the flavor, the stock should be strong tasting.
Ten minutes before serving, bring the stock to a boil, then pour over the couscous. Cover, and allow the couscous to swell for 10 to 15 minutes. Toss gently with a rice paddle or chopsticks to prevent lumps.
* *Chuba Iriko*, obtainable in Japanese food stores.

Couscous with Chickpeas

Serves: 4
Time: 6 minutes

1 cup cooked chickpeas
½ cup chickpea water
2 cups cooked couscous
½ teaspoon shoyu (natural soy sauce)

Place the chickpeas and water in a 2-quart saucepan over low heat; arrange the couscous on top. When the water starts to steam, mix the ingredients together. Add shoyu; cover, and heat for 5 minutes.

Stir-Fried Vegetables

Serves: 4
Time: 10 minutes; 5 minutes

1 teaspoon sesame oil
¼ head red cabbage, chopped
2 stalks celery, chopped
¼ head chicory, chopped
1 teaspoon brown rice vinegar
1 teaspoon shoyu (natural soy sauce)
1 tablespoon water

Wash and chop the vegetables. Heat the oil in a skillet or wok over medium heat; add the cabbage, celery, and chicory in that order, stirring well after each addition. Combine the vinegar, shoyu, and water; sprinkle over the vegetables. Cover and steam for 5 minutes.

Fish Salad in Pita Bread

Serves: 4
Time: 5 minutes

2 tablespoons parsley
3 scallions
1 cup watercress
1 tablespoon red pepper
1½ cups cooked fish
4 or 5 whole wheat pita breads
Alfalfa sprouts
Lettuce leaves

Chop the parsley, scallions, watercress, and red pepper. With a fork, flake the fish into a large bowl; add the chopped vegetables and mix well. Moisten with Tahini-Lemon Dressing to loosely hold the mixture together. Cut pita breads in half; stuff each half with 2 heaping tablespoons of the fish salad and top with sprouts. Serve 2 halves per person on a bed of lettuce.

Tahini-Lemon Dressing

Serves: 4
Time: 5 minutes

4 tablespoons tahini
4 tablespoons lemon juice (one lemon)
4 tablespoons water
¼ teaspoon salt or to taste

Combine the tahini and lemon juice in a small bowl, mixing well. Add water by the spoonful and blend until creamy; add the salt and use immediately.

Winter Meals

	Dinner	Breakfast	Lunch
Menu No. 1 PAGE 105	*Polish Mushroom Soup* *Bay Rice* *Aduki-Squash Stew* *Broccoli Bravado* *Apple Mousse*	*Kasha Cream with* *Sunflower Seeds*	*Rice and Beans with* *Mushroom Sauce* *Steamed Watercress*
Menu No. 2 PAGE 111	*Oden Stew* *Kasha-Rice* *Sauerkraut* *Baked Apples*	*Oden-Miso Soup* *Garlic Toast*	*Sauerkraut Casserole* *Chicory with Scallions*
Menu No. 3 PAGE 117	*Russian Soup* *Chapati (Flatbread)* *Miso-Tahini Spread* *Chicory Salad with* * Umeboshi Horse-* * radish Dressing*	*Puffed Corn Bread* *with Prune Butter*	*Baked Stuffed Calabaza* * or Pumpkin* *Steamed Broccoli* * with Pumpkin Seeds*
Menu No. 4 PAGE 123	*Millet Casserole* *Baked Squash and Turnips* *Turnip Greens Gomasio* *Coconut-Spice Cookies*	*Cracked Wheat with* *Walnuts and Raisins*	*Vegetable Soup with* * Millet* *Whole Grain Bread with* * Tofu-Miso Spread*
Menu No. 5 PAGE 129	*Lentil Soup* *Queen Yam Casserole* *Barley-Rice* *Celery Tarragon* *Apples Glacé*	*Oats with Shoyu* *(Natural Soy Sauce)*	*Cream of Vegetable Soup* *Rice-Lentil Loaf with* * Scallion-Kuzu Sauce* *Dill Pickles*
Menu No. 6 PAGE 135	*Roasted Sunflower Seeds* *Caraway Millet* *French Carrots* *Stuffed Fish Fillets* *Watercress Salad with* * Lemon-Mustard Dressing* *Hot Fruit Compote*	*Hot Peanut-Kuzu Cream* *with Stewed Fruit*	*Millet and Carrots* *Daikon with Miso*

Dinner	*Breakfast*	*Lunch*
Polish Mushroom Soup	*Kasha Cream*	*Rice and Beans with*
Bay Rice	*Sunflower Seeds*	*Mushroom Sauce*
	Aduki-Squash Stew	*Steamed Watercress*
Broccoli Bravado		
Apple Mousse		

Comments

The most important aspect of a winter meal is that it provides warmth. Although we live in heated houses, we still have to venture out into the cold and our bodies have to adjust quickly to the extreme change. Hearty meals that require longer cooking are the most effective protection against cold weather. Therefore, with a vegetarian regime, it is advisable to emphasize grains, beans, and vegetables such as roots and squash and to reduce the proportion of salads and fruits. The use of sea salt, miso and shoyu (natural soy sauce) will provide the weight and heartiness usually supplied by animal protein foods.

The dinner in this menu set is a hefty one; it will take a bit longer to prepare than the others because the soup requires work; if you're in a hurry, omit it. The rest of the dinner can be made within 1½ hours without undue effort.

Nutritional Values

The rice and aduki beans provide a complete protein combination, as do the kasha and sunflower seeds. Vitamin A is obtained from the squash, broccoli, and watercress; the B-complex vitamins from the mushrooms, grains, aduki beans, squash, kasha, sunflower seeds, and apples; and vitamin C from the broccoli, scallions, watercress, and apples. Calcium is supplied by the seeds, broccoli, kombu, and watercress; and iron by the rice, beans, kombu, kasha, kuzu, sunflower seeds, broccoli, and watercress.

Utensils

Dinner: Two 3-quart covered saucepans, 2-quart covered saucepan, 2-quart soup pot; 1½-quart saucepan, 4-quart pressure cooker, garlic press, wire whisk, slotted spoon, suribachi or mortar, fine grater.

Breakfast: Blender, coffee mill or hand mill, 2-quart covered saucepan.

Lunch: 1½-quart saucepan, two 2- or 3-quart pots, blender.

Polish Mushroom Soup

Serves: 4

Time: 15 to 20 minutes; 1 hour, 10 minutes

STOCK:
1 cup vegetables trimmings (onion skins especially, carrots,
   celery, cabbage leaves, parsley stems, et cetera)
6½ cups water

1. Prepare the stock; go on to aduki beans.

Place the vegetable trimmings and water in a 2-quart pot; bring to a boil, reduce heat, cover, and simmer for 30 minutes. Strain the stock, pressing all the liquid from the vegetable trimmings; return to pot.

6 cups vegetable stock
1 ounce dry, imported mushrooms (available in supermarkets)
1 bunch scallions
3 tablespoons corn oil
1 clove garlic
3 tablespoons whole wheat pastry flour
½ teaspoon sea salt
1 tablespoon shoyu (natural soy sauce) or to taste
1 handful of parsley, chopped

6. Chop and cook mushrooms; return to mousse.

8. Finish soup; move on to broccoli.

Heat the stock over medium heat; rinse and chop the mushrooms (no soaking necessary) and add to the stock; reduce heat and simmer for 30 minutes.

Chop the scallions, then heat the oil in a 3-quart saucepan over medium heat. Squeeze the garlic through a garlic press into the hot oil (or add it finely minced). When the garlic sizzles, add the scallions and stir for 3 to 4 minutes or until the scallions wilt; add the flour and continue stirring until the mixture has a nut-like aroma. Now slowly pour the hot stock into the flour mixture, beating with a wire whisk. Add the salt and shoyu; reduce heat, cover, and simmer for 10 minutes, stirring occasionally.

10. Chop parsley for the soup.

Serve the soup garnished with chopped parsley.

Aduki-Squash Stew

Serves: 4

Time: 5 minutes; 1¼ hours

1½ cups aduki beans, washed
5 cups water
3-inch piece kombu seaweed
1 small butternut squash (2 cups)
Shoyu (natural soy sauce) to taste

2. Start beans; move on to rice.

5. Cut up squash and add to beans; return to soup.

Place the beans, water, and kombu in a 2-quart pot and bring to a boil; reduce heat, cover, and simmer for 30 minutes.

Chop the squash into small chunks, discarding the seeds; arrange on top of the beans (make sure the beans are still covered with water), and continue cooking for another 30 minutes. Using a wooden spoon, mix the squash into the beans; add the shoyu, and cook for 15 minutes more. Ladle the bean mixture into serving bowls with a slotted spoon.

Bay Rice

Serves: 4
Time: 5 minutes; 45 minutes

3 cups short grain brown rice
5 cups water
1 bay leaf
1 teaspoon sea salt or to taste

Wash the rice by swirling it in a pot with water to cover; then strain through a fine mesh strainer. Dry-roast the rice in a 4-quart pressure cooker over medium-high heat, stirring constantly until it begins to turn color and has a nut-like aroma. Add the water, bay leaf, and salt; reduce to low heat, cover, bring to pressure, and cook for 40 minutes. (To cook in a regular pot, add ½ cup water and simmer covered over minimum heat for 1 hour and 10 minutes.)

3. Cook rice;
   go on to mousse.

Apple Mousse

Serves: 4
Time: 10 minutes; 30 minutes

3 pounds McIntosh apples
½ cup water
1 tablespoon vanilla
Grated rind of ½ lemon
A pinch of sea salt (optional)
3 tablespoons kuzu
½ cup water
Chopped roasted almonds

Peel, quarter, and core the apples. Place the pieces in a 3-quart covered pot with the water; cook over low heat for 20 minutes or until the apples fall apart. Stir occasionally to break up the pieces.
Add the vanilla and lemon rind to the apples; add salt if the apples are tart. Dissolve the kuzu or arrowroot in water and add to the apples, stirring constantly until mixture thickens and comes to a boil; then continue stirring for 2 minutes more. Remove from heat and allow to cool. Serve individual portions garnished with almonds.

4. Cook apples:
   return to beans.

7. Finish the mousse;
   go back to soup.

Broccoli Bravado

Serves: 4
Time: 10 minutes; 12 minutes

1 bunch broccoli
1 tablespoon oil
½ cup water
2 tablespoons roasted sesame seeds or sesame salt

9. **Prepare** the broccoli; return to soup.

Slice ½ inch from the bottom of the broccoli stalks; peel off the tough skin. Cut the broccoli flowerettes from the stems and chop the stems into fine pieces. Heat the oil in a 1½-quart saucepan, and sauté stems for 2 minutes; add the water, reduce heat to minimum, cover, and cook for 3 minutes. Now arrange the flowerettes on top of the stems; cover and steam for 5 minutes more or until broccoli is bright green. Lightly grind the sesame seeds in a mortar or suribachi. Transfer the broccoli to a serving platter and toss with the seeds. Serve immediately.

Breakfast

Kasha Cream with Sunflower Seeds

Serves: 4
Time: 5 minutes; 15 minutes

1 cup kasha (buckwheat groats)
4 cups water (or more for thinner consistency)
½ teaspoon sea salt
½ cup sunflower seeds
Shoyu (natural soy sauce) to taste

Grind the kasha in a blender, a coffee mill, or handmill. In a 2-quart saucepan, blend the kasha with 1 cup water until smooth, then add the remaining water and salt. Bring to a simmer, stirring constantly until it thickens. Cover and simmer for 15 minutes, stirring occasionally and adding water as needed. When the kasha has finished cooking, add the sunflower seeds and serve. Allow each person to season individual portions with shoyu to taste.

Rice and Beans with Mushroom Sauce

Serves: 4
Time: 5 minutes; 7 minutes

MUSHROOM SAUCE:

1 cup Polish mushroom soup
1 tablespoon rolled oats
1 tablespoon shoyu (natural soy sauce) or to taste
1 tablespoon tahini
½ teaspoon fresh grated ginger or horseradish

Place the soup and oats in a blender and purée until creamy; pour into a 1½-quart saucepan, and bring to a simmer; cook for 7 minutes, stirring constantly. Add the shoyu and ginger or horseradish. Turn off heat and stir in the tahini.

1. Make the sauce; go on to rice.

3 cups cooked rice
1 cup aduki-squash stew

In a 2- or 3-quart saucepan, combine the rice and aduki stew, mixing well. Warm thoroughly over low heat, stirring occasionally. Serve topped with Mushroom Sauce.

2. Prepare rice and beans; move on to watercress.

Steamed Watercress

Serves: 4
Time: 5 minutes

1 bunch watercress
3 tablespoons water

Take the watercress in one hand and wring with the other hand to break it in half; wash under cold running water. Place the wet watercress in a 1-quart saucepan; add water, cover, and cook over low heat for 3 to 4 minutes or until steam begins to escape from the pot and the watercress turns bright green. Serve immediately.

3. Cook the watercress.

Dinner	*Breakfast*	*Lunch*
Oden Stew	Oden-Miso Soup	Sauerkraut Casserole
Kasha-Rice	Garlic Toast	Chicory with Scallions
Sauerkraut		
Baked Apples		

Comments

Sauerkraut requires 10 days to 2 weeks to sour, therefore, you may want to prepare some at your leisure and keep it on hand. Sauerkraut is called for on the dinner menu, but it can be replaced with any green salad.

The oden stew, made only with root vegetables, is a strong, hearty dish that will warm you on a cold day. Some of the root vegetables suggested may not be available, but the stew also can be made with onions, carrots, turnips, parsnips, white or icicle radishes, and rutabaga or yellow turnip, all of which are carried by most supermarkets. Burdock may be the only root that is hard to find, but make the attempt because it makes a difference in the taste of the stew. Look for it in oriental food stores and health food stores that sell produce. Since it grows wild, it can be dug up from a field or garden if you recognize it when you see it. Some people say that burdock imparts its own hardiness and resistance to cold weather to those who eat it regularly.

The kasha-rice, incidentally, is a quick and easy way to extend your rice if you don't have enough for the meal at hand.

Nutritional Values

Protein is obtained from the kasha, rice, and root vegetables and is complemented by the protein in the tofu, miso, and sunflower seeds; vitamin A is provided by the stew and chicory; the B-complex vitamin by the grains, toast, vegetables, and apples; and vitamin C by the sauerkraut, parsley, and chicory. Calcium is supplied by the vegetables, sunflower seeds, and tofu; and iron by the stew, miso, chicory, and tofu.

Utensils

Dinner: 4-quart covered pot, wok for deep frying, 3-quart covered saucepan, 9-inch shallow baking dish, candy or deep fry thermometer, pickling setup for the sauerkraut, large crock or bowl with inside-fitting cover or plate and 10-pound weights.

Breakfast: 2-quart covered saucepan, pastry brush.

Lunch: 2-quart covered casserole dish, large bowl, 2-quart covered saucepan.

Dinner

Sauerkraut

Time: 15 minutes; 10 to 12 days

1 head white cabbage (8 cups)
8 teaspoons sea salt
1 tablespoon caraway seeds (optional)

1. Allow the sauerkraut 10 to 14 days to pickle.

Remove loose, green, outer leaves of the cabbage; rinse and quarter. Cut away the core and shred very fine crosswise. Spread a layer of cabbage (1 cup) on the bottom of a large earthenware crock, or glass or enamel bowl; sprinkle with 1 teaspoon salt and a few caraway seeds. Continue adding layers of cabbage, salt, and seeds and finish with a layer of salt. Press the cabbage down with a plate or cover that fits snugly inside the container. Place 10 pound stones or other well washed weights on top of the cover and allow the cabbage to stand undisturbed for at least 10 days—longer if you like strong sauerkraut. On the second day, check to make sure that the water drawn out by the salt has risen about 1 inch above the cabbage; if, for lack of pressure, it has not risen, add enough salted water (ratio: 1 teaspoon salt to 1 cup water) to reach that level. If the cabbage is not covered completely by water, it will decay. Formation of mold on the surface is normal; skim it off every three days or so with chopsticks or a slotted spoon.

Oden Stew

Serves: 6
Time: 20 minutes; 40 minutes

1 medium-sized yellow onion
2 tablespoons sesame oil
2 carrots
1 parsnip
1 white turnip
1 rutabaga, peeled
1 cup radish (white, black or daikon)
1 parsley root with top (reserve the greens)
2 burdock roots
1½ cups water
Fried tofu (see below)
3 tablespoons shoyu (natural soy sauce) or to taste

3. Make the stew;
go on to kasha-rice.

Peel and chop the onion. In a 4-quart pot, heat the oil over low heat and add the onion: as the onion sautés, dice and add the remaining vegetables in the order given, stirring well after each addition. The burdock should be slivered as if shaving a pencil. After all the vegetables have been added, pour in the water, cover, and simmer over low heat while preparing the fried tofu.

9. Finish the stew.

Add the fried tofu and the shoyu to the stew; continue to simmer for 10 minutes longer. Chop the reserved parsley greens and add to the stew just before serving.

Fried Tofu

Time: 15 minutes

Two 8-ounce cakes tofu
Oil for deep frying (sesame or safflower)

Press the tofu between two layers of cloth or paper toweling to remove excess water. Slice tofu in half, then crosswise in ¼-inch pieces. Heat 2 cups of oil in a wok until the oil starts to move or until it registers 290–300°F. on a candy thermometer. (If the oil is too hot the watery tofu will splatter excessively.)

Gently lower tofu pieces into the oil and fry for 10 to 15 minutes or until browned, turning once. Drain on brown paper.

5. Press the tofu and heat the oil;
return to kasha.

7. Fry the tofu;
check the kasha.

Baked Apples

Serves: 4
Time: 10 minutes; 30 minutes

4 red baking apples
15 to 20 raisins
10 almonds
Cinnamon to taste
1½ cups water

Preheat oven to 400°F. Wash the apples, then remove the cores, without cutting through the bottoms of the apples. Slit the skin around the middle of each apple to prevent bursting while they bake; place in a 9-inch shallow baking dish. Stuff each apple with 3 or 4 raisins and 2 almonds; sprinkle with cinnamon and fill with water. Pour the remaining water into baking dish to cover the bottom with ½ inch of water. Bake for 30 minutes or until apples are soft inside. Serve at room temperature or chill.

2. 1½ hours before serving, prepare and bake apples;
go on to stew.

Kasha-Rice

Serves: 4
Time: 5 minutes; 15 minutes

2 cups water
½ teaspoon sea salt or to taste
1 cup whole kasha
3 to 4 cups cooked rice

Bring the water to a boil in a 3-quart saucepan.
Add the salt to the boiling water, and pour in the kasha; reduce heat, cover, and cook for 10 to 12 minutes or until fluffy.
Add the cooked rice to the kasha; mix well, and heat thoroughly.

4. Put water on to boil;
return to stew, check apples.

6. Pour kasha in the water;
return to tofu.

8. When done, mix kasha and rice;
return to stew.

Oden-Miso Soup

Serves: 4
Time: 15 minutes

3 cups oden stew
2 cups water
1 handful parsley
1 tablespoon miso or to taste
½ cup water

In a 2-quart saucepan, bring the stew and water to a boil; reduce heat, cover, and simmer for 10 minutes to allow the flavors to blend.
Chop the parsley. Dissolve the miso in the water and add to the soup; simmer for 30 seconds more. Serve hot with chopped parsley on top and garlic toast on the side.

Garlic Toast

Time: 10 minutes; 8 to 10 minutes

10 slices whole grain bread
1 or 2 tablespoons corn or olive oil
1 or 2 cloves garlic, peeled

Brush one side of each slice lightly with oil. Toast in 375°F. oven until medium brown and crunchy, then rub with garlic.

Sauerkraut Casserole

Serves: 4
Time: 3 minutes; 20 minutes

3 cups cooked rice-kasha
1 cup sauerkraut
½ cup sunflower seeds
2 tablespoons chopped parsley

Preheat oven to 350°F. Combine the ingredients in a large bowl, mixing well. Spoon the mixture into an oiled, 2-quart casserole dish. Cover and bake for 20 minutes.

Chicory with Scallions

Serves: 4
Time: 7 minutes

1 bunch chicory
6 scallions, whites and greens
1 tablespoon corn or sesame oil
¼ teaspoon sea salt or to taste

Separate the leaves of the chicory and wash thoroughly; shake off the excess water and slice crosswise into thin pieces. Chop the scallions. In a 2-quart saucepan, warm the oil over medium heat and add the scallions, allowing them to sauté for 2 minutes. Stir in the chicory and sprinkle with salt. Cook, uncovered, for 4 to 5 minutes, stirring occasionally, until the chicory wilts. Serve immediately.

Dinner	*Breakfast*	*Lunch*

Russian Soup
Chapati (Flatbread)
Miso-Tahini Spread
Chicory Salad with Umeboshi-
  Horseradish Dressing

Puffed Corn Bread with
  Prune Butter

Baked Stuffed
  Calabaza or Pumpkin
Steamed Broccoli
  with Pumpkin Seeds

Comments

The Russian soup, a very hearty, all-in-one-pot dish, is balanced by the crunchy, round chapati and the crisp cool salad. This soup can easily be made in large amounts and is an ideal food for buffet parties or large families.

Lunch is a bit more elaborate than usual in this menu set, but the baked calabaza is simple to prepare and fun to serve at any time.

Nutritional Values

Protein is obtained from the barley and beans in the soup, miso-tahini spread, bread, cornbread, and pumpkin seeds; vitamin A from the chicory, prune butter, pumpkin, and broccoli; the B-complex by the grains, seeds, cornbread, and in varying amounts in all the vegetables; and vitamin C from the chicory and broccoli. Calcium is supplied by the tahini, chicory, eggs, broccoli, prunes, and both pumpkin and pumpkin seeds; and iron by the beans, miso-tahini spread, eggs, prune butter, and barley.

Utensils

Dinner: Two 2-quart covered pots, 4- to 6-quart pot, skillet or sautéing pan, one large and one small mixing bowl, baking sheet, 9-inch skillet or small saucepan, blender or suribachi.

Breakfast: 9-inch cast-iron skillet or pie plate, 1½-quart saucepan, blender, wire whisk or egg beater, two large mixing bowls.

Lunch: Shallow baking pan, 1½-quart saucepan, 2-quart pot.

Dinner

Russian Soup

½ cup chick peas (garbanzos)
½ cup kidney beans
1 cup barley
8 cups water
1 onion
1 carrot
1 turnip
¼ small head cabbage, shredded
2 tablespoons corn or sesame oil
1 teaspoon sea salt
2 tablespoons shoyu (natural soy sauce) or to taste
1 handful parsley, chopped

1. Soak beans and chickpeas 6 to 8 hours beforehand. Or bring to a boil for 2 minutes, and allow to soak for 2 hours.

Wash the beans and chickpeas separately, then soak each separately in 2 cups cold water for 8 hours; or bring to a boil, simmer for 2 minutes, and allow to soak in the warm water for 2 hours.

2. 1½ hours before serving, cook beans and chickpeas separately for 40 minutes; go on to chapati.

Drain beans; add fresh water to cover. Bring the beans and chickpeas to a boil; reduce heat, cover and simmer for 30 minutes. Then combine the beans and chickpeas with their cooking water in a 4- to 6-quart pot. Add the barley and remaining 4 cups of water; cover and bring to a simmer, cooking for 40 minutes. (Reserve 1½ to 2 cups of the beans and barley mixture for the pumpkin stuffing at lunch.)

4. Prepare the rest of the soup; go back to chapati.

Chop the onion, dice the carrot and turnip, and shred the cabbage. Heat the oil in a large skillet over medium heat; add the onion and sauté, then add the rest of the vegetables, stirring well after each addition. Continue to sauté for 10 to 15 minutes. Now stir the vegetable mixture into the beans and barley; add more water if needed, and simmer for 25 minutes. Season with the salt and shoyu, and simmer for 10 minutes more.

9. Chop parsley for soup.

Garnish the soup with chopped parsley and serve.

Miso-Tahini Spread II

½ cup tahini (sesame paste)
½ teaspoon marjoram
1 tablespoon barley miso
¼ cup water
1 tablespoon grated onion

6. Roast the tahini; while it cools, go to salad.

In a small saucepan, roast the tahini, stirring constantly until it turns the color of light coffee. Add the marjoram and continue stirring for 6 to 8 minutes, scraping the tahini off the bottom of the pan to avoid burning. Remove from heat and cool.

8. Finish the spread; go back to soup.

Dissolve the miso in the water; add grated onion and gently mix into the tahini. If the mixture curdles, add extra water, a tablespoon at a time, until it is smooth. Refrigerated, this spread will keep for 3 to 4 days.

Chapati (Flatbread)

Serves: 4
Time: 15 minutes; 25 minutes

1 cup water
1 tablespoon corn oil
½ teaspoon sea salt
3 to 4 cups whole wheat flour

Combine the water, oil, and salt in a large mixing bowl. Add the flour gradually, stirring with a wooden spoon until the batter is too thick to stir. Continue to add the flour, working it in with your hands until a soft dough forms. Turn the dough onto a floured board and knead vigorously; add flour if the dough is sticky; continue working the dough with the hands until it feels resilient and smooth (like the earlobe) and no longer sticks to the fingers when pinched.

Preheat oven to 375°F. Form the dough into 2-inch balls; flatten these into 4- to 5-inch circles either by hand or with a rolling pin. Make sure all the circles are of the same thickness to insure even baking. Place on an oiled baking sheet and bake for 15 minutes.

3. Make the chapati; return to soup.

Turn over the chapati and continue baking for 10 to 15 minutes more or until they sound hollow when tapped and are very lightly browned.

5. Turn over chapati; go on to spread.

Chicory Salad

Serves: 4
Time: 10 minutes

½ bunch chicory
2 stalks celery
4 radishes

Wash the chicory, separating all the leaves, then cut crosswise into thin slices. Cut the celery diagonally into thin pieces and add to the chicory; slice the radishes. Combine the vegetables in a salad bowl and toss well. Top individual servings with Umeboshi-Horseradish Dressing.

7. Prepare the salad and dressing; check chapati and remove from oven when done.

Umeboshi-Horseradish Dressing

2/3 cup water
2 umeboshi plums (pitted)
3 tablespoons olive oil
1 tablespoon fresh, grated horseradish

Combine the ingredients in a blender and purée for 2 minutes, or grind in a suribachi or mortar. Serve 1 or 2 tablespoons over individual servings of salad.

Prune Butter

Serves: 4
Time: 10 minutes; overnight

1½ cups pitted prunes
3 cups water

1. Soak prunes overnight.
2. Cook prunes;
   go to cornbread.
4. Finish the prune butter.

Combine the prunes and water in a saucepan and soak overnight.
The next morning, add water to cover and simmer for 10 minutes. Retain the cooking water.
Pit the prunes if necessary, then place in a blender with 2 or 3 tablespoons of cooking water and purée until smooth.

Puffed Corn Bread

Time: 10 minutes; 20 minutes

5 eggs, separated
½ cup water
½ teaspoon sea salt or to taste
2 cups stone ground cornmeal
Oil for skillet

3. Prepare the cornbread and bake;
   return to prunes.

Combine the egg yolks and water in a large mixing bowl, beating well with an egg beater or wire whisk until frothy. Add the salt, stir in the cornmeal, and allow to stand uncovered.
Preheat oven to 400°F. In a small bowl, beat the egg-whites until they stand in stiff peaks; gently fold the egg whites into the batter with a rubber spatula. Heat a 9-inch, oiled cast-iron skillet; pour the batter into the middle so it spreads evenly towards the sides. Immediately place the skillet in the oven and bake for 20 to 25 minutes or until puffy.

Baked Stuffed Calabaza or Pumpkin

Serves: 4
Time: 15 minutes; 1 hour

1 small onion
1 clove garlic
1 tablespoon sesame oil
1 teaspoon oregano
1 teaspoon dried basil
1½ cups cooked barley and beans
1 to 2 tablespoons shoyu (natural soy sauce)
  or to taste
1 calabaza or pumpkin, 7 to 8 inches in diameter

Preheat oven to 450°F. Chop the onion and mince the garlic. Heat the oil in a 1½-quart saucepan over medium heat; add the garlic, onion, oregano, and basil, stirring continuously until lightly browned and aromatic. Now add the barley-bean mixture and shoyu; reduce heat and continue cooking for 8 to 10 minutes.

Cut the top off the calabaza or pumpkin, scoop out the seeds, and stuff with the barley-bean mixture. Replace the top and place in a shallow, oiled baking pan. Bake for 1 hour or until it feels soft when pierced with a sharp knife.

Steamed Broccoli with Pumpkin Seeds

Serves: 4
Time: 7 minutes; 6 minutes

1 bunch broccoli
½ cup water
½ cup pumpkin seeds
A dash of salt (optional)

Separate the broccoli flowerettes from the stems and trim ¼ inch from the stem bottoms; peel off the thickest part of the skin and slice the stems crosswise in thin pieces. Combine the broccoli pieces in a 2-quart pot with the water and steam for 3 minutes; place the pumpkin seeds and flowerettes on top, sprinkle with salt, cover, and steam for 3 minutes more or until bright green.

Dinner	*Breakfast*	*Lunch*
Millet Casserole	Cracked Wheat with	Vegetable Soup with
Baked Squash and	Walnuts and Raisins	Millet
Turnips		Whole Grain Bread with
Turnip Greens Gomasio		Tofu-Miso Spread
Coconut-Spice Cookies		

Comments

It is always desirable, although not always possible, to eat the greens of a root vegetable at the same meal as the root itself. Other green leaves may be substituted when necessary.

The whole grain bread at lunch can be store-bought or home-made.

Nutritional Values

Protein is obtained from the millet, wheat, bread, spread, sesame seeds, walnuts, and cookies, and in lesser amounts from the squash and greens; vitamin A from the squash, turnips, and greens; the B-complex vitamin from the vegetables, millet, oats, wheat, nuts, seeds, and spread; and vitamin C from the vegetables, especially the greens. Iron is supplied by the millet, greens, wheat, walnuts, raisins, and miso; and calcium is supplied by the greens, tofu, sesame seeds, walnuts, and vegetables.

Utensils

Dinner: 3-quart covered saucepan, cast-iron or stainless steel skillet, 2- or 3-quart casserole dish with cover, 2-quart covered saucepan, two mixing bowls (one large and one small), baking sheet.

Breakfast: 2-quart covered pot.

Lunch: 2- or 3-quart soup pot, garlic press, suribachi and pestle or bowl and fork.

Dinner

Coconut-Spice Cookies

Yields: 2 to 2½ dozen
Time: 15 minutes; 30 minutes

2 cups whole wheat pastry flour
1 cup rolled oats
A dash of sea salt
½ cup grated coconut
½ cup corn oil
2/3 cups barley malt or rice syrup
  or ½ cup honey or maple syrup
½ cup water
¼ teaspoon each allspice, nutmeg, and ginger powder
½ teaspoon cinnamon

1. Make the cookies;
   move on to millet.

Combine the flour, oats, salt, and coconut in a large mixing bowl; add the oil. Rub the mixture between your hands until it has the consistency of wet sand. In a small bowl, combine the syrup, water, and spices; add to the flour mixture, blending well. Form the dough into a ball and allow it to rest for 10 minutes.

Preheat the oven to 375°F. Shape pieces of dough into flat, 2-inch cookies, and bake for 10 minutes.

3. Turn cookies;
   go on to squash.

Turn the cookies over and bake for 10 minutes more.

Millet Casserole

Serves: 4
Time: 20 minutes; 40 minutes

3 cups millet
1 medium onion
1 tablespoon corn oil
½ red bell pepper
3 stalks celery
5 cups water
1 teaspoon sea salt or to taste

2. Prepare millet casserole;
   return to cookies.

Wash and drain the millet and chop the onion. Place the millet in an iron skillet and dry roast, stirring constantly until the millet becomes fragrant; remove from heat. Heat the oil in a 3-quart saucepan over medium heat; add the onion and sauté for 2 to 3 minutes; chop the red pepper and the celery; add to the onion, stirring well before each addition. Now add the millet, water, and salt and bring to a boil. Reduce heat, cover, and simmer for 40 minutes or until millet is done.

Baked Squash and Turnips

Serves: 4
Time: 5 minutes; 40 minutes

2 small or 1 large butternut squash
1 teaspoon sesame oil
4 to 5 medium turnips with tops
¼ teaspoon sea salt or to taste
1 bay leaf

Preheat oven to 350°F. Wash and scrub the squash and cut into chunks. Heat the oil in a 3-quart casserole dish over low heat and sauté the squash for 3 minutes. Cut the turnips into chunks and add to the squash, sautéing for 1 more minute. Sprinkle the mixture with salt and add the bay leaf. Remove from stove, cover, and place in the oven. Bake for 30 to 40 minutes or until the vegetables are tender.
NOTE: If the casserole dish cannot be used on top of the stove, sauté the vegetables first in a 2-quart saucepan, then transfer to oiled casserole dish.

4. Prepare squash and turnip, remove cookies if they're still in the oven, and bake vegetables;
in 15 minutes, go on to greens.

Turnip Greens Gomasio

Serves: 4
Time: 10 minutes; 7 minutes

1¼ pounds turnip greens (or any other green)
¼ cup water
1 to 2 tablespoons gomasio (sesame salt)

Wash the greens well and place in a 2-quart saucepan; add the water and cover. Place the pan over medium heat until the pot begins to hiss; then reduce heat and steam gently for 7 minutes. Make sure the bottom greens don't burn. When the greens have finished cooking, drain well and chop into pieces. Toss with Gomasio and serve immediately.

5. Prepare greens.

Cracked Wheat with Walnuts and Raisins

Serves: 4
Time: 40 minutes

1 cup cracked wheat
½ cup raisins
½ cup walnuts
4 cups water
¼ teaspoon sea salt
½ teaspoon ground cinnamon (optional)

Combine the ingredients in a 2-quart pot and bring to a boil; stir once or twice, then reduce heat, cover, and simmer for at least 35 to 40 minutes. Stir occasionally. (The cereal improves with longer cooking.) If a thinner mixture is desired, add more water. Stir in the cinnamon 3 minutes before serving.

Vegetable Soup with Millet

Serves: 4
Time: 10 minutes; 10 minutes

1 to 1½ cups leftover millet casserole
2 cups baked squash or turnips
Cooked turnip greens
5 cups water
1 clove garlic
2 tablespoons shoyu (natural soy sauce) or to taste
1 handful parsley

Place the millet, vegetables, and water in a 2-quart soup pot; bring to a boil, reduce heat, cover, and simmer for 10 minutes. Squeeze the garlic through a garlic press into the soup; add the shoyu and simmer for 5 minutes more. Chop the parsley into fine pieces and place a teaspoonful on top of each serving of soup.

Tofu-Miso Spread

Serves: 4
Time: 5 minutes

1 8-ounce cake tofu
1 tablespoon barley or
   brown rice miso
1 tablespoon sesame oil

Mash the tofu in a bowl or suribachi; add the miso and oil, and blend until the mixture is creamy. Serve with homemade whole grain bread, or store-bought sourdough, whole wheat, or rye.

Dinner	*Breakfast*	*Lunch*
Lentil Soup	*Oats with Shoyu*	*Cream of Vegetable Soup*
Queen Yam Casserole	*(Natural Soy Sauce)*	*Rice-Lentil Loaf with*
Barley-Rice		*Scallion-Kuzu Sauce*
Celery Tarragon		*Dill pickles*
Apples Glacé		

Comments

The oats require soaking and the lunch-time pickles must ripen from 10 to 14 days. Pickling creates antibiotic acids that appear to have a highly beneficial effect on the digestive system. This is true only of those pickling methods that use salt and time to allow bacteria to sour the vegetables. The use of vinegar in pickling provides taste, but not the quality provided by natural pickling. Mimi Sheraton writes in *The New York Times* regarding the proper way to make pickles: "Brine always; vinegar never."

Nutritional Values

Protein is obtained from the lentils, barley, rice, oats, root vegetables, miso, and shoyu; vitamin A from the yams, carrots, celery, and fresh parsley; the B-complex from the rice, barley, oats, lentils, and from smaller amounts in the vegetables; and vitamin C from the celery, parsley, apples, pickles, and root vegetables. Calcium is supplied by the yams, parsnips, pickles, lentils, celery, and kuzu sauce; and iron by the lentils, miso, barley, pickles, oats, and parsley.

Utensils

Dinner: 4-quart covered pot or pressure cooker, medium skillet, blender or suribachi, 3-quart soup pot, small mixing bowl, 2-quart covered saucepan, covered 2- or 3-quart casserole dish, large skillet.

Breakfast: Two 2-quart covered saucepan.

Lunch: Blender, 2-quart saucepan, large mixing bowl, loaf pan, small saucepan, and pickling setup: 1-quart sterilized jar, 1½-quart pot, measuring cup.

Dinner

Lentil Soup

Serves: 4
Time: 10 minutes; 45 minutes

2 cups lentils
8 cups water
1 medium onion
1 tablespoon corn oil
2 medium carrots
2 bay leaves
2 tablespoons barley miso
Chopped parsley

1. Wash and simmer lentils;
   go on to barley-rice.

Wash the lentils and place in a 3-quart soup pot with water; bring to a boil, reduce heat, cover, and simmer.

3. Slice, sauté, and add vegetables to the soup;
   move on to casserole.

Chop the onion. Heat the oil in a skillet over medium heat; add the onion, and sauté. Slice the carrots; add to the onions, stir once or twice, and allow to cook for 4 to 5 minutes. Now add the vegetables and bay leaves to the simmering lentils and cook for 30 minutes more or until the lentils are tender.

7. Season and finish soup;
   go back to celery.

Dissolve the miso in ½ cup of the lentil broth and add to the soup; discard the bay leaves. Reserve 2 cups of the thickest part of the soup for lunch. Place another 2 cups of the soup in a blender or suribachi and purée; then return soup to the pot over low heat to keep warm (the puréeing gives the soup body without having to add flour or cream). Serve in individual soup bowls garnished with ½ teaspoon chopped parsley.

Queen Yam Casserole

Serves: 4
Time: 15 minutes; 40 minutes

2 yams
4 parsnips
1 medium yellow onion
1 clove garlic
2 tablespoons corn or sesame oil
½ teaspoon oregano
2 tablespoons tahini
1 tablespoon shoyu (natural soy sauce)
½ cup water

4. Prepare casserole and bake;
   go on to celery.

Preheat oven to 350°F. Wash, scrub, and dice the yams and parsnips; chop the onion and mince the garlic. Heat the oil in a large skillet over medium heat; add garlic, then the onion, and sauté for 1 minute. Stir in the yams and parsnips and continue cooking for 5 minutes; now add the oregano and sauté for 2 minutes more.

Combine the tahini, shoyu and water in a small bowl, blending until a liquid sauce is obtained. Transfer the vegetables to a lightly oiled 2-quart casserole dish and cover with the sauce. Cover and bake for 35 to 40 minutes.

Barley-Rice

Serves: 4
Time: 2 minutes; 45 minutes

2 cups short grain brown rice
1 cup barley
5 cups water
1 teaspoon sea salt or to taste
½ cup sunflower seeds

Wash the rice and barley together; place grains, water, salt, and sunflower seeds in a pressure cooker, and cook at minimum pressure over low heat for 40 minutes. (If a 4-quart covered pot is used, simmer the grains over low heat for 1 hour and 10 minutes.)
Remove from heat and allow the pressure to come down; uncover and toss with a wooden paddle or spoon.

2. Prepare barley-rice; return to soup.

9. Remove grain dish from stove and fluff; serve dinner, then return to dessert.

Celery Tarragon

Serves: 4
Time: 5 minutes; 15 minutes

1 bunch celery
1/3 cup water
1 tablespoon shoyu (natural soy sauce)
½ teaspoon tarragon

Wash the celery thoroughly; chop the leaves and stems into pieces. Combine the water, shoyu, and tarragon in a small bowl.
Place the celery in a 2-quart saucepan; pour in the shoyu mixture, cover, and steam over low heat for 10 minutes or until all the liquid is absorbed. Uncover, toss gently, and serve.

5. Cut up the celery; go on to dessert.
8. Cook the celery; return to barley-rice.

Apples Glacé

Serves: 4
Time: 10 minutes

5 tart red apples
1 tablespoon corn oil
¼ cup water
2 tablespoons maple syrup
¼ teaspoon vanilla

Core the apples; slice into ¼-inch thick circles.
Heat the oil in a large skillet over low heat; add the apples and fry for 2 to 3 minutes, turning once, until they begin to soften. Combine the water, syrup and vanilla in a small bowl; pour over the apples and continue cooking for 4 to 5 minutes over low heat until mixture becomes syrupy. Serve immediately.

6. Core the apples; return to soup.
10. Slice and cook apples just before serving.

Breakfast

Oats with Shoyu

Serves: 4
Time: overnight; 20 minutes

1½ cups rolled oat groats or steel cut oats
1 teaspoon salt
6 cups cold water
Shoyu (natural soy sauce) to taste
Roasted almonds or sunflower seeds

Place the oats in a 2-quart pot with cold water; cover, and soak overnight. In the morning, add salt and bring to a boil; reduce heat and cook uncovered for 20 minutes, stirring often. Allow each serving to be seasoned individually with shoyu and roasted nuts to taste.

Lunch

Dill Pickles

Serves: 6 to 8
Time: 10 minutes; 10 to 14 days

6 to 8 unwaxed small cucumbers (Kirby's)
2 sprigs fresh dill
2 cloves garlic, peeled
Water to cover
1 teaspoon sea salt per cup of water

1. Allow 10 to 14 days for pickles.

The cucumbers should be as fresh as possible, otherwise the pickles will have a hole through the center. Wash the cucumbers well, and pack them very tightly in a 1-quart sterilized jar or crock. Add the dill and garlic, and fill the container with water. Then pour the water out of the container into a measuring cup in order to gauge the amount of salt needed. In a 1½-quart pot, bring the water and salt to a boil; pour the hot water over the cucumbers, cover, and allow them to stand undisturbed at room temperature for 10 to 14 days. After 8 or 9 days, sample the pickles; when they taste right to you, place them in the refrigerator. They will keep several weeks. (When buying pickles, be sure they are made only with cucumbers, water, salt, and spices.)

Rice-Lentil Loaf

Serves: 4
Time: 30 minutes

2 cups cooked, thick lentil soup
3 cups cooked barley-rice
½ teaspoon fresh grated ginger

Preheat oven to 375°F. Combine the ingredients in a large mixing bowl, blending well. Pack the mixture firmly into an oiled loaf pan. Bake, uncovered, at 350°F. for 25 to 30 minutes. Slice and serve topped with Scallion-Kuzu Sauce.

2. Prepare casserole; go on to soup.

Cream of Vegetable Soup

Serves: 4
Time: 5 minutes; 5 minutes

1 cup leftover queen casserole
1 cup leftover celery tarragon
Water
Sea salt to taste
1 handful parsley

Place the leftovers in a blender; add water (approximately 3 cups) to 1½ inches above vegetable mixture, and purée. Transfer to a 2-quart soup pot and heat thoroughly over medium-low heat; add salt to taste. Chop the parsley, garnish the soup, and serve.

3. Make the soup; go on to sauce.

Scallion-Kuzu Sauce

Serves: 4
Time: 10 minutes

1 tablespoon sesame oil
3 tablespoons shoyu (natural soy sauce) or to taste
1 cup water
4 teaspoons kuzu
3 scallions, whites and greens

In a small saucepan, bring the oil, shoyu, and 3/4 cup water to a boil. Dissolve kuzu in remaining water; add to boiling liquid, stirring until thickened. Remove from heat; chop scallions very finely and add to the sauce. If the sauce is too liquid, allow it to stand; it will thicken as it cools.

4. Make the sauce.

Dinner	*Breakfast*	*Lunch*
Roasted Sunflower Seeds	*Hot Peanut-Kuzu Cream*	*Millet and Carrots*
Caraway Millet	*with Stewed Fruit*	*Daikon with Miso*
French Carrots		
Stuffed Fish Fillets		
Watercress Salad with		
Lemon-Mustard Dressing		
Hot Fruit Compote		

Comments

This is a nice dinner to serve on special occasions; the stuffed fillets make it rather festive. Once again, it is possible to omit the fish and still have a balanced and satisfying meal. The sunflower seeds, incidentally, make a good snack at any time. The dry-roasting technique used for the seeds and the millet should be done in a metal (cast iron or stainless steel) pot or skillet. If enamel pans are used, the porcelain may crack and pop out of the pan. Glass and corning-ware pots may also crack if heated while dry.

Nutritional Values

Protein is provided by the seeds, millet, fish, peanut butter, and miso; vitamin A by the carrots, parsley, watercress, and dried fruits; the B-complex vitamins by the millet, seeds, and fish; and vitamin C by the parsley, watercress, daikon, and lemon juice. Abundant calcium is obtained from the fish, seeds, watercress, carrots, cauliflower, kuzu, and dried fruits; and iron from the fish, dried fruit, seeds, parsley, watercress, and millet.

Utensils

Dinner: Small metal pot or skillet, pressure cooker or 4-quart covered pot, 3-quart covered saucepan, skillet, toothpicks, shallow baking dish, salad bowl, lemon juicer, small mixing bowl, one heavy 3- to 4-quart covered pot.

Breakfast: Small saucepan, measuring cup.

Lunch: Steamer or pot-and-colander setup, 2-quart covered pot, small bowl.

Dinner

Hot Fruit Compote

Serves: 4
Time: 5 minutes; 90 minutes

1 cup dried California apricots (unsulphured)
2 cups prunes
1 cup dried apples
2 cinnamon sticks
10 cups water
½ cup almonds

1. Prepare fruit compote; go on to seeds.

Place the ingredients in a 3-quart pot and bring to a boil; reduce heat, cover, and simmer, for 1½ hours. Add more water, if necessary, to keep the fruits covered. Serve the fruits with juice spooned over the top.
NOTE: Reserve 1½ cups fruits and 2 cups juice for breakfast.

Roasted Sunflower Seeds

Serves: 4
Time: 8 minutes

1 cup sunflower seeds
1/8 teaspoon sea salt in 1 tablespoon water

2. Roast the seeds; move on to fish.

Wash the seeds and place in a small skillet over medium heat; dry-roast, stirring continuously, until they begin to brown. Now sprinkle in the salted water and stir quickly to coat the seeds; continue roasting until the seeds are dry. The seeds are done roasting when their weight on a spoon is very light, and they make a hollow sound when dropped into the pot from a height of 2 to 3 inches. The oil in the seeds keeps them very hot; allow them to cool for 15 to 20 minutes before tasting.

Caraway Millet

Serves: 4
Time: 10 minutes; 20 minutes

3 cups millet
1 teaspoon caraway seeds
5 cups water
1 teaspoon sea salt or to taste

4. Prepare and cook millet; return to fillets.

Wash and drain the millet; place the millet and caraway seeds in a pressure cooker over medium heat. Dry-roast until the mixture begins to turn color and becomes fragrant. Slowly add the water (the pot is hot so it will sizzle) and salt; pressure-cook for 20 minutes over minimum heat. If a pressure-cooker is not used, roast the millet and seeds in a metal skillet, then transfer to a 4-quart pot with water and salt; cook for 40 minutes.

9. Remove millet from heat and remove fish from oven.

Allow the pressure in the pressure cooker to come down naturally; uncover, and toss the millet with a wooden spoon or paddle.

Stuffed Fish Fillets

5 short, wide fillets of sole or flounder
Coarse sea salt (if available)
1 small onion
2 cloves garlic
2 tablespoons sesame oil
½ teaspoon each tarragon and basil
1 cup homemade whole wheat breadcrumbs (see Bread Chapter)
2 tablespoons shoyu (natural soy sauce)
2 tablespoons water or stock
1 tablespoon sake, optional
1 egg
½ cup water
½ cup sake

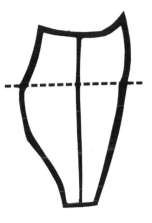

Wash the fillets and pat dry; place in a colander, sprinkle with coarse salt, and set aside. Mince the onion and garlic. Heat the oil in a small skillet over low heat; add the garlic, onion, and herbs; stir and cook until the mixture begins to turn brown and is very aromatic. Now add the breadcrumbs, mixing well. Remove from heat and add the shoyu, 2 tablespoons water or stock, and 1 tablespoon sake. Taste, add salt if needed, and allow to cool.

In a small bowl, beat the egg and add it to bread crumb stuffing, blending well. Preheat oven to 400°F. Rinse the fillets again and pat dry. Cut a strip from the widest point of the neck section to even out the shape; mince the strips and stir into the bread crumb filling, mixing well. Place a tablespoon of filling on the widest part of the fillet, then roll toward the tail, securing with 2 toothpicks, one on each side of the center seam. With a sharp knife, carefully cut the rolled fillets in half along the seam line. Place the pieces cut-side-down in a shallow baking pan. Add ½ cup each water and sake, and bake for 30 minutes.

3. Salt the fillets and prepare stuffing;
   go on to millet.

5. Prepare and bake fillets;
   move on to carrots.

Watercress Salad

Serves: 4
Time: 10 minutes

2 bunches watercress

7. Prepare the salad and
   dressing;
   return to carrots.

With a firm twist, break each bunch of watercress in two. Pick over and discard the toughest stems. Wash, drain, and pat dry. Place in individual bowls and toss with Lemon-Mustard Dressing.

Lemon-Mustard Dressing

Time: 5 minutes

4 tablespoons lemon juice
2 tablespoons tahini
2 tablespoons olive oil
2 tablespoons barley miso
2 teaspoons French or Polish mustard
4 tablespoons water

In a small bowl, combine lemon juice and tahini and blend for 2 to 3 minutes. Add the remaining ingredients, one at a time, mixing well after each addition until the dressing is light and creamy.

French Carrots

Serves: 4
Time: 8 to 10 minutes; 5 minutes

2 pounds carrots
½ inch water
2 tablespoons corn oil
1 small handful parsley

6. Start the carrots;
   go on to salad.

8. Finish the carrots;
   return to millet.

Scrub and cut the carrots diagonally into thin slices. Pour ½ inch water into a 2-quart pot (the exact quantity of water will vary with the diameter of the pot); add the carrots. Cover and steam over low heat for 8 to 10 minutes or until just soft.
Uncover the carrots and drain off excess water. Add the corn oil to the carrots and sauté for 4 to 5 minutes, stirring carefully once or twice until the carrots have a rich, sweet fragrance. While the carrots sauté, chop the parsley. When carrots are done, remove them from heat. Add the parsley, toss gently, and serve at once.

Hot Peanut-Kuzu Cream with Stewed Fruit

Serves: 4
Time: 15 minutes

1½ cups drained, leftover fruit compote
  (reserve the juice)
2 cups fruit compote juice
7 tablespoons kuzu
1 cup water
5 tablespoons peanut butter
A dash of sea salt

Pit the fruit and chop into small pieces; set aside. Pour the compote juice into a pan and place over medium heat. Dissolve the kuzu in the water; then add the peanut butter, salt, and kuzu mixture to the saucepan, stirring constantly until it thickens to a pudding-like consistency. Reduce heat and simmer for 4 to 5 minutes, stirring constantly. Pour into bowls and serve with 2 tablespoons of fruit as a topping.

Daikon with Miso

Serves: 4
Time: 5 minutes; 25 minutes

3 cups daikon chunks
1 cup water
1 tablespoon barley miso

Chop enough daikon to make 3 cups. Place daikon and water in a 2-quart pot and bring to a boil; reduce heat, cover, and simmer for 20 to 25 minutes. Add more water if needed. Just before serving, dissolve the miso in a few tablespoons of the cooking water and add to the pot. Stir well, allowing the liquid to bubble for 30 seconds. Serve hot.

Millet and Carrots

Serves: 4
Time: 15 minutes

1 bunch watercress
3 cups cooked millet
2 cups cooked carrots

Wash the watercress and discard tough stems; chop coarsely. In a 2-quart bowl, combine the carrots, watercress, and millet, mixing well. Transfer to a steamer or a pot and colander and steam until heated through.

Spring Meals

Spring Menus

	Dinner	Breakfast	Lunch
Menu No. 1 PAGE 143	Zucchini Cream Soup Sesame Rice Stir-fried Vegetables Cold Tofu with Garnish	Tofu-Sprout Spread on Toast	Norimaki (Rice and Seaweed Rolls) Salted Cuke and Watercress
Menu No. 2 PAGE 149	Polenta Curried Beans Dandelion Salad with Sesame Dressing Pears with Raisin Sauce	Fried Cornmeal Mush Steamed Dandelion Greens	Bean Salad on Tortillas Apricot Kuzu
Menu No. 3 PAGE 155	Watercress Soup Roasted Bulghur Sukiyaki Tofu Cream Pie	Scrambled Tofu with Rice Cakes	Vegetable Aspic Bulghur Croquettes
Menu No. 4 PAGE 161	Noodles in Broth Broccoli Tempura Cucumber-Wakame Salad Baked Pears	Raisin Oatmeal	Noodles with Tofu and Bean Sprouts Mustard Greens and Onions
Menu No. 5 PAGE 167	Sauteed Mushrooms on Toast Whole Wheat Macaroni with Tomato Sauce Spinach Fritters Celery Salad with Plum- Basil Dressing Apple-Strawberry Kanten	Granola with Apple- Strawberry Kanten	Celery Vichyssoise Macaroni and Bean Salad with Miso-Dill Dressing
Menu No. 6 PAGE 173	Clams Marinière Multicolored Rice Chinese Cabbage Salad with Tahini-Onion Dressing Mocha Mousse	Crêpes with Sprouts	Escarole-Garlic Soup Rice and Vegetable Salad with Creamy Parsley Dressing

Dinner	*Breakfast*	*Lunch*
Zucchini Cream Soup *Sesame Rice* *Stir-fried Vegetables* *Cold Tofu with Garnish*	*Tofu-Sprout Spread* *on Toast*	*Norimaki (Rice and* *Seaweed Rolls)* *Salted Cuke and* *Watercress*

Comments

As the weather gets warm, meals become lighter and cooler. The norimaki are a perfect picnic or lunch-bag food. They keep well, unrefrigerated, for a day or two. Lunch requires no cooking and is quick and easy to make if you have cooked rice on hand.

Nutritional Values

Protein is obtained from the rice, sesame seeds, tofu, miso, oatmeal, bread, and, in lesser amounts, from the zucchini and cauliflower; vitamin A from the parsley, red pepper, cauliflower, watercress, and cabbage; the B-complex vitamin from the rice, sesame seeds, bread, cauliflower, and mushrooms, and vitamin C from the parsley, cabbage, mushrooms, pepper, sprouts, cucumbers, and scallions. Calcium is supplied by the sesame seeds, tofu, nori, watercress, cabbage, cauliflower, parsley, and zucchini; and iron is supplied by the sesame, miso, rice, watercress, parsley, tofu, and nori seaweed.

Utensils

Dinner: 3-quart soup pot, blender, 4-quart covered saucepan, wok or large skillet with cover, small bowl, serving bowl, ginger grater.

Breakfast: Small bowl or suribachi.

Lunch: Sushi mat or several wet paper towels, small bowls, salad bowl.

Cold Tofu with Garnish

Serves: 4
Time: 10 minutes; 1 hour

1½ cakes tofu (10 to 12 ounces)
Ice cubes
½ bunch watercress
6 scallions
Fresh ginger root
Shoyu (natural soy sauce) to taste

1. Place tofu in the freezer;
   move on to rice.
6. Cube tofu and set on ice;
   return to vegetables.
8. Chop scallions and grate
   ginger.

Chill tofu in the freezer for 1 hour.
Put ice cubes into a bowl; cut tofu into 1-inch cubes and place atop ice. Garnish the border of the bowl with watercress.

Chop scallions; grate 1 tablespoon ginger. To serve, provide each person with several cubes of tofu, garnished with a few sprigs of watercress, 1 teaspoon scallions, and ¼ teaspoon ginger. Season with a few drops of shoyu.

Sesame Rice

Serves: 4
Time: 5 minutes; 1 hour

2½ cups medium grain brown rice
½ cup unhulled sesame seeds
4½ cups water
1 teaspoon sea salt or to taste

2. Cook the rice;
   move on to soup.

Wash the rice, then the seeds, in a fine-mesh strainer. Place rice, seeds, water, and salt in a 4-quart saucepan and bring to a boil; cover, reduce heat, and simmer for 1 hour. Mix seeds back into rice with a wooden paddle before serving.

Zucchini Cream Soup

Serves: 4
Time: 10 minutes; 20 minutes

1 small onion
1 tablespoon corn oil
3 or 4 medium zucchini (about 1½ pounds)
6 cups water or stock
½ cup oatmeal or rolled oats
½ teaspoon sea salt
2 tablespoons chopped parsley

3. Make soup;
   move on to vegetables.

5. Blend and season soup;
   go back to tofu.

Peel and chop the onion. In a 3-quart soup pot, heat the oil, then add onion and sauté over medium heat. Chop the zucchini, add to onion and sauté for 2 to 3 minutes. Now add water, oatmeal, and salt, and stirring constantly, bring to a boil; reduce heat and simmer for 15 minutes.
Transfer to a blender and purée, then strain to remove the fibers and seeds. Garnish each serving with chopped parsley. Serve hot or cold.

Stir-fried Vegetables

Serves: 4
Time: 10 minutes; 5 minutes

1 small head cauliflower
¼ small green cabbage, or bok choy
½ red pepper
1 cup mushrooms
1 cup bean sprouts
1 tablespoon dark sesame oil
1½ tablespoons shoyu (natural soy sauce)
1½ tablespoons brown rice vinegar
1½ tablespoons water

Wash vegetables carefully. Cut cauliflower into very small flowerettes (reserve stems for use in soup stock); chop cabbage into thin strips crosswise, slice red pepper into strips, then dice; trim bottoms off mushroom stems, then slice caps vertically.

Heat the oil in a large wok or skillet. Add the vegetables one at a time in the order given, sautéing for 1 minute after each addition. In a small bowl, mix shoyu, vinegar, and water and sprinkle over vegetables. Reduce heat to minimum, cover, and steam for 4 minutes. Now uncover and stir. Serve immediately.

4. Chop all the vegetables; return to soup.

7. Stir-fry vegetables; while they steam, go back to tofu.

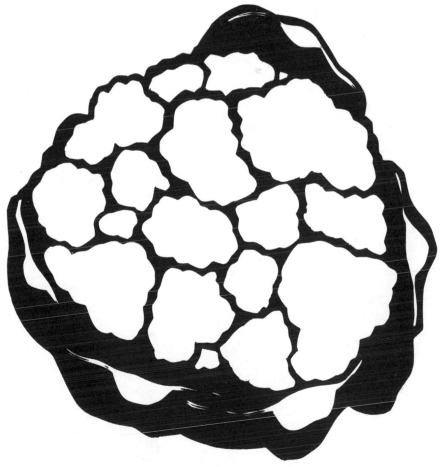

Tofu-Sprout Spread on Toast

Serves: 4
Time: 3 to 4 minutes

2 8-ounce cakes tofu
1 tablespoon white or brown rice miso
4 tablespoons tahini
2 tablespoons lemon juice
1 cup alfalfa sprouts
10 slices toasted whole grain bread

In a small bowl or suribachi, mash tofu, miso, tahini, and lemon juice together with a fork until thoroughly mixed. Lightly chop sprouts, then fold into tofu mixture. To serve: spread thick on toast. Top with extra sprouts. (Refrigerated in a covered jar, this spread will keep for 2 days.)

Salted Cuke with Watercress

Serves: 4
Time: 5 minutes; 20 minutes

5 small unwaxed cucumbers (Kirby's)
1 teaspoon sea salt
½ bunch watercress
1 tablespoon lemon juice
1 teaspoon olive oil

Wash and score the cucumbers lengthwise with a fork (or peel, if waxed), then cut crosswise into thin slices, discarding the tips. Spread cucumber slices over a chopping board and sprinkle them with salt. Now transfer to a salad bowl and allow them to stand for 20 minutes.
Squeeze the cucumbers to extract excess water, and discard the water. Chop off and discard the thickest stems from the watercress, chopping the leaves coarsely. Combine the vegetables and toss with lemon juice and olive oil. Serve in individual bowls.

1. Prepare cucumbers; move on to norimaki.

3. Finish cucumber dish.

Norimaki (Rice and Seaweed Rolls)

Serves: 4
Time: 20 minutes

2 cups cooked brown rice
4 sheets of nori seaweed
4 long, thin strips of celery
1 red pepper, cut into long thin strips
2½ teaspoons umeboshi plum paste

Toast each nori sheet by holding it over a flame, by spreading it out in a 250°F. oven for 2 minutes or by putting it in a toaster oven at the lowest setting. The nori is done when it crisps and turns green. Set out a small bowl filled with cold water, and a sushi mat or wet paper towel. Moisten the palm of one hand and rub it quickly against the palm of the other; now take a sheet of nori and flatten it on the sushi mat or paper towel. Remoisten your hands. Spread about 1/3 cup rice on the lower half of the nori sheet, packing rice down tightly and making sure it reaches to the edges of the nori in an even layer. Arrange a celery strip across the center of the rice layer, then place red pepper strips alongside the celery, making sure the vegetable strips reach the edges. Now brush or spread 1/4 teaspoon plum paste next to the strips. Remoisten your hands and lift the sushi mat or paper towel, with your fingers on top of the rice and your thumbs beneath; roll mat forward as tightly as you can, pushing with your fingers and guiding with your thumbs (make sure the mat or paper does not get rolled into the norimaki). When you reach the end of the rice, lightly moisten the remaining edge of nori and continue rolling to seal. Squeeze the roll gently and evenly to firm, then remove mat. With a sharp moistened knife carefully slice the roll into six equal pieces. To serve, stand each piece on its side. Repeat with each nori sheet until all ingredients are used.

2. Make norimaki; return to salad.

Dinner	*Breakfast*	*Lunch*

Polenta
Curried Beans
Dandelion Salad with
   Sesame Dressing
Pears with Raisin Sauce

Fried Cornmeal Mush
Steamed Dandelion Greens

Bean Salad on Tortillas
Apricot Kuzu

Comments

Although the word "polenta" is Italian, corn is, of course, the classic grain of the Americas. Fried mush has been a staple in America since colonial times, and tortillas with beans in one form or another are still widely consumed.

There is a dramatic difference between freshly ground cornmeal and cornmeal that has been sitting on the shelf for a while: the older it is, the more bitter it becomes, although it is possible to remove some of the bitterness by dry-roasting. Ideally, one could grind fresh corn meal before using it, but corn is very hard and not all grinders or blenders can handle it. Try to buy cornmeal where it is sold in bulk or where there is a big turn-over, and be sure it's whole and not de-germed.

The texture of the grain is also important: some cornmeal has the texture of coarse corn flour, and some the texture of grits. It is the latter that makes the best polenta; if unobtainable, use the former, but dissolve it in cold water first, and add another cup of cornmeal to the ingredients.

Note that the kidney beans must be soaked for 2 to 8 hours or longer (depending on method) before cooking.

To roast sesame seeds, be sure to use a small (¾-quart) metal pot. The seeds should form a 1-inch-thick layer on the bottom of the pot so they will not pop out during roasting.

Nutritional Values

Complementary proteins are obtained from the corn, beans, and sesame seeds; abundant vitamin A from the dandelion and yellow corn-meal; the B-complex vitamin from the cornmeal, beans, pears, and celery; and abundant vitamin C from the dandelion, sprouts, lettuce, parsley, pears, radishes, lemon and apricot juices. Calcium is supplied by the dandelion, onions, beans, radishes, celery, sesame seeds, and kuzu; and iron by the beans, dandelion greens, raisins, sesame seeds, radishes, and kuzu.

Utensils

Dinner: 4- to 6-quart pot, wire whisk, pyrex loaf pan, two 2-quart sauce-pans, metal pot or skillet, small saucepan, salad bowl, lemon juicer, small bowl, blender. A suribachi is optional.

Breakfast: Skillet, 2-quart saucepan with cover.

Lunch: Large bowl, skillet, small bowl or blender, 1½-quart saucepan.

Curried Beans

Serves: 4
Time: 1 hour, 15 minutes; 2 to 8 hours soaking

2 cups kidney beans
8 cups water
1 teaspoon sea salt or to taste
1 medium yellow onion
2 cloves garlic
2 tablespoons corn oil
½ teaspoon curry or to taste

1. Soak beans 6 to 8 hours or 2 hours,
   depending on process used.

2. Cook beans;
   move on to polenta.

8. Finish the bean dish.

Place the beans in a 2-quart saucepan, then wash and pick them over. Cover beans with water and soak for 6 to 8 hours. (Or, to save time, bring beans to a boil, reduce heat, and simmer for 2 minutes; turn off heat, cover, and soak in the hot water for 2 hours.)

To cook, make sure the beans are covered with water, then simmer for 1 hour or until tender. Add the salt, and simmer for 5 minutes more. Strain, reserving the liquid for use in soup.

Chop the onion; crush and mince the garlic. In a 2-quart saucepan, heat oil and sauté garlic, then onion; add curry, stirring well, then add 2 cups cooked beans. Cook for 10 minutes over low heat, stirring occasionally. Add some bean liquid if the mixture is too dry. Serve atop the polenta.

Polenta

Serves: 4
Time: 5 minutes; 1 hour plus

7 cups water
1 teaspoon sea salt
2 cups gritty yellow cornmeal (not flour)

3. Prepare polenta;
   move on to dessert.

In a 4- to 6-quart pot, bring water and salt to a boil. Slowly add cornmeal in a gentle stream while beating constantly with a wire whisk. Reduce heat to medium low and continue beating for a few minutes until cornmeal has thickened. Now reduce heat to absolute minimum, cover the pot, and simmer for as long as it takes to make the rest of the dinner (at least 1 hour). Stir polenta once in a while to avoid burning; a crust will naturally form on the bottom of the pot. Just before serving, pour part of the polenta into a Pyrex loaf pan and set it aside, uncovered, to use for breakfast. Pour the remainder into a serving bowl or serve from the pot. As it cools, the polenta will thicken and jell.

Pears with Raisin Sauce

Serves: 4
Time: 10 minutes; 10 minutes

5 firm green pears (Packham)
1½ cups water
1 cinnamon stick

Wash, quarter, and core the pears, and slice each quarter into three sections. In a 2-quart saucepan, bring water, pears, and cinnamon stick to a boil. Cover, reduce heat, and simmer for 8 to 10 minutes or until just soft (do not overcook).

4. Prepare pears;
   move on to raisin sauce.

Raisin Sauce

Time: 10 minutes; 5 minutes

1 cup raisins
1¼ cups water
1 tablespoon kuzu

In a small saucepan, cook the raisins in 1 cup water for 10 minutes. Transfer to a blender and purée, then return to saucepan. In a small bowl, dissolve kuzu in remaining 1/4 cup of water and add to raisin purée. Cook over medium heat, stirring constantly, until sauce thickens and becomes translucent; allow to cool, stirring occasionally. Pour over pears and serve chilled or at room temperature.

5. Prepare sauce;
   go on to the salad.

Dandelion Salad with Sesame Dressing

Serves: 4
Time: 5 minutes

4 cups dandelion leaves
5 large radishes
2 stalks celery

Separate dandelion greens from the stalks and wash greens well (they tend to be gritty); pat dry and chop crosswise. Slice radishes into thin rounds. Dice celery. Now toss ingredients together in a serving bowl. Serve Sesame Dressing separately.

6. Prepare salad;
   move on to dressing.

Sesame Dressing

Time: 15 minutes

½ cup sesame seeds
2 tablespoons sesame oil
3 tablespoons lemon juice
2 tablespoons shoyu (natural soy sauce)
½ cup water

In a metal pot or skillet, toast seeds over medium heat, stirring constantly for about 10 minutes or until fragrant. Grind seeds in a suribachi, then add remaining ingredients one by one, grinding the mixture together. Or, combine ingredients in a blender and blend for 1 minute.

7. Prepare dressing;
   return to beans.

Breakfast

Fried Cornmeal Mush

Serves: 4
Time: 15 to 20 minutes

1 loaf of cooked polenta
Oil for frying
Shoyu (natural soy sauce) or maple syrup to taste

1. Fry mush;
   move on to greens.

Cut cornmeal loaf into 1/4- to 1/2-inch slices. Heat 1/4 inch of oil in a skillet and fry the slices for 8 to 10 minutes or until crisp and golden on one side, then turn over and fry other side for 5 to 7 minutes. Serve slices sprinkled with shoyu, or serve with maple syrup and omit the steamed greens from the menu.

Steamed Dandelion Greens

Serves: 4
Time: 5 minutes

4 cups dandelion greens
A dash of lemon juice

2. Steam greens.

Wash and trim greens and place them, still wet, in a 2-quart pot over medium heat. When the pot starts to hiss, reduce heat, cover, and steam the greens for 2 to 3 minutes. Serve hot, with a sprinkle of lemon juice.

Lunch

Apricot Kuzu

Serves: 4
Time: 5 minutes

10 tablespoons kuzu
3 cups apricot juice
1 cup water
2 tablespoons tahini
1 teaspoon vanilla
4 to 5 tablespoons chopped roasted almonds

1. Make the dessert;
   go on to tortillas.

In a 1½-quart saucepan, dissolve kuzu in 1/4 cup water; stir in the apricot juice. In a small bowl, dissolve tahini in 1/4 cup of water; add to the juice mixture along with the remaining water and vanilla. Cook over medium heat, stirring constantly. When the mixture becomes thick and creamy, stir for 1 minute more, then pour into individual dessert bowls. Serve hot or cold, topped with almonds.

Bean Salad on Tortillas

Serves: 4 (2 per person)

DRESSING:

Time: 3 minutes

3 tablespoons lemon juice
2 tablespoons shoyu (natural soy sauce)
1 teaspoon prepared mustard
1 tablespoon tahini
3 tablespoons water

Combine the ingredients for the dressing in a small bowl or blender; mix well. Add to bean mixture.

2. Prepare and assemble tortillas in the order given.

FILLING:

Time: 10 minutes

2½ cups cooked kidney beans
2 medium yellow onions, chopped
½ bunch parsley (2 to 3 tablespoons chopped)
¼ to 1/3 cup mustard dressing

Place the beans in a large bowl. Chop the onions and parsley and add to beans, mixing well. Add the dressing, toss well, and allow the mixture to marinate while you prepare tortillas.

TORTILLA:

Time: 15 minutes

¼ head iceberg lettuce
8 to 10 whole corn tortillas
Oil
½ cup scallions
1 cup alfalfa sprouts

Shred the lettuce very fine. Brush a skillet with oil and heat tortillas for 2 to 3 minutes on each side. Pile tortillas on a plate covered with a napkin to keep warm. Assemble by placing a layer of lettuce and 3 tablespoons bean mixture on each tortilla. Top with scallions and sprouts, and fold.

Dinner	Breakfast	Lunch

Watercress Soup
Roasted Bulghur
Sukiyaki
Tofu Cream Pie

Scrambled Tofu
    with Rice Cakes

Vegetable Aspic
Bulghur Croquettes

Comments

This easy dinner is also quite light because there is almost no oil in the main part of the meal. Thus, the tofu pie makes a pleasant complement and can be digested easily. For lunch, the cool aspic is a fine balance for the yang, fried croquettes. Allow at least 2 hours for the aspic to chill and set, or prepare it the night before.

Notice that there are two tofu dishes in this menu set; a dessert and a main dish. Tofu is a versatile food that is becoming more and more popular as a dairy substitute and source of vegetable protein. However, it is not advisable to use it in the same amount and proportion that animal food is normally consumed. To find out how much is appropriate, it is always wise to take a look at the traditional way food is prepared. Tofu generally is served cubed or fried in soups, stews, or as an appetizer with garnishes. It is served in small amounts, certainly no more than a cake per day per person, preferably less. For those who have stopped eating dairy foods or meat, there is a tendency to treat tofu as a substitute for butter or cheese and even as the main part of a meal. Please remember that tofu is a *partial* food; the soybean solids, *okara*, are taken out in the manufacturing process. Therefore, tofu should be used only as a complement or secondary food.

Nutritional Values

Protein is obtained from the bulghur, tofu, pie crust, and rice cakes; vitamin A from the watercress and carrots; the B-complex vitamin from the bulghur, cauliflower, mushrooms, and zucchini; and vitamin C from the watercress, onion, celery tops, sprouts, zucchini, cauliflower, and Chinese cabbage. Calcium is supplied by the watercress, zucchini, tofu, kanten, and cabbage; and iron by the bulghur, watercress, mushrooms, and kanten as well as by the shoyu (natural soy sauce) and miso used as condiments.

Utensils

Dinner: Soup pot, large stainless steel or cast iron saucepan or skillet, 2-quart pot, small bowl, 4-quart covered saucepan or pot, two large bowls, 9-inch pie plate, blender.

Breakfast: Medium skillet, small bowl.

Lunch: 5- to 6-cup mold or bowl, 2-quart mixing bowl, 2-quart saucepan, heavy skillet.

Dinner

Tofu Cream Pie

Serves: 4
Time: 15 minutes; 35 to 40 minutes

CRUMBLE CRUST:
¼ cup corn oil
4 tablespoons water or maple syrup
Pinch of sea salt
1½ cups whole wheat flour

1. Make the pie in the order given;
move on to bulghur.

Preheat oven to 375°F. In a large bowl, beat together oil, water or syrup, and salt; add flour, mixing well with a fork or wire whisk. Rub the mixture between your hands to insure even blending, then turn into the center of an oiled pie plate. Working from the center outwards, press down with your fingers to form a crust, going up the sides and guiding the edges with your thumb placed flat along the border of the plate. Pre-bake for 8 minutes.

FILLING:
3½ cakes tofu (8 ounces each)
4 tablespoons tahini
1 tablespoon lemon juice
Grated rind of 1 lemon
½ cup maple syrup or barley malt
2 teaspoons vanilla

Crumble the tofu into a blender. Add remaining ingredients and blend at low speed, scraping the mixture down the sides of the blender with a spatula; blend until smooth and creamy. Pour tofu mixture into the center of a pre-baked crust, allowing the filling to radiate outward. Bake at 350°F. for 35 to 40 minutes. Allow to cool before slicing.

Roasted Bulghur

Serves: 4
Time: 10 minutes; 45 minutes

3 cups bulghur (wheat pilaf)
5 cups water
1 teaspoon sea salt

2. Prepare the bulghur;
move on to soup.

In a large stainless steel pot or cast iron skillet, dry-roast bulghur over medium heat, stirring constantly until the bulghur begins to exude a nut-like aroma. (Watch closely, it burns fast). Transfer the roasted bulghur to a large bowl and allow to cool. In a 2-quart pot, bring water to a boil, add salt, then pour over the cooled bulghur. Cover the bowl, and allow to stand for 45 minutes to 1 hour.

Watercress Soup

Serves: 4
Time: 10 minutes; 8 minutes

1 medium yellow onion
1 teaspoon sesame oil
1 clove garlic
1 cup celery tops
6 cups water
½ teaspoon sea salt
1 tablespoon white (shiro) or barley miso
1 bunch watercress

Chop the onion. Heat the oil in a soup pot; mince the garlic and sauté for 30 seconds, then immediately add onion. Sauté onion and garlic over medium heat until they begin to brown. Chop the celery tops, add, and sauté for 2 or 3 minutes more. Now add the water and salt, and bring to a boil; reduce heat and simmer for 5 to 6 minutes. Pour the soup into a blender with miso; purée, then return to the soup pot.
Slice the watercress crosswise and drop into soup. Bring just to a boil, and serve.

3. Prepare soup;
move on to sukiyaki.
Check pie, remove from
oven if ready.

5. Finish soup.

Sukiyaki

Serves: 4
Time: 10 minutes; 5 to 6 minutes

2 carrots
1 head chinese cabbage
2 zucchini
1 red pepper
1 cup bean sprouts
1 cup fresh mushrooms
3 tablespoons shoyu (natural soy sauce)
2/3 cup water

Scrub, then cut the carrots into thin slices on the diagonal; place carrot slices in a 2-quart pot. Wash the cabbage, chop into thin strips crosswise, and arrange above carrots. Scrub and dice the zucchini and add to the pot. Cut the red pepper into thin strips, chop crosswise, and sprinkle over zucchini. Wash sprouts and add. Finally, wash the mushrooms, trimming away the stems and slicing the caps lengthwise; place mushrooms in a mound atop the sprouts. In a small bowl, mix water and shoyu and slowly pour over vegetables; cover the pot and turn heat to high. When the pot begins to hiss, reduce the heat and steam for 5 minutes or until vegetables shrink to about half their original volume. Toss gently with wooden spoons. Serve over bulghur.

4. Prepare sukiyaki;
while it steams, return
to soup.

Scrambled Tofu

Serves: 4
Time: 10 minutes

½ cup alfalfa sprouts
¼ cup fresh parsley tops
2 tablespoons sesame oil
2 8-ounce cakes tofu
1 tablespoon shoyu (natural soy sauce) or to taste

Lightly chop sprouts three or four times and set aside. Chop the parsley very fine and place in a bowl.
Barely heat the oil in a medium skillet, then crumble in the tofu. Using a fork, scramble the tofu and cook over medium heat for 3 to 4 minutes; add the shoyu, mix in the alfalfa sprouts and parsley and continue cooking for another 3 to 4 minutes. Serve immediately. Delicious with rice cakes or whole rye Swedish crispbread.

Vegetable Aspic

Serves: 4
Time: 10 minutes; 3 hours

2 bars kanten (agar) or 5 tablespoons agar flakes
4 cups water or stock
1½ tablespoons shoyu (natural soy sauce) or to taste
1 teaspoon fresh grated ginger or horseradish
2 cups cooked vegetables (leftover sukiyaki)
Lettuce, parsley, radishes

Rinse kanten bars under running water until soft. In a 2-quart saucepan, add kanten bars or flakes to water or stock, season with shoyu, and bring to a boil; reduce heat and simmer for 2 to 3 minutes or until agar is dissolved, then add the ginger or horseradish. Cool in the refrigerator for 15 to 20 minutes or until kanten begins to thicken. Now fold in vegetables and transfer to a 5- to 6-cup mold or bowl. Chill until set (about 2 hours). Unmold and serve on a bed of lettuce decorated with parsley sprigs and radishes.

1. Make the aspic several hours in advance.

Bulghur Croquettes

Serves: 4
Time: 10 minutes; 20 to 30 minutes

3 cups cooked bulghur
½ cup whole wheat flour
2 tablespoons arrowroot
1 teaspoon sea salt
Oil for frying

In a 2-quart mixing bowl, combine the bulghur, flour, arrowroot, and salt, squeezing the mixture through your fingers to form a thick paste. Working with lightly moistened hands, shape the mixture into 2-inch patties. Heat 1/2 inch of oil in a heavy skillet and fry patties on both sides until nicely browned. Drain on brown paper and keep warm until ready to serve.

2. Prepare croquettes.

Dinner	*Breakfast*	*Lunch*
Noodles in Broth Broccoli Tempura Cucumber-Wakame Salad Baked Pears	*Raisin Oatmeal*	Noodles with Tofu and Bean Sprouts Mustard Greens and Onions

Comments

The cucumbers for the dinner salad require salting beforehand that will extract excess water; the water is then discarded. Don't be concerned that nutrients will be drawn out with the water. Cucumbers are rich in phosphoric and sulphuric acids that some people find hard to digest: the the contractive salt attracts and draws out the expansive acids and water thereby making the cucumber more balanced and digestible.

The tempura, also on the dinner menu, is a delicious dish but it is rich in oil, and if served too often will tax the liver. Therefore it is best not to eat tempura more than once every two or three weeks. Opinion is divided as to what to do with the tempura cooking oil after use: some people re-use it— at most—three more times; others use it to grease baking pans; and still others believe that oil heated over 350°F. (the temperature necessary for deep-frying) for more than 8 minutes can be carcinogenic. Use your own judgment in this matter, but in any case, discard the oil if it smells heavy, burnt, or looks much darker than before heating.

Nutritional Values

Protein is obtained from the buckwheat noodles, oatmeal, and tofu, as well as smaller amounts from all the vegetables; abundant vitamin A from the broccoli and mustard greens; the B-complex vitamin from the noodles, oatmeal, broccoli, and pears; and vitamin C from the broccoli, cucumbers, pears, greens, sprouts, and onions. Calcium is supplied by the broccoli, wakame, oatmeal, raisins, tofu, and greens; and iron by the grains, broccoli, raisins, wakame, and mustard greens.

Utensils

Dinner: 4-quart pot, colander, 2-quart covered saucepan, 1-quart mixing bowl, wok, deep-fry or candy thermometer, salad bowl, small bowl, shallow baking pan, fine mesh skimmer, apple corer, 2 pair cooking chopsticks or 2 pair tongs (if both unavailable, use wooden spoons).

Breakfast: 2-quart covered saucepan.

Lunch: Large covered skillet, small bowl, 1-quart covered saucepan.

Dinner

Baked Pears

Serves: 4
Time: 10 minutes; 30 to 40 minutes

5 hard, green pears (Bartlett)
Raisins
10 almonds
Cinnamon to taste
2 cups water

1. Prepare pears;
    go on to noodles.

Preheat oven to 375°F. Wash the pears, and slice 1/2 inch off the top of each; reserve tops. Core the pears with an apple corer but do not puncture the bottom of the pear. Stuff each pear with raisins, two almonds, and a dash of cinnamon, then fill with water and replace the tops. Stand the pears in a shallow baking pan and pour in 1/2 inch of water.

7. Check pears,
    remove from oven if done;
    move on to tempura dip-
    ping sauce.

Bake for 30 to 40 minutes or until soft. The baking time will vary with the size and hardness of the pears.

Cucumber-Wakame Salad

Serves: 4
Time: 15 minutes; 30 minutes

1 pound cucumbers, unwaxed
1 teaspoon sea salt
1 ounce wakame seaweed
1 cup water
2 tablespoons lemon juice
1 tablespoon sesame oil
1 teaspoon brown rice vinegar
½ red pepper

3. Prepare cucumbers,
    soak wakame;
    return to noodles.

Wash cucumbers and, if unwaxed, score them lengthwise with a fork; if waxed, peel them. Cut the cucumbers into thin slices, then spread slices on a chopping board and sprinkle with salt. Transfer to a bowl and allow the cucumbers to stand for 30 minutes. In a separate bowl, soak wakame in the water for 15 minutes or until it softens and expands.

11. Chop wakame and finish
    salad;
    return to tempura.

Remove wakame from soaking water and squeeze to rid of excess water; chop into small pieces. In a small bowl, combine the lemon juice, oil, and vinegar. Squeeze water from the cucumbers and discard; taste the cucumbers: if too salty, rinse with fresh water. Slice the pepper into thin strips, then dice crosswise. Combine the ingredients, add lemon juice mixture, and toss.

Noodles in Broth

Serves: 4
Time: 10 minutes; 30 minutes

3 quarts water
1 teaspoon sea salt
1 pound buckwheat noodles

In a 4-quart pot, bring water and salt to a rolling boil.
Add the noodles to the boiling water. (For a shorter noodle, break in half inside the package.) Reduce heat to medium (the water should bubble gently) and cook for 20 to 25 minutes or until cooked to taste.
Drain the noodles in a colander, reserving the water for use in soup or bread. Rinse noodles under cold running water, cover, and set aside.

2. Set the water to boil;
   move on to salad.
4. Add noodles to boiling water;
   move on to broth.
10. Drain noodles;
    go on to salad.

Broth

Time: 5 minutes; 20 minutes

4 cups water
1 3-inch piece of kombu seaweed
½ cup leftover vegetable parings (onion skins, carrot ends, et cetera)
3 tablespoons shoyu (natural soy sauce)
¼ teaspoon sea salt or to taste
2 scallions

In a 2-quart saucepan, bring water, kombu, and vegetable parings to a boil. Reduce heat, cover, and simmer for 15 minutes, then strain, discarding vegetable pieces. Season with shoyu and salt and simmer for 2 minutes more.
Chop the scallions. Add noodles to the broth and serve at room temperature or reheat. Ladle into individual serving bowls and garnish with chopped scallions and 2 or 3 pieces of tempura.

5. Prepare broth;
   move on to broccoli.

13. Chop scallions and finish noodle dish.

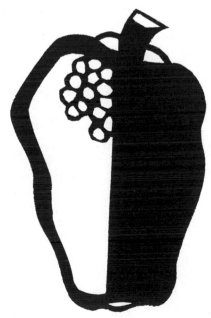

Broccoli Tempura

Serves: 4
Time: 30 minutes

1 bunch broccoli
1 cup whole wheat pastry flour
1 cup water
1 tablespoon kuzu or arrowroot
¼ teaspoon sea salt
2 cups cold pressed oil

6. Cut broccoli;
   return to pears.

9. Prepare batter;
   go back to noodles.

12. Make tempura;
    go back to noodles.

Cut the broccoli flowerettes from the stems and separate into small clusters; reserve stalks for lunch.

In a 1-quart mixing bowl, combine the flour, water, kuzu or arrowroot, and salt to form a loose batter (kuzu or arrowroot, will make the tempura crisp and non-oily); add half the amount of flowerettes, coating well with flour mixture.

In a wok, heat the oil to 350°F. on a candy or deep-fry thermometer or until a little of the batter dropped into the hot oil rises to the surface within 15 to 20 seconds. With chopsticks, tongs, or wooden spoons, gently lower coated flowerettes, one by one, into the hot oil. Do not crowd them. The flowerettes will hiss and bubble and rise to the surface in less than 1 minute. Regulate the heat—medium high seems to work best—so the tempura will cook in 3 to 4 minutes. A higher heat and shorter cooking time will burn but not cook the pieces; a lower heat and longer cooking time will not present a problem (the kuzu or arrowroot prevents any sogginess) except spending more time than is necessary at the stove. The tempura should be light brown, and crisp. Remove the pieces with a clean pair of chopsticks or wooden spoons and drain on 2 or 3 layers of brown paper or paper towels; keep warm in a 150°F. oven. Clean the oil with a fine mesh skimmer between batches. Add the rest of the flowerettes to the flour mixture, then fry. Tempura should be served hot as soon after preparation as possible with individual portions of dipping sauce.

DIPPING SAUCE:

Time: 5 minutes

¼ cup shoyu (natural soy sauce)
¼ cup water
½ teaspoon grated ginger
1 tablespoon grated daikon or onion

8. Prepare sauce; return to tempura.

Combine the ingredients in a small bowl. Pour into individual serving dishes.

Raisin Oatmeal

Serves: 4
Time: 15 minutes

1½ cups rolled oats
4 cups water
½ cup raisins
½ teaspoon cinnamon
¼ teaspoon sea salt
4 tablespoons sunflower seeds

Combine the first 5 ingredients in a 2-quart saucepan and bring to a boil. Cover pan, reduce heat, and simmer for 10 to 15 minutes, stirring often. Serve garnished with sunflower seeds.

Noodles with Tofu and Bean Sprouts

Serves: 4
Time: 15 minutes

1 8-ounce cake tofu
½ teaspoon grated fresh ginger
½ cup bean sprouts
4 cups cooked noodles
1 heaping teaspoon white (shiro) or brown rice miso

Cut tofu into ½-inch cubes and place in a 1-quart saucepan with water to cover. Add ginger and boil for 5 minutes.
Drain the tofu, reserving water. In a large bowl, mix tofu with bean sprouts and noodles. Dissolve the miso in ¼ cup reserved cooking water. Pour miso over noodle mixture, and toss.

1. Prepare tofu; move on to greens.
3. Finish noodle dish.

Mustard Greens and Onions

Serves: 4
Time: 15 minutes

1 large red onion
1 tablespoon corn oil
2 to 3 broccoli stalks
1 bunch mustard greens (about ½ pound)
¼ cup water
1 tablespoon shoyu (natural soy sauce) or to taste

Peel and chop the onion. Heat the oil in a large skillet over medium heat, then sauté onion for 2 to 3 minutes or until transparent. Trim coarse ends from broccoli stalks, slice stalks thin on the diagonal, and add to onions. Trim ends from mustard greens, chop coarsely and stir into mixture. Combine water and shoyu and pour over vegetables; then reduce heat to a minimum, cover, and steam for 5 minutes or until cooked to taste. Toss gently. Serve immediately.

2. Prepare greens; return to noodles.

Dinner	*Breakfast*	*Lunch*
Sautéed Mushrooms On Toast	Granola with Apple-Strawberry Kanten	Celery Vichyssoise
Whole Wheat Macaroni with Tomato Sauce		Macaroni and Bean Salad with Miso-Dill Dressing
Spinach Fritters		
Celery Salad with Plum-Basil Dressing		
Apple-Strawberry Kanten		

Comments

If you are in a cooking mood, this dinner is ideal. Although it appears complicated, only the fritters will take work; the rest of the preparations are quite easy since there is a lot of unattended cooking and cooling. Note that the breakfast granola requires about 1 hour and 15 minutes to make from scratch: you may want to prepare it at some time other than breakfast. The vichyssoise will need to cool for 4 to 6 hours and can be made the night before if there isn't time to make it in the morning. You will need cooked beans for the luncheon salad.

Matzoh meal, a ground meal that is pre-cooked, is used in the fritters because the cooking time of a fritter is not long enough to thoroughly cook a raw flour such as whole wheat pastry. The matzoh meal has a tendency to absorb liquid quickly which is desirable in this dish because you can never drain all the water from the spinach. The arrowroot flour helps keep the oil out of the spinach, and the fritters crisp.

The breakfast granola, delicious as it is, should be used with caution; it has a very high fat content: commercial varieties contain up to 40 percent fat; homemade varieties about 20 percent. The oat flakes, encased in a mixture of sweetener and oil, are literally "fried" as they bake. Unless it's thoroughly chewed, granola can be difficult to digest.

Nutritional Values

Abundant protein is obtained from the pasta, oats, eggs, seeds, miso, beans, and some of the vegetables; vitamin A from the spinach, tomatoes, strawberries, Romaine lettuce, watercress, and parsley; the B-complex vitamins from the mushrooms, pasta, celery, oats, beans, nuts, and egg; and vitamin C from the raw salad vegetables and parsley, as well as the tomatoes, apple juice, strawberries, and spinach. Calcium is supplied by the grain, lettuce, watercress, nuts, beans, and agar-agar; and iron by the oats, pasta, spinach, nuts, seeds, agar-agar, parsley, watercress, lettuce, and mushrooms.

Utensils

Dinner: Medium-sized skillet, baking sheet, 4-quart pot, two 2-quart covered saucepans, colander, one small and two large mixing bowls, salad bowl, blender, 9-inch shallow, rectangular baking pan.

Breakfast: Large baking pan, one large and one small mixing bowl, blender.

Lunch: 2- or 3-quart soup pot, 2-quart saucepan, blender, Foley food mill or strainer, large salad bowl, small mixing bowl.

Dinner

Apple-Strawberry Kanten

Serves: 4
Time: 8 minutes; 2 hours

3 bars kanten (agar-agar) or 8 tablespoons flakes
4½ cups apple juice
1½ cups water
2 teaspoons vanilla
1½ pints strawberries
2 tablespoons tahini
6 almonds

1. Make the kanten;
go on to tomato sauce.

In a 2-quart saucepan, combine kanten, juice and water, and bring to a boil; simmer for 4 to 5 minutes until dissolved, then stir in vanilla. While mixture simmers, wash and clean strawberries, then cut each one lengthwise into several slices. Line the bottom of a 9-inch shallow rectangular baking pan with 2/3 of the strawberries, setting the remainder aside in another pan or bowl. Gently pour the hot kanten mixture over the strawberries in the first pan to a depth of about 1½ inches; pour the remaining kanten over the strawberries in the second pan. Chill until firmly set.

14. Finish kanten.

To serve, slice the kanten in the baking pan into six pieces. Break up the kanten in the second pan and transfer to a blender; add tahini and purée until smooth. Serve as a sauce over the kanten squares. Top with almonds. Reserve remaining kanten purée for breakfast.

Spinach Fritters

Serves: 4
Time: 15 minutes; 15 to 20 minutes

2 pounds fresh spinach
¼ teaspoon sea salt
1 egg
¼ to ½ cup matzoh meal
2 tablespoons arrowroot or 1 tablespoon kuzu powder
Oil for frying

3. Wash and steam spinach;
go on to salad.

Try to buy spinach plants rather than packaged leaves. Trim 2 inches from the bottom of the plant and discard, then wash spinach in a sinkful of water, fishing out the leaves and leaving the grit on the bottom of the sink. Repeat three times. Place wet spinach in a 4-quart pot, cover, and bring up the heat. As soon as the pot starts to hiss, reduce heat and steam for 5 to 7 minutes or until spinach shrinks to about 1/4 of its original volume.

5. Drain spinach;
return to macaroni.

Drain the spinach in a colander, then squeeze to extract as much water as possible; allow to cool.

10. Make half of the fritters;
return to macaroni.

Chop the spinach fine and transfer to a mixing bowl. Add the next 4 ingredients, mixing gently to form a thick batter. Heat 1/4 inch of oil in a skillet, until oil begins to move. Gently lower the spinach mixture into the hot oil by the spoonful. When the edges of the fritters turn light brown, carefully turn fritters with a flat spatula. Cook until lightly browned and firm. Drain thoroughly on brown paper, and keep fritters warm in the oven until ready to serve.

Tomato Sauce

Serves: 4
Time: 10 minutes; 1 hour

Boiling water
1 pound deep red, ripe tomatoes
1 or 2 cloves garlic
1 large yellow onion
2 tablespoons olive oil
½ teaspoon oregano
½ teaspoon dried basil
½ teaspoon sea salt or to taste
1½ tablespoons kuzu powder (optional)
¼ cup water (optional)

Prepare tomatoes by dipping them for 30 seconds into boiling water, then peeling away the skin; cut tomatoes into quarters, then cut each quarter in half. Place tomatoes in a bowl or deep plate and set aside. Peel and mince garlic, then peel onion and chop fine. Heat the oil in a 2-quart saucepan over medium heat and sauté garlic, then onion. Add the oregano and basil and continue cooking, stirring constantly for 3 to 4 minutes until strongly fragrant. Now add tomatoes and salt, and continue stirring for 2 minutes or until tomatoes begin to release some liquid; cover pan, reduce heat to minimum and simmer, stirring occasionally, for as long as it takes to make the rest of the dinner (at least one hour). This sauce, traditionally cooked for 12 hours, needs no water; there's enough in the tomatoes themselves. Before serving, check consistency; if sauce is too watery, stir in kuzu dissolved in a little water and simmer until thickened and clear. Refrigerated, this sauce will keep for several days.

2. Make the tomato sauce; move on to fritters.

Whole Wheat Macaroni

Serves: 4
Time: 20 minutes

1 pound whole wheat macaroni
3 quarts water
½ teaspoon sea salt

In a 4-quart pot, bring the water and salt to a rolling boil.
Add pasta to the water, return to a boil, and cook over medium heat for 15 to 20 minutes. The macaroni will swell to more than double its dry size. Drain the noodles (reserving the water for use in soup), and rinse quickly under cold running water to prevent sticking. When ready to serve, reheat by steaming noodles over a little water (¼ to ½ inch) in the bottom of the pot.

6. Start water for the macaroni (in the spinach pot); go back to salad.
9. Cook the macaroni; return to fritters.
11. Drain and rinse macaroni; go back and finish fritters.

Celery Salad

Serves: 4
Time: 10 minutes; 15 minutes

3 celery stalks
3 to 4 radishes
3 scallions
2 tablespoons shoyu (natural soy sauce)
2 leaves Romaine lettuce

4. Prepare salad;
   return to spinach.

13. Toss salad;
    return to dessert.

Cut celery into 2-inch matchsticks; slice radishes crosswise into disks; chop scallions. Combine vegetables in a salad bowl and sprinkle with shoyu; marinate for 15 minutes or more.
Just before serving, shred lettuce and toss with vegetables and Plum-Basil Dressing.

Plum-Basil Dressing

Time: 3 minutes

½ teaspoon umeboshi paste
2 tablespoons olive or safflower oil
2 tablespoons water
4 to 5 fresh basil leaves

7. Make the salad dressing;
   move on to mushrooms.

In a small bowl, cut the oil into the umeboshi paste, then mix in the water. Now chop basil very fine and add.

Sautéed Mushrooms on Toast

Serves: 4
Time: 5 minutes; 10 minutes

Whole wheat bread slices
1 pound mushrooms
3 tablespoons sesame oil
¼ to ½ teaspoon sea salt
1 tablespoon chopped parsley

8. Slice the mushrooms and
   toast the bread;
   return to macaroni.

12. Sauté mushrooms;
    go on to salad.

Preheat oven to 375°F. Cut bread slices into rounds, squares, and triangles (allow 2 or 3 per person). Place on a baking sheet and bake for 5 to 6 minutes or until crisp.
Wash the mushrooms, trimming away the bottoms, and cut into thin slices lengthwise. Heat oil in a skillet over medium heat; add the mushrooms, sprinkle with salt, and stir. The salt will draw out the water and after a few minutes of dryness, the mushrooms will release their juice. Cook for 4 to 5 minutes, then drain or spoon the juice into a cup and continue sautéing until mushrooms shrink to about half their original size. Serve on toast slices with a small amount of mushroom juice spooned over the top. Garnish with chopped parsley.

Granola

4 cups rolled oats
½ cup sunflower seeds
½ cup chopped walnuts
¼ cup unrefined safflower oil
¼ cup maple syrup or honey
1½ teaspoons vanilla
Leftover apple-strawberry kanten

Preheat oven to 350°F. Combine solid and liquid ingredients separately, then mix them together. Spread on a large, shallow baking pan, and bake for 20 minutes, stirring often. The granola is ready when uniformly light golden brown. It will crisp as it cools; allow 20 minutes. Serve 2/3 cup per person, topped with Apple-Strawberry Kanten. Store remaining granola in an air-tight container.

Lunch

Celery Vichyssoise

1 medium yellow onion
3 tablespoons corn oil
4 stalks celery
½ teaspoon sea salt or to taste
½ cup rolled oats
5 cups water
2 tablespoons chopped parsley

Peel and chop the onion. Heat the oil in a 2-quart soup pot, add onion and saute until translucent. Chop the celery, add to the pot and saute for 2 minutes more. Now add salt, oats, and water, and bring to a boil. Reduce heat and simmer for 30 minutes, stirring occasionally. Transfer to a blender and puree, then pass through a sieve or food mill to remove celery strings. Chill for 2 to 6 hours. Serve garnished with parsley.

1. Make soup 4 to 6 hours in advance.

Macaroni and Bean Salad

3 cups cooked whole wheat macaroni
1½ cups cooked kidney beans
4 scallions, whites and greens
½ bunch watercress

In a large salad bowl, combine macaroni and beans (if you do not have cooked beans, soak 1 cup overnight in 3 cups water, then simmer for an hour or so before leaving for work in the morning). Chop the scallions very fine and the watercress very coarse, and add to the macaroni mixture. Add Miso-Dill Dressing, toss, and allow to stand for 15 minutes or more.

2. Prepare salad.

Miso-Dill Dressing

Time: 5 minutes

1 tablespoon white (shiro) or brown rice miso, or 2 teaspoons shoyu
  (natural soy sauce)
2 tablespoons lemon juice
2 tablespoons olive oil
1 tablespoon fresh chopped dill
1 teaspoon shoyu (natural soy sauce) optional

In a small bowl, combine all ingredients, mixing well. Use either the miso
or the shoyu, but not both together.

Dinner	*Breakfast*	*Lunch*
Clams Marinière	*Crêpes with Sprouts*	Escarole-Garlic Soup
Multicolored Rice		Rice and Vegetable Salad with
Chinese Cabbage Salad with		Creamy Parsley Dressing
Tahini-Onion Dressing		
Mocha Mousse		

Comments

The dinner and lunch menus assume you have some cooked rice already on hand. If you do not and decide to make some, adjust your timing accordingly by preparing the rice first. Since both the multicolored rice and the garlic-seasoned clams are mixed dishes, the simple cabbage salad provides a leafy contrast. The breakfast crêpes are fun to make for a Sunday brunch with friends or family.

For those who live along the seashore as well as for seasonal visitors there, spring and summer are wonderful for clamming. This clam recipe is the classic way of preparing mussels in my home town of Mar del Plata, Argentina. I find it unequalled in taste and simplicity.

Nutritional Values

Protein is obtained from the clams, and complementary proteins from the rice, tofu, miso, sunflower seeds, and vegetables; vitamin A from the parsley, red pepper, carrot, broccoli, escarole, watercress, and squash; the B-complex vitamins from the clams, rice, tofu, miso, escarole, onions, parsley, and mushrooms; vitamin C from all the raw vegetables as well as in the parsley, garlic, escarole, onion, pepper and squash. Calcium is supplied by the clams, agar (kanten), tofu, broccoli, escarole, squash, and onions; and iron by the clams, agar, miso, parsley, escarole, and broccoli.

Utensils

Dinner: Short strong knife, pail or bucket or bowl, large pot, two serving bowls per person (for clams and broth), 2-quart saucepan, salad bowl, small mixing bowl, 1½-quart saucepan, wire whisk, shallow baking pan, blender.

Breakfast: Blender or mixing bowl, 2 medium skillets, metal spatula.

Lunch: 2-quart soup pot, salad bowl, blender.

Clams Marinière

Serves: 4
Time: 15 minutes; 1 hour

4 dozen fresh clams
1 tablespoon flour or cornmeal
2 handfuls parsley (about 1½ cups loosely packed)
2 to 3 cloves garlic
Water
Shoyu (natural soy sauce) to taste

1. Clean and soak clams;
move on to dessert.

Wash and scrub the clams or scrape them with a paring knife to remove any weeds that may protrude. Discard open clams that do not close when you tap them. Place clams in a pan or bucket with water to cover, and sprinkle flour or cornmeal over the surface: this will cause the clams to open and expel any sand and grit. Soaking time should be a minimum of one hour.

7. Prepare clams;
while they steam, return to mousse.

Shortly before serving time, chop the parsley and mince the garlic. Place clams in a large pot on the stove, sprinkle on parsley and garlic and half cover the clams with water. Bring to a boil, then reduce heat, cover, and steam for 5 to 7 minutes or until all the clams open. Place the clams in one set of individual serving bowls; swirl the broth and pour into a second set of serving bowls. Dip the clams in the broth or add a sprinkle of shoyu to the broth and serve the clams immersed in the steaming liquid.

Mocha Mousse

Serves: 4
Time: 15 minutes; 1 to 1½ hours

3 cups apple juice
1 cup water
2 bars kanten or 5 tablespoons agar flakes
1½ teaspoons vanilla
4 tablespoons instant cereal coffee
2 tablespoons tahini
6 split whole almonds

2. Prepare kanten and chill;
go on to salad.

In a 1½-quart saucepan, bring apple juice and water to a boil; add kanten bars or sprinkle agar over the liquid, and simmer until dissolved. Using a wire whisk, gradually beat in vanilla, then cereal coffee. Pour mixture into a shallow baking pan and cool; when the liquid has ceased steaming, place in the freezer for 30 to 40 minutes or until firmly set.

8. Blend mousse.

Remove mocha mixture from the freezer and slice into small pieces, with a spatula; place half of the mocha pieces in a blender with 1 teaspoon tahini and purée, working contents towards the center with a spatula; repeat the process with remaining half. When mixture is smooth, pour into individual dessert bowls. Garnish each serving with almond halves.

Chinese Cabbage Salad

Serves: 4
Time: 10 minutes

1 small Chinese cabbage (about 4 cups)

Cut away the bottom of the cabbage, separate the leaves, and wash well. Stack the leaves and chop very fine.
Toss with Tahini-Onion Dressing about 10 minutes before serving.

3. Chop salad;
   move on to dressing.
6. Toss salad;
   return to clams.

Tahini-Onion Dressing

Time: 5 minutes

2 tablespoons tahini
1 tablespoon shoyu (natural soy sauce)
¼ teaspoon umeboshi paste
3 tablespoons water
1 tablespoon grated onion

In a small mixing bowl, combine tahini and shoyu, then add plum paste. Gently stir in the water, add the grated onion, and mix well.

4. Make dressing;
   go on to rice.

Multicolored Rice

Serves: 4
Time: 5 minutes; 15 minutes

½ green pepper
½ red pepper
1 tablespoon corn oil
1 small yellow squash
1 teaspoon shoyu (natural soy sauce)
1 tablespoon water
3 cups cooked brown rice

Slice the peppers lengthwise into strips, then dice. Heat oil in a 2-quart saucepan, and sauté peppers gently over medium heat. Cut squash lengthwise, then dice and add to peppers. Continue to sauté until squash is limp. Combine shoyu and water and sprinkle over vegetables. Stir for 1 minute more. Now add cooked rice, breaking up any lumps; mix well. Cover pan, reduce heat to minimum, and heat through for 5 to 6 minutes.

5. Prepare rice;
   return to salad.

Crêpes with Sprouts

Serves: 4
Time: 1 hour

2 cups water
1 fertile egg
¼ teaspoon sea salt
2 cups whole wheat pastry flour
1 cup sprouts

Place the first 4 ingredients in a blender and blend for 1 to 2 minutes until smooth. Chop sprouts and stir into mixture by hand. Lightly oil a skillet with a paper towel and warm over medium heat. Pour in or ladle just enough batter to cover the bottom of the skillet. As the edges start to shrink and curl, turn the crêpe over, press down with a spatula and cook for 2 minutes more. The first one or two crêpes may be imperfect, but they will improve with practice. Make two or three crêpes per person and serve with Pimento-Olive Spread or any miso or tofu dip.

Pimento-Olive Spread

Time: 10 minutes

5 to 6 Spanish olives, stuffed with pimento
1 8-ounce cake tofu
1 teaspoon shoyu (natural soy sauce)
1 tablespoon olive oil
2 tablespoons tahini

Chop the olives and pimento very fine and place in a small mixing bowl. Add the remaining ingredients and mash thoroughly with a fork. Spread thickly across the middle of each crêpe, then gently roll.

Rice and Vegetable Salad

Serves: 4
Time: 15 minutes

1 carrot
½ bunch watercress
4 scallions
2 celery stalks
2 cups cooked brown rice

Shred carrot with a potato peeler. Remove the stems from the watercress; chop scallions and celery stalks. Now combine the vegetables in a salad bowl, stir in the rice, and toss with Creamy Parsley Dressing.

1. Make rice salad; go on to soup.

Creamy Parsley Dressing

Time: 5 minutes

2 ounces soft tofu
2 tablespoons tahini
½ cup water
2 tablespoons brown rice vinegar (or lemon juice)
½ teaspoon sea salt or to taste
1 handful washed parsley

Place all ingredients in a blender and purée until creamy. Pour approximately ¼ cup of the dressing on the rice-vegetable salad. Toss well.

3. Prepare dressing and toss salad.

Escarole-Garlic Soup

Serves: 4
Time: 5 minutes; 10 minutes

½ bunch escarole
1 or 2 cloves garlic
1 tablespoon corn or sesame oil
½ teaspoon sea salt or to taste
5 cups water
Shoyu (natural soy sauce) to taste

Wash and slice the escarole and mince the garlic. Heat the oil in a 2-quart soup pot; add the garlic, stirring briefly until it begins to brown, then stir in the escarole and salt. Cook over medium heat until the escarole wilts. Add the water and bring to a boil, then reduce heat, cover, and simmer for 10 minutes. Season to taste with shoyu.

2. Prepare soup; return to salad.

Summer Meals

	Dinner	Breakfast	Lunch
Menu No. 1 PAGE 181	*Long-grain Brown Rice with Parsleyed Nut Sauce Sautéed Greens Chickpeas Garni Beets with Tofu Mayonnaise Peach Compote*	*Lemon-Miso Soup Waldorf Rice*	*Humus on Pita Bread Orange-Tahini Ices*
Menu No. 2 PAGE 187	*Savory Bulghur White Beans Vinaigrette Spinach with Sesame Sauce Strawberry Custard Pie*	*Whole Grain Toast or Crackers with choice of spreads: White Bean, Avocado-Olive, Peanut-Apple Miso, Tofu-Pickle*	*Eggplant Appetizer Tabouli with Mint Dressing*

Menu No. 3
 	
PAGE 193
	*Cream of Cucumber Soup
	Pasta al Pesto
	Russian Salad
	Cantaloupe Royale*
		*Herbed Scrambled Eggs
		Chilled Russian Salad*
			*Noodle-Cucumber-Arame
			   Salad with Sour Dressing
			Leeks and Cauliflower
			   Sesame*

Menu No. 4
 	
PAGE 199
	*Torta Pascualina
	   (Spinach Pie)
	Corn, Peas, and Carrots
	Caraway Baked Potatoes
	Bibb Salad with Tahini-
	   Parsley Dressing
	Couscous Pudding*
		Muesli	*Empanadas (Vegetable
			   Turnovers)
			Green Rainbow Salad with
			   Miso-Vinegar Dressing*

Menu No. 5
 	
PAGE 205
	*Cold Artichokes with Corn
	   Dipping Sauce
	Fancy Barley Loaf with
	   Green Sauce
	Baked Tomatoes with Miso
	String Beans Vinaigrette
	Tahini Candy*
		*Raw Vegetable Plate
		   with Dips*
			*Cold Tomato Soup
			String Bean-Barley Salad
			   with Tahini-Tofu Dressing*

Menu No. 6
 	
PAGE 211
	*Escabeche (Pickled Fish)
	Baked Corn-on-the-Cob
	Watercress Salad with Tofu-
	   Mustard Dressing
	Cherries in Apricot Sauce*
		*Corn Fritters with
		   Apple Butter*
			*Split Pea Aspic
			Curried Vegetables on
			   Rice*

Dinner	*Breakfast*	*Lunch*
Long-Grain Brown Rice with Parsleyed Nut Sauce *Sautéed Greens* *Chickpeas Garni* *Beets with Tofu Mayonnaise* *Peach Compote*	*Lemon-Miso Soup* *Waldorf Rice*	*Humus on Pita Bread* *Orange-Tahini Ices*

Comments

When the weather is hot, the tendency is to cook less, and indeed summer meals should be lighter, cooler, greener, and crunchier than winter repasts. Many people, however, find it more conducive to year-round health if they also eat some cooked grains in the summertime along with fruits and salads. Thus in the summer menu sets, whole grains are still the main source of protein but are lightened by cooling preparation methods, flavorings, and temperature as well as by the type of accompanying legumes, vegetables, and desserts. Also, and perhaps even more importantly, the choice of grains reflects the season; long grain brown rice is the primary grain used—together with bulghur wheat, corn, and barley—since all these grains are grown in warmer climates. Kasha, millet, and cooked oatmeal are reserved for the cold winter months.

Note that the chickpeas on the dinner menu must be soaked 2 to 8 hours in advance and the ices for lunch must be prepared the night before.

Nutritional Values

Protein is obtained from the rice and chickpeas and is complemented by the tofu, miso, walnuts, chard, and beets; vitamin A from the parsley, chard and carrots; the B-complex vitamin from the rice, chickpeas, tofu, miso, nori, and walnuts; and vitamin C from the chard, parsley, sprouts, peaches, celery, lettuce, and orange juice. Calcium is supplied by the chard, chickpeas, beets, tofu, nori, and tahini; and iron by the chard, beets, chickpeas, miso, nori, raisins, and tahini.

Utensils

Dinner: 4-quart covered pot, small saucepan, small bowl, 3-quart pot, medium skillet, two 2-quart covered saucepans, 1½-quart covered saucepan, blender, lemon juicer.

Breakfast: Two 2-quart pots, small bowl.

Lunch: Blender, grater, 1-quart bowl, small paper cups for the ices.

Dinner

Chickpeas Garni

Serves: 4
Time: 5 minutes; 1 hour
Soaking: 2 to 8 hours

2 cups chickpeas
8 cups water
1 small whole onion, peeled
1 stalk celery with leaves
1 bay leaf
1 teaspoon olive oil
1 teaspoon sea salt

1. Soak the chickpeas 2 to 8 hours in advance.

2. 1½ hours before serving time, bring chickpeas to a boil;
go on to beets.

12. Finish chickpeas; return to chard.

Wash the chickpeas well, pick out any stones, then cover with 6 cups cold water. Soak in cold water for 6 to 8 hours; or bring to a boil, simmer two minutes, and allow to soak for 2 hours.

Add the onion, celery, bay leaf, and oil to the chickpeas and simmer, covered, for 1 hour or until soft. Add water if necessary to keep the chickpeas covered.

During the last 10 minutes of cooking, salt the chickpeas and discard the celery, onion, and bay leaf. Place a hefty spoonful of chickpeas on top of the rice. Serve topped with Parsleyed Nut Sauce.

Beets

Serves: 4
Time: 1½ hours; 5 minutes

1 bunch beets with tops (or 1 beet per person)
Water to cover
Watercress

3. Trim and cook beets; move on to rice.

10. Drain and cool beets; return to chard.
14. Peel and slice beets.

Cut the greens from the beets leaving 1 inch of stalk connected to the beet; retain the long root end. Scrub the beets, taking care not to puncture the skin, and place in a 1½-quart saucepan with water to cover. Bring to a boil, reduce heat, cover, and simmer for 1 hour.

Drain the beets and allow them to cool for 30 minutes.

Slip off the skin from the beets with your fingers. (Wash your hands immediately after peeling to remove any stain.) Slice the beets into rounds. Serve a row of beet slices on a bed of watercress topped with Tofu Mayonnaise.
NOTE: Retain the beet greens to make Sautéed Greens. Or make a soup with the greens and the cooking water from the beets.

Tofu Mayonnaise

Time: 5 minutes

1 8-ounce cake tofu
¼ cup water
2 tablespoons olive oil or cold-pressed corn oil
2 tablespoons brown rice vinegar or lemon juice
1 teaspoon sea salt or to taste
¼ teaspoon ground coriander

Combine the ingredients in a blender and purée until creamy, pushing contents down with a rubber spatula. Refrigerated, this mayonnaise will keep for 2 days. If the mixture separates, stir well to combine.

6. Make the mayonnaise;
go on to chard.

Long-Grain Brown Rice

Serves: 4
Time: 2 minutes; 1 hour

3 cups long-grain brown rice
6 cups water
1 teaspoon sea salt or to taste

Wash rice thoroughly. Place in a 4-quart pot with the water and salt; bring to a boil, reduce heat, cover, and simmer for 1 hour. When the rice has finished cooking, fluff with a wooden spoon or paddle. Serve topped with Parsleyed Nut Sauce.

4. Cook rice;
go on to dessert.

Parsleyed Nut Sauce

Time: 10 minutes

6 scallions
1 handful of parsley
1 tablespoon corn or sesame oil
½ cup walnut pieces
1 cup water
1 tablespoon kuzu
1 tablespoon shoyu (natural soy sauce) or to taste

Wash, trim, and chop the scallions very fine; chop the parsley. In a small saucepan, heat the oil, then add the scallions; reduce heat to medium low and sauté for 2 to 3 minutes. Add the nuts and sauté for 2 minutes longer. In a small bowl, dissolve kuzu in the water; add to the scallions, then add the parsley. Stir over medium heat until the sauce is clear and thick. Season with shoyu and serve over rice. (If the sauce is not served immediately, cover and stir occasionally to avoid formation of a film.)

9. Make parsleyed nut sauce;
return to beets.

Peach Compote

Serves: 4
Time: 10 minutes; 5 minutes

2 pounds ripe, fresh peaches
2 cups water or to cover
1 teaspoon vanilla
Roasted nuts (optional)

Scrub peaches thoroughly then cut longitudinally, gently separating the pulp from the pit; cut each half in 3 wedges. Place the peaches in a 2-quart saucepan with water and vanilla; bring to a boil, reduce heat, cover and simmer for 5 minutes.
Serve chilled or at room temperature with a sprinkling of roasted nuts.

5. Make the compote;
return to beets.
8. Remove compote from heat;
go on to rice.

Sautéed Greens

1 bunch chard (or beet tops, mustard greens or kale)
1 or 2 cloves garlic
1 tablespoon sesame or safflower oil
¼ teaspoon sea salt or to taste

7. Wash chard;
   return to compote.

11. Prepare chard;
    return to chickpeas.

13. Sauté chard;
    return to beets.

Wash the greens thoroughly in several changes of water to remove all the grit.

While still wet, place the greens in a 2-quart saucepan over very low heat; cover, and allow them to steam in their own moisture for 10 minutes until completely wilted. (Add water if needed to prevent burning.) Drain the greens well and chop very fine.

Peel and mince the garlic. Heat the oil in a medium skillet; add the garlic and allow it to sizzle for 5 seconds, then add the chopped greens. Sprinkle salt over the mixture and sauté over medium heat for 5 minutes, stirring constantly. Serve immediately.

Breakfast

Waldorf Rice

1 cup water
1 cup raisins
½ cup crushed walnuts
2 celery stalks
3 cups cold cooked rice

1. Prepare salad;
   move on to soup.

In a 2-quart pot, simmer the raisins and walnuts in the water; chop the celery very fine. Remove pot from the heat; add the celery first, then the rice. Mix well and allow to stand for 10 minutes or longer before serving.

Lemon-Miso Soup

Serves: 4
Time: 10 minutes; 6 to 7 minutes

4 ounces fresh mushrooms
2 scallions
1 cup water
2 sheets nori seaweed
1½ tablespoons white or brown rice miso
½ cup water
2 tablespoons lemon juice
3½ cups cold water
5 thin, round lemon slices

Wash mushrooms, trim bottoms of stems, and cut vertically in thin slices; chop the scallions. Place mushrooms in a 2-quart soup pot with water; bring to a boil, reduce heat, cover, and simmer. Roast the nori over medium heat, and crumble into the mushrooms; simmer for 1 minute more. In a small bowl, dissolve the miso in ½ cup water and stir into the soup; allow the soup to come to a boil, then remove from heat. Stir in the lemon juice and cold water. Serve with a sprinkling of chopped scallions and a floating lemon slice.

2. Prepare soup.

Lunch

Humus on Pita Bread

Serves: 4
Time: 10 to 15 minutes

2 cups cooked chickpeas
2/3 cups chickpea water
3 tablespoons tahini
1 or 2 cloves garlic
½ teaspoon sea salt
2 tablespoons olive oil
2 tablespoons lemon juice
5 whole wheat pita or 10 slices bread
Shredded lettuce
Grated carrot
Alfalfa sprouts

Place the first 7 ingredients in a blender, food mill or meat grinder and purée until creamy. Split the pita breads in half and spread each half thickly with the humus; top with lettuce, carrot, and sprouts. Serve open-faced or as a closed pouch.

2. Prepare humus.

Orange-Tahini Ices

Serves: 4
Time: 15 minutes; freeze overnight

10 oranges
2 tablespoons tahini
½ teaspoon vanilla

1. Prepare ices the night before; freeze overnight.

Extract 2 cups juice from the oranges. Combine ½ cup orange juice and the tahini in a blender for 1 to 2 minutes; transfer to a 1-quart bowl and stir in the remaining juice and vanilla. Pour into small paper cups and freeze overnight.
NOTE: To make popsicles, place ice cream sticks in the cups once the mixture has started to thicken.

Dinner	*Breakfast*	*Lunch*
Savory Bulghur	*Whole Grain Toast or*	*Eggplant Appetizer*
White Beans Vinaigrette	*Crackers with choice of*	*Tabouli with Mint*
Spinach with Sesame Sauce	*spreads: White Bean,*	*Dressing*
Strawberry Custard Pie	*Avocado-Olive,*	
	Peanut-Apple-Miso,	
	Tofu-Pickle	

Comments

Spinach generally is served with some form of protein (eggs, cheese, bacon, et cetera) to counterbalance its sharpness. In the dinner meal, sesame sauce will provide the necessary protein and oil to serve as a balancing element to the spinach. The proof is in the taste; it will make a difference whether you eat the spinach plain or with the sauce.

Eggplant is a strongly expansive vegetable. The traditional way to make eggplant more contractive is to press it with salt over a two or three day period during which time the acids and water are drawn out by the salt. Since the lunch menu calls for eggplant, allow several days for its preparation. The tabouli with mint dressing should be prepared 1 hour in advance to allow it to marinate.

Nutritional Values

Complementary proteins are obtained from the bulghur, beans, sesame seeds, pie crust, avocado, toast, peanut butter miso, and tofu spreads; vitamin A from the parsley, spinach, red pepper, avocado, and watercress; the B-complex vitamin from the bulghur, beans, seeds, toast, pie crust, celery, avocado, and eggplant; and vitamin C from the parsley, spinach, watercress, beans, strawberries, red pepper, celery, scallions, chives, and avocado. Calcium is supplied by the seeds, spinach, beans, watercress, parsley, kuzu, tofu, and eggplant; and iron by the beans, sesame seeds, miso, tofu, spinach, olives, watercress, and eggplant.

Utensils

Dinner: 3-quart pot, two 2-quart saucepans, 1½-quart saucepan, wire whisk or fork, mixing/serving bowl, small bowl, 2-quart serving bowl, small metal pot or skillet, suribachi or mortar and pestle, blender, 9-inch pie plate.

Breakfast: Four medium bowls and a fork.

Lunch: Crock or bowl with inside cover and weights, 1½-quart pot, salad bowl, small bowl or jar.

White Beans Vinaigrette

Serves: 4
Time: 10 minutes; 3 hours, 15 minutes

2 cups dry baby lima beans
8 cups water
1 small onion
1 small carrot
2 parsley sprigs
1 teaspoon sea salt
2 tablespoons chives
½ red bell pepper
1 handful parsley
2 whole scallions

1. Soak the beans 6 to 8 hours in advance.
2. Cook beans; go on to dessert.
9. Drain and cool beans; go on to spinach dish.
11. Finish bean dish; go back to spinach.

Place the beans and water in a 3-quart pot; bring to a boil, reduce heat, and simmer for 2 minutes. Turn off heat, cover, and soak for 2 hours.

Add the whole carrot and onion and the parsley sprigs to the beans; simmer for 1 hour. Add salt 10 minutes before removing beans from heat. Discard the carrot, onion, and parsley sprigs; drain the beans and cool to room temperature.

Chop the chives, red pepper, parsley, and scallions. In a 1-quart bowl, combine 3 cups cooked beans, chives, red pepper, parsley and scallions. Toss with Vinaigrette Dressing, and marinate for at least 15 minutes.

VINAIGRETTE:

Time: 3 minutes

1 teaspoon umeboshi plum paste
4 tablespoons brown rice vinegar
2 tablespoons olive oil

8. Make vinaigrette; return to beans.

Combine the ingredients, mixing well with a fork.

Strawberry Custard Pie

Serves: 12
Time: 40 minutes; 2 hours to chill

CRUMBLE CRUST:

Time: 15 minutes; 15 minutes

¼ cup corn oil
3 tablespoons water
A dash of sea salt
1½ cups whole wheat flour

3. Make pie crust; move on to bulghur.

5. Remove pie crust from oven; return to bulghur.

Preheat oven to 375°F. In a small bowl, beat the oil, water, and salt with a fork or wire whisk. Place the flour in a 2-quart bowl and pour the oil mixture over the flour, rubbing lightly between the hands until the flour is thoroughly moistened. (The mixture should hold its shape when squeezed.) Place the flour mixture in a lightly oiled 9-inch pie plate and pat down firmly as you would a graham cracker crust. Form the edge by applying pressure with the thumb along the rim of the pie plate. Bake for 12 to 15 minutes or until the edges and center are lightly browned.
Remove pie crust from oven and allow to cool.

STRAWBERRY FILLING: Time: 20 minutes

1 pint strawberries
2 cups apple juice
1 cup water
3 tablespoons tahini
¼ cup maple syrup or 2/3 cup rice syrup
2 teaspoons vanilla
8 tablespoons kuzu

Wash the strawberries and remove leaves and stems. Place all but 7 of the strawberries in a blender; add the remaining ingredients and purée until smooth. Transfer the mixture to a saucepan over high heat, stirring continuously until it thickens and becomes creamy. Pour into a pre-baked pie crust.

Slice 6 of the remaining strawberries in half. Place along the outer circle of the pie like numerals on a clock; place the last strawberry in the center. Transfer pie to the refrigerator and allow it to jell. Serve by slicing between the strawberry halves.

7. Make filling, fill pie and chill;
go back to bean dish.

Savory Bulghur
Serves: 4
Time: 15 minutes; 45 minutes

2 cloves garlic
2 medium yellow onions
2 tablespoons corn oil
1 teaspoon thyme
6 cups boiling water
1 teaspoon sea salt
4 cups bulghur

Peel and mince the garlic; peel and chop the onion. Heat oil in a 2-quart saucepan; add the garlic and sauté for 30 seconds; add the onion and the thyme, and sauté over medium heat for 4 minutes. In another 2-quart pot, bring the water and salt to a boil. Add the bulghur to the onions and continue sauteing for 3 to 4 minutes more, or until the water boils in the other pot.

Turn off heat under both pots. Using a ladle, slowly add the boiling water to the bulghur (it will sizzle and foam up); cover, and allow to stand for 45 minutes or until all the water is absorbed. Fluff the bulghur with a wooden spoon just before serving.

NOTE: Reserve 3 cups of bulghur for lunch.

4. Prepare bulghur;
return to pie.

6. Add water to bulghur;
return to pie.

Spinach with Sesame Sauce

Serves: 4
Time: 5 minutes; 5 minutes

1½ pounds spinach

12. Finish spinach dish.

Wash the spinach thoroughly (if whole plants, trim 1½ inches off the bottom); chop into coarse pieces. Place the wet spinach in a 2-quart saucepan over medium-low heat; cover, and steam in its own moisture for 5 minutes or until spinach shrinks and turns bright green. Serve topped with a large spoonful of Sesame Sauce.

Sesame Sauce

Time: 20 minutes

1 cup unhulled sesame seeds
½ cup water
1½ tablespoons shoyu (natural soy sauce) or to taste

10. Roast seeds and make sauce;
return to beans.

Wash the seeds and drain well. Place a 1- to 1½-inch-thick layer of seeds in a small stainless steel saucepan or skillet and dry-roast over high heat, stirring constantly until the seeds are fragrant and begin to pop. Grind the seeds in a suribachi; add the water and shoyu and continue blending until creamy. Or, place all ingredients in a blender and purée.

Breakfast

Avocado-Olive Spread

Serves: 4
Time: 10 minutes

1 ripe avocado
2 tablespoons lemon juice
6 black Greek olives
Sea salt to taste
Sliced radishes

Scoop the avocado pulp into a bowl; add the lemon juice and mash with a fork. Pit and finely chop the olives; stir into the avocado. Add salt to taste. Garnish with sliced radishes and serve with whole grain toast or crackers.

Peanut-Apple-Miso Spread

Serves: 4
Time: 5 minutes

½ cup peanut butter
4 tablespoons apple butter
1 to 2 tablespoons miso
3 tablespoons water
Roasted peanuts

Combine the first 4 ingredients in a bowl, mixing with a wooden spoon until creamy. Garnish with roasted peanuts and serve with whole grain toast or crackers.

Tofu Pickle Spread

Serves: 4
Time: 10 minutes

1 8-ounce cake tofu
2 tablespoons sesame oil
1 cucumber dill pickle
1 tablespoon sesame salt (gomasio) or to taste
Sprouts
1 red pepper

Using a fork, mash the tofu in a bowl or suribachi; blend in the sesame oil. Chop the pickle very fine and add to the tofu, mixing well; add sesame salt to taste. Garnish with sprouts and strips of red pepper and serve with whole grain toast or crackers.

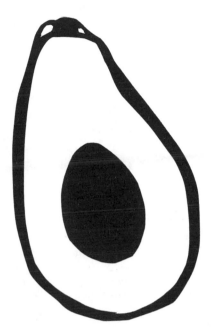

White Bean Spread

Serves: 4
Time: 5 minutes

Leftover white beans vinaigrette
3 to 4 tablespoons water
Shoyu (natural soy sauce) to taste
Parsley

Using a fork, mash the beans thoroughly in a mixing bowl. Moisten with the water and continue mashing until smooth. Add shoyu to taste. Garnish with parsley and serve with whole grain toast or crackers.

Lunch

Eggplant Appetizer

Serves: 4
Time: 15 minutes, 30 hours; 15 minutes, 30 minutes

1 medium-sized eggplant
Sea salt
2 to 3 cups water
½ teaspoon oregano
½ teaspoon basil
2 tablespoons lemon juice
2 tablespoons olive oil

Wash the eggplant and cut into ½-inch round slices. Sprinkle each slice liberally with salt and stack in a crock or bowl. Place a plate on top of the slices with stones or other weights on top of the plate; allow to stand for at least 30 hours. Discard the water that has been extracted from the eggplant and cut the eggplant into bite-size chunks.
Combine the eggplant, oregano, and basil in a 2-quart pot with water to cover; simmer for 15 minutes. Drain the eggplant and allow to cool. Combine the lemon juice and olive oil; add to the eggplant and toss well. Allow to marinate for at least 30 minutes. The mixture will keep for 5 to 6 days in the refrigerator.

1. Prepare eggplant two or three days in advance.

Tabouli with Mint Dressing

Serves: 4
Time: 10 minutes; 45 minutes

1 handful of parsley
1 stalk celery
3 whole scallions
5 medium radishes
3 cups cooked bulghur
5 large romaine lettuce leaves
Alfalfa sprouts

3. Make tabouli 1 hour before serving time.

Chop the parsley, celery, and scallions; slice the radishes into thin rounds. Combine the vegetables in a salad bowl and stir in the bulghur. Add the Mint Dressing, toss and allow to marinate for 45 minutes. Serve on lettuce leaves topped with sprouts.

Mint Dressing

2 tablespoons lemon juice
1 tablespoon shoyu (natural soy sauce)
2 tablespoons olive oil
5 leaves fresh mint

2. Prepare mint dressing; go on to tabouli.

Combine the first 3 ingredients in a small bowl or jar, mixing well. Chop the mint very fine and add to the liquid mixture. To improve the flavor, allow the dressing to stand for 10 to 15 minutes.

Dinner	*Breakfast*	*Lunch*
Cream of Cucumber Soup	Herbed Scrambled Eggs	Noodle-Cucumber-Arame
Pasta al Pesto	Chilled Russian Salad	Salad with Sour
Russian Salad		Dressing
Cantaloupe Royale		Leek and Cauliflower
		Sesame

Comments

The soup for dinner is served warm to take advantage of the water left over from boiling the vegetables; it also is excellent when served chilled. The Russian salad and the soup can be made in advance to allow time for them to chill. The dessert, pasta, and dressing for the salad should be prepared 45 minutes before serving time.

Nutritional Values

Protein is obtained from the pasta, walnuts, eggs, miso, sesame, and most of the vegetables; vitamin A from the basil, carrot, cantaloupe, cauliflower, peas, and red pepper; the B-complex vitamins from the pasta, walnuts, eggs, leek, and peas; and vitamin C from the basil, peas, cantaloupe, cucumbers, daikon, zucchini, cauliflower, cucumbers, and red pepper. Calcium is supplied by the cauliflower, cucumbers, zucchini, daikon, arame, leek, and sesame seeds; and iron by the pasta, miso, basil, daikon, cucumbers, eggs, arame, leek, raisins, and sesame seeds.

Utensils

Dinner: 4-quart pot, 3-quart pot, colander, one medium and one small mixing bowl, suribachi if available, blender, 1½-quart saucepan, slotted spoon, salad bowl.

Breakfast: Mixing bowl, whisk or fork, skillet, serving bowl.

Lunch: One small and one large bowl, 2-quart covered saucepan.

Dinner

Cantaloupe Royale

Serves: 4
Time: 10 minutes; 30 minutes

1 ripe cantaloupe
1 cup raisins
1 cup water
1 mint tea bag
1 tablespoon kuzu
¼ cup cold water

1. Make the dessert;
   go on to salad.

Cut the cantaloupe in quarters, scooping out the seeds; slice each quarter in half, remove skin, and dice. Place the cantaloupe pieces in a large serving bowl. Boil the raisins in water for 4 to 5 minutes in a small saucepan; turn off heat and add the tea bag. Dissolve the kuzu in cold water; remove the tea bag from the raisins. Add the kuzu to the raisins and bring heat to medium, stirring continuously until the mixture is clear and thick. Pour immediately over the cantaloupe and allow to cool for at least 30 minutes.

Russian Salad

Serves: 4
Time: 20 minutes; 30 to 40 minutes

2 quarts water
1 teaspoon sea salt
2 large carrots
8 ounces daikon or white radish
2 small zucchini
½ pound fresh peas
1 head cauliflower

2. Prepare vegetables, then
   drain and cool;
   go on to soup.

Bring the water and salt to a boil in a 2-quart pot. Wash the vegetables, then dice the carrots, daikon, and zucchini. Shell the peas and separate the cauliflower into small flowerettes. Parboil the carrots, daikon, and cauliflower separately for 4 minutes each; parboil the zucchini and peas separately for 2 minutes. Remove the vegetables from the pot with a slotted spoon and place in an uncovered colander to drain and cool. (Reserve the vegetable water for soup.) Transfer the vegetables to a salad bowl. Add Miso-Dill Dressing, toss, and serve.

Miso-Dill Dressing with Tahini

Time: 10 minutes

1 tablespoon white (shiro) or brown rice miso
2 tablespoons lemon juice
2 tablespoons olive oil
1 tablespoon fresh chopped dill
1 tablespoon tahini

Combine the ingredients in a small bowl, blending well. (1 teaspoon shoyu [natural soy sauce] may be used in place of the shiro or brown rice miso.)

8. Make salad dressing; go back to the noodles.

Cream of Cucumber Soup

Serves: 4
Time: 10 minutes; 25 minutes

¼ green pepper
2 tablespoons corn or sesame oil
2 stalks celery
1 pound cucumbers, peeled and chopped
6 cups water or vegetable cooking broth
½ cup rolled oats
½ teaspoon sea salt or to taste
1 tablespoon lemon juice
2 teaspoons chopped fresh dill

Chop the green pepper. Heat the oil in a 2-quart soup pot over medium heat; add the pepper and sauté for 3 to 4 minutes. Chop the celery and stir into the pepper; reduce heat and simmer while peeling and chopping the cucumbers. Add the cucumbers to the pot, stirring constantly for 2 minutes.

3. Prepare soup; go on to pasta.

Add the water, oats, and salt to the cucumbers; cover and simmer for 20 minutes more.

5. Continue with the soup; go back to pasta.

Transfer the soup to a blender and purée; then strain through a food mill or colander into a large bowl. Add the lemon juice and stir well. Just before serving, chop the dill and garnish individual servings of the soup. (If cold cucumber soup is desired, chill for 4 to 6 hours.)

10. Finish the soup.

Pasta al Pesto

Serves: 4
Time: 15 to 20 minutes; 20 minutes

2 quarts water
1 teaspoon sea salt
1 pound buckwheat or whole wheat noodles

Combine the water and salt in a 4- to 6-quart pot and bring to a boil. Add the noodles to the water and cook for approximately 20 minutes. Drain the noodles in a colander, then rinse in cold water and return to the pot. Cover until ready to serve.

4. Boil water for pasta; return to soup.
6. Cook the pasta; go on to pesto.
9. Drain and rinse the pasta; return to soup.

Pesto

1 bunch fresh basil (3 to 4 cups loosely packed)
4 tablespoons olive oil
1 or 2 cloves garlic, minced
2 tablespoons barley miso
½ cup walnuts

7. Make the pesto; return to salad.

Wash the basil and chop very fine; combine the basil and the oil in a suribachi, grinding well. Add the minced garlic, then the miso, blending to form a thick paste. Grind the walnuts into the paste, leaving an occasional crunchy piece. Or combine the ingredients and ¼ cup walnuts in a blender at low speed for 2 minutes; add the remaining walnuts and blend for 1 minute more. Since the mixture is very strong, serve only a teaspoon over each mound of pasta.

Breakfast

Herbed Scrambled Eggs

Serves: 4
Time: 5 minutes

5 organic eggs
¼ teaspoon sea salt or to taste
1 tablespoon sesame oil
2 cloves garlic, minced
½ teaspoon oregano
½ teaspoon basil
Toast or rice cakes

Break the eggs into a mixing bowl; add the salt and beat gently with a fork or wire whisk. Heat the oil in a skillet over medium heat; add the minced garlic, oregano, and basil and stir for 1 minute. Pour in the eggs and stir until they reach the desired consistency. Serve immediately with toast or rice cakes and chilled Russian salad or cantaloupe.

Noodle-Cucumber-Arame Salad

Serves: 4
Time: 10 minutes; 25 minutes

¼ cup arame (or hiziki) seaweed
¾ cup water
2 unwaxed cucumbers
1 teaspoon sea salt
3 cups cooked pasta or whole wheat macaroni

Soak the arame in water for 10 minutes or until refreshed. Peel or score the cucumbers; slice into thin rounds, discarding the tips. Spread the slices out on a chopping board or table and sprinkle with salt, then transfer to a large bowl and allow to stand for 15 minutes or more.

Squeeze the cucumber slices to express any remaining water, then drain; pour off the water from the arame. In a large bowl, combine the pasta, cucumbers, and arame. Add the Sour Dressing, toss, and serve.

1. Soak the arame and salt the cucumbers; go on to vegetable dish.

4. Finish preparing salad.

Sour Dressing

Time: 2 minutes

2 tablespoons lemon juice
1 tablespoon brown rice vinegar
1 teaspoon shoyu (natural soy sauce)
2 tablespoons water

Combine the ingredients in a small bowl and blend well with a fork or chopsticks.

3. Make the dressing; go back to cucumbers.

Leeks and Cauliflower Sesame

Serves: 4
Time: 15 minutes; 8 minutes

2 leeks
1 head cauliflower
2/3 cup water
2 tablespoons roasted sesame seeds or gomasio (sesame salt)

Cut the roots from the leeks and slice in half lengthwise; wash thoroughly, then slice crosswise in thin pieces. Wash the cauliflower, separating the flowerettes. Place the leeks and water in a 2-quart saucepan over medium heat; arrange the flowerettes over the leeks. Cover and steam for 8 minutes. Using a slotted spoon, transfer the vegetables to a large bowl. Sprinkle with roasted sesame seeds or gomasio and serve.

2. Prepare the vegetables; return to salad.

Dinner	*Breakfast*	*Lunch*
Torta Pascualina (Spinach Pie)	*Muesli*	*Empanadas (Vegetable Turnovers)*
Corn, Peas, and Carrots		*Green Rainbow Salad with Miso-Vinegar Dressing*
Caraway Baked Potatoes		
Bibb Salad with Tahini-Parsley Dressing		
Couscous Pudding		

Comments

Two dishes in this menu set will require advance preparation. Prepare the Torta Pascualina 5 to 6 hours before dinner or one day in advance. The muesli for breakfast must be prepared the evening before and allowed to stand overnight.

Since potatoes do not combine well with a grain-based diet, they are not included often on the menu sets. Potatoes, however, are the only food that provides an alkaline starch; they are good for the digestive system when it is over-acidic from eating too much animal protein.

Nutritional Values

Complete protein is obtained from the eggs, and complementary protein from the spinach, crust, tahini, couscous, corn, nuts, peas, and oats; vitamin A from the spinach, yellow corn, carrots, and peas; the B-complex vitamin from the whole wheat flour, oats, miso, couscous, peas, potatoes, and corn; and vitamin C from the raw vegetables, potatoes, and apples. Calcium is supplied by the spinach, oats, nuts, watercress, tahini, and peas; and iron by the spinach, watercress, peas, raisins, arugula, oats, and walnuts.

Utensils

Dinner: One small and two large mixing bowls, 4-quart pot, small pot, large strainer, 9-inch lasagna-type shallow baking pan or pie plate, pastry brush, rolling pin, garlic press, baking sheet, corn scraper or large knife, mixing bowl, two 2-quart covered saucepans, salad bowl, small mixing bowl, individual custard cups.

Breakfast: 1-quart pot, bowl with cover, coarse grater.

Lunch: Rolling pin, 4-inch diameter bowl to cut rounds in dough, 1½-quart saucepan, salad bowl, small mixing bowl.

Torta Pascualina (Spinach Pie)

Serves: 6 to 8
Time: 45 minutes; 45 minutes

3 pounds spinach
2 bunches Swiss chard (3 pounds)
½ teaspoon sea salt or to taste
½ teaspoon nutmeg
2 eggs
Parsley and radishes

1. Make spinach pie at least 5 or 6 hours in advance. Steam the greens; go on to crust.

Trim 2 inches from the stems of the spinach and chard. Wash the chard leaves several times in water to remove the dirt and sand. Place the wet spinach and chard in a 4-quart pot over medium heat; cover and steam for 10 minutes or until thoroughly wilted. Transfer the greens to a colander or strainer; place a plate on top of the greens to press out the water. Prepare the crust while the greens drain.

3. Prepare filling; go back to crust.

Preheat the oven to 350°F. Chop the drained spinach and chard very fine and place in a large mixing bowl; add salt and nutmeg to taste. Beat the eggs in a small bowl; reserve 2 teaspoons of beaten egg in a cup with ½ teaspoon water. Pour the remaining beaten egg over the greens and mix thoroughly.

4. Roll out crust and fill pie.

Divide the dough into three balls. Roll out one ball on an unfloured board; lift the dough, turn it over, and roll again. Repeat this process until the dough is very thin. (Rolling and turning the dough obviates the need for flour on the board, but the dough should not be sticky.) Place the sheet of dough in an oiled 9-inch shallow baking pan, pressing it up the sides; fill the crust with the spinach mixture. Roll out another ball of dough, rolling and turning until dough is thin; cover the pie. Press down the edges of the pie with a fork; trim the excess dough and decorate the pie with pastry strips. Place the remaining ball of dough in a plastic bag and store in the refrigerator. (Use for breakfast Empanadas.)

5. Bake pie.

Bake the pie for 20 minutes; open oven and brush the pie with the reserved beaten egg and bake for another 25 minutes or until the crust is firm and the edges are well done. Allow the pie to cool. When ready to serve, carefully run a knife around the sides to loosen the pie, transfer to a platter, and surround with mounds of parsley and thinly sliced radishes.

CRUST:

Time: 10 minutes

¾ cup unrefined corn oil
2 cups water
½ teaspoon sea salt
6 cups whole wheat flour

2. Prepare dough for crust; while it rests, make filling.

In a small pot, bring the oil, water, and salt to a boil; remove from heat and pour into a large mixing bowl. Beat the mixture with a whisk until it has a milky appearance; pour in the flour, stirring quickly to form a ball of dough. Add more water if the dough is too dry or more flour if too wet. Knead lightly, press into a ball, and allow to rest.

Caraway Baked Potatoes

Serves: 4
Time: 3 minutes; 40 minutes

5 potatoes
1 teaspoon caraway seeds
1 tablespoon shoyu (natural soy sauce)
1 tablespoon olive oil

Preheat the oven to 375°F. Wash the potatoes, cut out the eyes, and slice in half lengthwise. Sprinkle the seeds on a baking sheet; place the potatoes cut side down on top of them. Bake for 40 to 50 minutes or until done. Combine the oil and shoyu in a cup; brush on the seeded side of the potato and serve.

6. 1 hour and 15 minutes before serving time, begin to bake potatoes; then go on to dessert.

Couscous Pudding

Serves: 5 to 6
Time: 5 minutes; 30 minutes

1 cup couscous
2 cups apple juice
1 cup water
A dash of salt
½ cup raisins
½ cup chopped walnuts
1½ teaspoons vanilla
Grated rind of one lemon
Juice of ½ lemon
5 fresh cherries to garnish

Combine the ingredients in a 2-quart saucepan; bring to a boil, reduce heat, cover, and simmer for 10 to 15 minutes until all the liquid is absorbed. Pour the pudding into individual custard cups or dessert bowls. Decorate with a cherry and chill.

7. Start the pudding; while it cooks, go to vegetables.
9. Finish pudding; go back to vegetables.

Corn, Peas, and Carrots

Serves: 4
Time: 15 minutes; 15 minutes

6 ears corn
4 carrots
1½ pounds fresh green peas
1 tablespoon corn oil
¼ cup water
A dash of sea salt

Shuck the corn; using a corn scraper or the blunt edge of a kitchen knife, scrape the kernels from the cob into a bowl. Dice the carrots and shell the peas.
Heat the oil in a 2-quart saucepan over medium heat; add the corn and stir for 1 to 2 minutes. Add the carrots and sauté for 2 minutes more; reduce heat to minimum, cover, and steam for 8 minutes.
Add the peas and stir for 1 minute; then add the water and salt, cover, and simmer for 2 to 3 minutes or until the peas are bright green. Serve immediately.

8. Shuck corn and dice carrots; return to pudding.
10. Sauté the vegetables; while they steam, go on to salad.
12. Finish the vegetables; remove potatoes from oven.

Bibb Salad

Serves: 4
Time: 5 minutes

1 head Bibb lettuce

11. Make the salad and dressing; return to vegetables.

Separate the lettuce leaves; wash thoroughly, pat dry, and shred very fine. Place in individual serving bowls.

Tahini-Parsley Dressing

Time: 5 minutes

½ cup water
2 tablespoons tahini
1 tablespoon lemon juice
2 pitted umeboshi plums or 2 teaspoons
  umeboshi plum paste
1 handful of parsley

Combine the ingredients in a blender and purée at low speed until creamy, pushing the contents down with a spatula. Pour 1 teaspoon over each serving of Bibb lettuce. This dressing will keep for two days when refrigerated.

Breakfast

Muesli

Serves: 4
Time: Overnight; 5 minutes

2 cups rolled oats
½ cup sunflower seeds
½ cup chopped almonds
½ cup raisins
3 cups water
2 apples

Combine the first 4 ingredients in a large bowl; boil the water and pour over the dry mixture, mixing lightly. Cover, and allow to stand at room temperature overnight. In the morning, grate the apples into the muesli; mix well and serve.

Empanadas (Vegetable Turnovers)

Serves: 4
Time: 20 minutes; 40 minutes

1 tablespoon kuzu
¼ cup water
1 cup leftover corn, peas, and carrots
1 tablespoon shoyu (natural soy sauce) or to taste
Leftover dough from spinach pie

Preheat oven to 375°F. Dissolve the kuzu in water. Place the vegetable mixture in a 1½-quart saucepan; add the kuzu and place over medium heat, stirring constantly until thickened. Add shoyu to taste. On a flat surface, roll out the dough, turning and rolling until very thin. Cut the dough into 4- to 5-inch diameter circles. Place a spoonful of vegetable mixture in the center of each circle; bring the edges together and pinch shut; scallop the border by pressing the dough between the thumb and two fingers. (Make at least 2 empanadas per person.) Place the empanadas on a baking sheet; poke steam vents in the dough with a fork. Bake for 30 to 40 minutes or until the edges are lightly browned and the empanadas feel firm and sound hollow when tapped.

1. Prepare empanadas; while baking move on to salad.

Green Rainbow Salad

Serves: 4
Time: 10 minutes

1 bunch arugula or lettuce
½ bunch watercress
½ pound fresh peas
½ avocado
1 small zucchini

2. Make salad.

Wash the arugula and watercress; remove the thick stems, break the leaves into small pieces, and place in a salad bowl. Shell the peas and dice the avocado; add to the greens. Slice the ends from the zucchini, cut in half lengthwise, then cut crosswise into 2-inch chunks; cut the chunks into thin slices and add to the salad. Toss with Miso-Vinegar Dressing just before serving.

Miso-Vinegar Dressing

Time: 3 minutes

1 tablespoon brown rice miso
1 tablespoon olive oil
2 tablespoons brown rice vinegar
3 tablespoons water

Combine the miso and oil in a small mixing bowl. Add the remaining two ingredients, one at a time, mixing well after each addition.

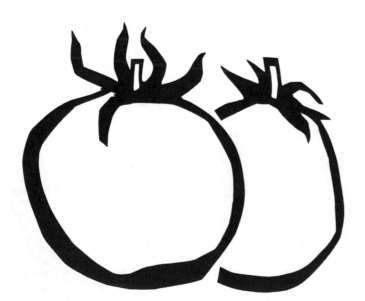

Dinner	*Breakfast*	*Lunch*
Cold Artichokes with Corn Dipping Sauce *Fancy Barley Loaf with Green Sauce* *Baked Tomatoes with Miso* *String Beans Vinaigrette* *Tahini Candy*	*Raw Vegetable Plate with Dips*	*Cold Tomato Soup* *String Bean-Barley Salad with Tahini-Tofu Dressing*

Comments

Various people, who have changed their diet to one consisting mainly of grains and vegetables, have found themselves reacting adversely to tomatoes and therefore tend to avoid them. Tomatoes, however, are a very yin food that will help to balance strong yang forces such as meat, hot summer days, a very active and energetic constitution or a surplus of physical activity. The method of preparation in this dinner is designed to balance the tomatoes, that is, to yangize them and make them less acidic and yin.

Some readers might find it odd to eat raw vegetables for breakfast, but if raw fruit is an acceptable breakfast food, why not raw vegetables? They are quick, easy, and refreshing, especially when it looks as though the thermometer will reach 96°F. by noon.

Nutritional Values

Complementary proteins are obtained from the barley, red lentils, sunflower seeds, tahini, miso, tofu, string beans, and roasted almonds; vitamin A from the parsley, tomatoes, string beans, cucumber, broccoli, celery, and carrot; the B-complex vitamin from the barley, red lentils, seeds, miso, celery, zucchini, broccoli, whole wheat, string beans, and tahini; and abundant vitamin C from the raw vegetables, parsley, tomatoes, and string beans. Calcium is supplied by the red lentils, seeds, string beans, tahini, carob, and sprouts; and iron by the barley, red lentils, parsley, miso, tahini, and broccoli.

Utensils

Dinner: 3-quart pot, small mixing bowl, 2-quart pot, 9-inch loaf pan, small saucepan, garlic press, blender, 3 small mixing bowls, serving bowl, small saucepan or skillet, shallow baking pan or baking sheet.

Breakfast: Blender, small saucepan, two small serving bowls, serving platter.

Lunch: Blender, strainer, salad bowl, small mixing bowl.

Dinner

Cold Artichokes

Serves: 5
Time: 45 minutes

5 artichokes
Water
1 teaspoon sea salt

1. Start the artichokes;
   go on to string beans.

Rinse the artichokes and place in a 4- to 6-quart pot; pour in enough water to half fill the pot. Add the salt and bring to a boil; then reduce heat, cover, and simmer for 40 to 45 minutes or until the artichokes are olive green and a leaf will detach easily. Cool artichokes and serve with Corn Dipping Sauce.

Corn Dipping Sauce

Time: 5 minutes

4 tablespoons lemon juice
3 tablespoons shoyu (natural soy sauce)
6 tablespoons raw unfiltered corn oil

5. Drain artichokes, and make dipping sauce;
   move on to tomatoes.

Combine the ingredients in a small bowl, mixing well.

String Beans Vinaigrette

Serves: 4
Time: 15 minutes; 30 minutes

1½ pounds string beans
1 quart water
½ teaspoon sea salt
1 tablespoon lemon juice
1 tablespoon brown rice vinegar
1 tablespoon shoyu (natural soy sauce)
1 tablespoon olive oil
1 hard boiled egg (optional)

2. Parboil the string beans;
   go on to barley loaf.

Wash the beans; remove the tips and snap or slice the beans into 1½-inch pieces. Bring the water and salt to a boil in a 2-quart pot. Add the beans, reduce heat, and simmer for 10 minutes.

4. Drain string beans;
   make vinaigrette, then
   return to artichokes.

Drain the beans and place in an uncovered serving bowl (reserve the cooking water for the lunch soup). In a small mixing bowl, combine the lemon juice, vinegar, shoyu, and oil; strain the egg through a sieve and add. Pour the dressing over the string beans and toss well. Marinate for at least 30 minutes. Turn the beans with a spoon once or twice to allow the dressing to reach all the beans. Cool and serve.

Fancy Barley Loaf

Serves: 4
Time: 10 minutes; 1 hour

1 cup barley
½ cup red lentils
¼ cup sunflower seeds
5 cups water
½ teaspoon sea salt
1 bay leaf

Preheat the oven to 350°F. Wash the barley and red lentils separately. Place the barley and lentils in a 2-quart pot with the remaining ingredients and bring to a boil; reduce heat and simmer for 2 minutes. Pour the mixture into a 9-inch oiled glass loaf pan, cover with aluminum foil, and bake for 1 hour. Serve in slices with Green Sauce on top.

3. Make the barley loaf; return to string beans.

Green Sauce

Time: 5 minutes; 2 minutes

6 scallions
1 tablespoon corn oil
1 tablespoon kuzu or arrowroot
1 cup water
1 handful parsley
1 tablespoon shoyu (natural soy sauce) or to taste

Chop the whole of each scallion; heat the oil in a saucepan and add the scallions, stirring over low heat for 2 minutes. Dissolve the kuzu or arrowroot in the water and add to the scallions; bring to a boil. Reduce heat and simmer for 2 minutes; meanwhile, chop the parsley. Add the shoyu to the sauce; then add the parsley. Serve immediately.

8. Make the green sauce; remove loaf and tomatoes from oven.

Baked Tomatoes with Miso

Serves: 4
Time: 10 minutes; 15 minutes

2 tablespoons brown rice or barley miso
2 tablespoons white miso (optional)
4 tablespoons water
½ cake tofu (4 ounces)
1 clove garlic, minced
1 teaspoon oregano
1 teaspoon basil
5 deep red tomatoes

Preheat the oven to 400° F. Combine the two misos in a small mixing bowl, blending well (if not using white miso, omit, but do not replace). Add the water and continue blending to form a smooth paste. Mash the tofu into the mixture, then add the minced garlic, oregano, and basil. Wash the tomatoes and slice in half crosswise; spread the miso mixture thickly on the cut side of each half. Stand the tomatoes side by side in a shallow baking pan or baking sheet and bake for 15 minutes. Serve one half to each person. Reserve the remaining halves to make soup for lunch.

6. Prepare tomatoes and bake them together with the barley loaf for the last 15 to 20 minutes before serving; move on to candy.

Tahini Candy

Serves: 4
Time: 10 minutes

¼ cup almonds
½ cup tahini
4 tablespoons maple syrup
¼ teaspoon almond extract
1 tablespoon carob flour
¼ cup grated coconut

7. Make the candy;
   return to barley loaf.

Preheat oven to 425°F. Spread the almonds on a baking sheet and roast in the oven for 5 minutes. In a small mixing bowl, blend the tahini, maple syrup, and almond extract, beating vigorously for 3 minutes until a stiff ball forms and the oil begins to separate; stir in the carob flour. As the mixture stiffens, press the dough against the sides of the bowl with a spoon to express the oil, then pour off. Allow the dough to sit for 1 to 2 minutes. Remove the almonds from the oven. Press and drain the dough again and place in a napkin or paper towel; squeeze to absorb excess oil. Chop the almonds and add to the mixture. Place the mixture on a piece of wax paper (so it won't stick to the chopping board) and roll into a cylinder shape. Slice the roll into bite-sized pieces and cover with grated coconut.

Breakfast

Raw Vegetable Plate with Dips

Serves: 4
Time: 10 minutes

2 carrots
3 to 4 stalks celery
1 zucchini squash
2 stalks broccoli

Cut the vegetables into sticks 2- to 3-inches long by ¼-inch thick. Arrange on a platter and serve with a dipping sauce.

Tofu Dip

Time: 5 minutes

1 8-ounce cake tofu
1 tablespoon sesame oil
½ to 1 teaspoon sea salt to taste
2 tablespoons water
½ teaspoon grated ginger

Place all the ingredients in a blender and purée, pushing mixture down the sides with a spatula, until smooth and creamy. Serve immediately.

Miso Dip

Time: 3 minutes; 10 minutes

3 tablespoons barley miso
5 tablespoons water
2 tablespoons lemon juice
1 tablespoon sake (rice wine) or dry sherry

Combine the miso and water in a small saucepan, mixing well; add the remaining ingredients. Bring to a boil, stirring constantly; reduce heat, cover, and simmer for 2 to 3 minutes. Cool before serving.

Lunch

String Bean-Barley Salad

Serves: 4
Time: 10 minutes

1½ to 2 cups leftover barley loaf
1½ to 2 cups string beans vinaigrette
1 carrot
1 stalk celery
Watercress

Crumble the barley loaf into a salad bowl; add the string beans. Grate the carrot very coarse and chop the celery; add to the mixture. Pour in Tahini-Tofu Dressing, toss, and allow salad to marinate for at least 15 minutes. Serve decorated with watercress.

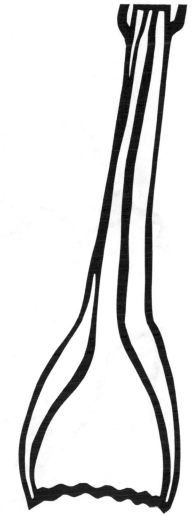

Tahini-Tofu Dressing

Time: 5 minutes

4 ounces tofu
2½ tablespoons tahini
½ teaspoon sea salt or to taste
3 tablespoons brown rice wine vinegar
4 tablespoons water
2 scallions
1 tablespoon sesame oil

Combine the ingredients in a blender and purée at medium speed until creamy.

Cold Tomato Soup

5 leftover baked tomato halves with miso
2 cups water
1 tablespoon tahini
Chopped chives or parsley

Chop the tomato halves into pieces; place in a blender with the water and tahini and purée until smooth. Strain to remove seeds. Pour into individual serving bowls and garnish each with ¼ teaspoon chopped chives or parsley.

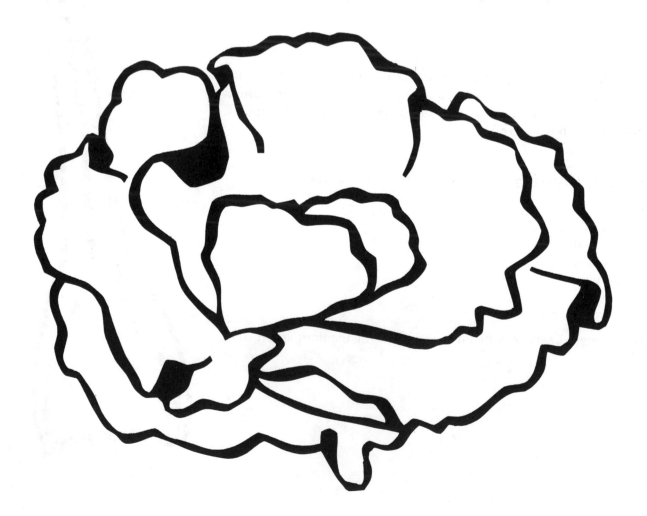

Dinner	*Breakfast*	*Lunch*

Escabeche (Pickled Fish)
Baked Corn-on-the-Cob
Watercress Salad with
   Tofu-Mustard Dressing
Cherries in Apricot Sauce
	Corn Fritters with
	  Apple Butter
		Split Pea Aspic
		Curried Vegetables on Rice
		Frozen Bananas

Comments

Both the dinner and lunch menus have dishes that require advance preparation. The escabeche should be prepared at least 8 hours in advance or even the day before; the aspic for lunch will take 2 to 3 hours to jell, and the bananas have to freeze overnight. Both the dinner and lunch menus work well for parties precisely because these dishes require advance preparation. For dinner, make as much corn as your oven will hold, and since everyone will shuck their own ear(s) of corn, the only work left to do before dinner time is to prepare the salad.

The corn fritters also make an excellent luncheon dish; omit the apple butter and serve with soup and salad for balance and color. For those with either a constant or an occasional ice cream craving, the frozen bananas are a nice alternative. Make sure you eat them before they thaw.

The escabeche is an example of how a yang (animal quality) food can be made more yin by the manner of preparation (sour flavoring, cold temperature), thus serving to balance the yang heat of summer.

Nutritional Values

Complete protein is obtained from the fish and the eggs in the breakfast fritters; complementary proteins from the corn, split peas, tofu, and brown rice; vitamin A from the carrots, watercress, corn, red pepper, lettuce, and eggs; the B-complex vitamins from the fish, corn, cherries, whole wheat flour, split peas, squash, daikon, and rice; and vitamin C from the onion, lemon juice, watercress, lettuce, cherries, apricot juice, squash, red pepper, daikon and bananas. Calcium is supplied by the corn, watercress, lettuce, cherries, kuzu, tofu, eggs, split peas, and kanten in the aspic; iron by the fish, lettuce, watercress, eggs, peas, kanten, rice, and bananas.

Utensils

Dinner: Two 2-quart saucepans, large skillet, paper bag, brown paper or paper towels, 2-inch deep serving dish (large enough to accommodate the fish), salad bowl, blender, 1-quart pot, cherry pitter, if available.

Breakfast: Large bowl or suribachi, large skillet, metal spatula.

Lunch: 6-cup ring mold or bowl, 2-quart covered saucepan, fine ginger grater, covered saucepan (with steamer if rice preferred hot).

Escabeche (Pickled Fish)

Serves: 4
Time: 30 minutes; 6 hours (optional)

1 large onion
1 tablespoon corn oil
1 large or 2 small carrots
2 cloves garlic
2 bay leaves
1 teaspoon thyme
1 cup water
1 teaspoon sea salt
1½ pounds scrod or other thick fillet
½ cup whole wheat pastry flour
Oil for frying (sesame or safflower)
4 tablespoons lemon juice
¼ cup sake (optional)

1. Make the escabeche, either in advance to serve chilled or 1½ hours before serving time to serve warm; go on to dessert.

Peel the onion; cut in half lengthwise and slice very thin. Heat the oil in a saucepan; add the onions and sauté over low heat. Cut the carrots into thin matchsticks and stir into the onions. Mince the garlic, then add the garlic, bay leaves and thyme to the saucepan. Continue sautéing for 2 to 3 minutes; add the water and ½ teaspoon salt. Cover and simmer for 10 minutes more.

Wash the fish and pat dry; cut into 2-inch pieces. Place the pieces in a paper bag with the flour and the remaining ½ teaspoon salt; shake until well coated. Heat ½ inch of oil in a large skillet and fry the fish until lightly browned on both sides. Using a spatula, remove the fish carefully from the pan and drain on brown paper; transfer to a 2-inch-deep serving dish. Add the lemon juice and sake to the sautéed vegetable mixture; simmer 1 minute more then pour over the fish. Serve hot or cold. The fish tastes best when allowed to marinate overnight.

Cherries in Apricot Sauce

Serves: 4
Time: 10 minutes

1½ pounds fresh cherries
1 cup apricot juice
1 cinnamon stick
1½ tablespoons kuzu
½ cup water
Rind of one lemon, grated

2. Simmer the cherries; go on to corn.

4. Finish the sauce for the cherries; move on to salad.

Pit the cherries (if possible) and place in a 1-quart saucepan; add the juice and cinnamon stick and place over medium heat; cover and simmer for 5 minutes.

Dissolve the kuzu in water; stir in the grated lemon rind, and pour into the cherries, stirring constantly over medium heat until clear and thick. Serve chilled or at room temperature.

Baked Corn-on-the-Cob

Serves: 4
Time: 30 minutes

2 unhusked ears of corn per person
(Plus 5 additional ears for breakfast fritters)

Preheat the oven to 350°F. Trim any loose pieces from the corn husks (the husks should be unopened, completely covering the corn). Stack the unhusked ears in the oven and bake for 30 minutes.
Remove the corn from the oven and serve piled on a platter or in a bowl or basket.

3. Put the corn in the oven; return to cherries.

6. Remove corn from the oven.

Watercress Salad

Serves: 4
Time: 10 minutes

1 bunch watercress
1 head red leaf lettuce

Wash the watercress and remove the thick stems. Wash the lettuce, trim the bottom, and pat dry with paper towels. Tear the greens into bite-sized pieces and place in a salad bowl. Toss with Tofu-Mustard Dressing.

5. Make the salad and dressing; return to the corn.

Tofu-Mustard Dressing

1 8-ounce cake tofu
¼ cup water
½ teaspoon sea salt
2 tablespoons olive oil
2 tablespoons lemon juice
½ to 1 teaspoon prepared mustard

Combine the ingredients in a blender and purée until creamy.

Breakfast

Corn Fritters

Serves: 4
Time: 30 minutes

5 ears corn, cooked
¼ teaspoon sea salt or to taste
1 tablespoon arrowroot
2 eggs, beaten
½ cup whole wheat flour
Oil for frying

Using a corn scraper or the blunt edge of a knife, scrape the corn from the cob into a bowl or suribachi; mash until pulpy (making 2 to 2½ cups). Stir in the salt, arrowroot, eggs, and flour, mixing well to form a thick batter. Heat ¼ inch oil in a skillet over medium heat. Lower spoonfuls of batter into the oil; flatten each one slightly with the spoon. Fry until the edges are brown, then turn over and fry the other side; drain on brown paper. Serve immediately with apple butter or maple syrup.

Lunch

Frozen Bananas

Serves: 4
Time: 5 minutes; overnight

4 bananas
Chopped walnuts (optional)

1. Freeze the bananas overnight.

Peel the bananas; cut the larger ones in half. Wrap the bananas in wax paper bags, close tightly, and place in the freezer; allow to freeze overnight. Serve the bananas sliced in individual bowls topped with walnuts.

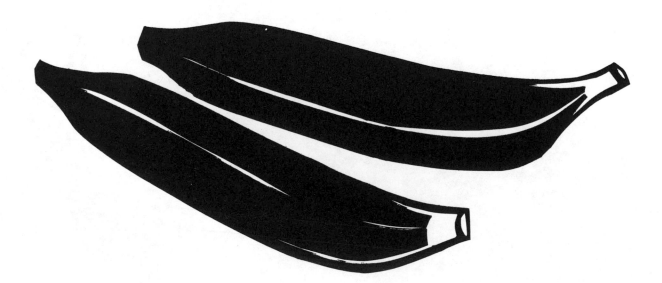

Split Pea Aspic

Serves: 4
Time: 1½ hours; 5 minutes; 2 hours

2 cups split green peas
6 cups water
2 bars kanten or 5 tablespoons agar flakes
1 teaspoon sea salt or to taste
½ teaspoon fresh grated ginger or to taste
1 carrot
1 bunch parsley

Wash the peas and place in a 2-quart saucepan with 5 cups of water over medium heat; bring to a boil, reduce heat, cover, and simmer for 1½ hours, stirring occasionally until the peas are soft.

Rinse the kanten bars; place the remaining cup of water in a small saucepan and shred the bars into it (if using flakes, sprinkle them over the water). Bring to a simmer for 2 to 3 minutes until dissolved. Add the salt and ginger to the peas. Shred the carrot with a potato peeler and place shreddings in the bottom of a 6-cup ring mold or bowl. Stir the kanten mixture into the peas, blending for 2 to 3 minutes until the kanten is completely dissolved. Remove the peas from heat and slowly pour the mixture into the mold; place the mold inside a bowl of cold water and allow to cool until no longer steaming. Refrigerate, or place in the freezer for 1½ to 2 hours.

When the aspic is firm, run a knife around the edge and place in hot water for a minute; turn over carefully onto a large serving plate. Decorate with parsley.

2. Prepare the aspic at least 2 to 3 hours beforehand.

Curried Vegetables on Rice

Serves: 4
Time: 10 minutes

1 red bell pepper
1 tablespoon unrefined corn oil
2 medium carrots
1 5-inch piece daikon
¼ teaspoon curry or to taste
A dash of salt
½ cup water
1 zucchini (1½ inches in diameter)
2 cups cooked long grain rice

Slice the pepper into thin strips and then chop crosswise. Heat the oil in a skillet over medium heat; add the pepper and sauté for 2 minutes. Cut the carrots diagonally into thin slices; stir into the pepper. Slice the daikon into ¼-inch rounds; stack the slices and cut straight down to form matchsticks; add to the sautéing vegetables. Sprinkle in the curry and salt, stirring for 1 minute; then add the water, reduce heat, cover, and steam for 3 minutes. Trim the ends from the zucchini, cut lengthwise in half, then cut crosswise. Add to the vegetables; stir, cover, and steam 1 minute longer.

Steam the rice in another pot or serve cold. Place 2 heaping tablespoonfuls of vegetables over each serving of rice.

3. Cook the vegetables and steam the rice (if desired hot).

Basic Beverage Recipes

There are several coffee substitutes on the market made of various roasted grains and roots such as barley, chicory, soybean, or dandelion. A grain coffee that has to simmer is preferable to instant coffee as a daily beverage because it is closer to the original nature of the plant. The process that makes it "instant" is highly technological. Try the following easy recipe if you want to make your own coffee substitute.

Hot Drinks

Coffee Substitute

1 cup dry soybeans
1 cup barley

Place the soybeans and the barley in 2 separate shallow, metal roasting pans and roast at 375°F. for 45 to 50 minutes, stirring every 10 minutes. The beans and barley should smell slightly burnt. Grind separately in a blender or coffee mill until fine; then mix and store in a closed jar.
For Daily Use: Place approximately 1 teaspoon of the grain mixture to a cup (more if you like) in a coffee pot and percolate for 20 minutes. Or pour teaspoons of the mixture into the amount of boiling water needed; remove pan from heat and allow the mixture to settle for 1 to 2 minutes, then pour through a paper coffee filter. If the grounds are very thick, the latter method is preferable, but do not make more than 2 cups at a time because the water will not drip through.

Apple-Mu Cider
Serves: 5

1 cup water
1 teabag Mu tea
1 cinnamon stick
1 quart apple juice

In a small pan, simmer together the water, tea, and cinnamon stick for 10 minutes; add the apple juice, and remove the teabag and cinnamon. Now heat thoroughly and allow to remain on low heat until ready to serve. Float orange slices on top.

Hot Carob Toddy
Serves: 4

4 cups water
4 tablespoons tahini
4 tablespoons carob powder
4 tablespoons rice or maple syrup

Combine the ingredients in a blender and whip for 1 minute. Pour into a 1½-quart pot and heat just to the boiling point (do not boil or the tahini will curdle). Serve immediately.

Hot Kuzu Ginger Broth (Ume-Syo-Kuzu)

Serves: 1

1 tablespoon kuzu
1 cup water
1 umeboshi plum, pitted or ½ teaspoon plum paste
1/8 teaspoon fresh grated ginger
1 teaspoon shoyu (natural soy sauce) or to taste

In a small pan, dissolve the kuzu in the water; add the plum and ginger. Stir over medium heat until thickened and clear. Now add shoyu; stir, and serve.
(For a milder drink, omit the plum and ginger. Both ingredients are used medicinally since they are soothing and helpful for most disorders of the respiratory and digestive systems.)

Cold Drinks

Bancha-Mint

Serves: 4

1 quart water
1 tablespoon Bancha or Kukicha tea
1 mint teabag

In a 1½-quart pot, combine the Bancha or Kukicha and water and simmer for 2 minutes. Turn off heat; add the mint teabag, and allow to steep for 3 to 4 minutes. Cool before serving.

Apple Soda

Serves: 8

1 quart apple juice
1 quart naturally carbonated mineral water
Juice of 1 lemon

Combine the ingredients in a 2-quart pan or pitcher and serve chilled. If you are serving this for a party, float lemon and strawberry slices on top.

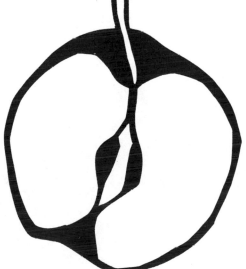

Fruit Shakes

Serves: 4

2 cups chopped fruit
2 cups water
2 tablespoons tahini (optional)

Place the ingredients in a blender and purée, then serve. The variations of fruit shakes are as wide as the imagination; apple-pear; peach-banana; apricot-peach-apple; apple-banana; watermelon, et cetera. Fruit shakes should be served as a snack and not as an accompaniment to food.

Homemade Bread

"Eat bread and salt and speak the truth"
Russian proverb

Few things are as satisfying as making your own bread: it fills the house with wondrous aromas, gives the breadmaker a chance to catch up with all the mudpies never made, brings joy to the children allowed to create their own loaf of bread or crackers, and above all, it is inexpensive. In addition, it is an excellent exercise, especially for the triceps in the back of the arms, an area too often neglected.

Breadmaking is not as difficult as you might think, especially when whole grain flours are used. White flour breads must rise high and fluffy in order to be edible; they can fall easily and therefore are more delicate in the pre-baked stages, while whole grain bread is edible even when it has not risen, albeit with extra chewing. Also, whole grain bread will rise less and weigh more per volume than white bread, which is why some people consider it heavy. However, a bread that feels heavy in weight, when well chewed, is light and easy on the digestion whereas a chocolate soufflé with whipped cream, all air and lightness, may weigh quite heavily on your stomach.

Like many other traditional foods, bread is a fermented product. Yeasts and bacteria break down the protein, starches, and fat present in the dough, turning them into amino acids, simple sugars, and fatty acids. This activity further creates gases and alcohols that account for the rising of the dough and its aroma. Because of the fermentation process, bread—especially old fashioned sourdough—falls roughly into the same category as yoghurt, cheese, pickles, miso, shoyu soy sauce, and tempeh. The quality of the fermentation process is important; fermentation helps to pre-digest the food as does cooking, a factor that leads many people to prefer unyeasted or naturally rising breads, since the enzymes and bacteria present in unyeasted bread may be more favorable to digestion.

Be cautious, however, about excessive bread eating; it causes bloating and gas in some people, not to mention unwanted weight. Also, flour products, as opposed to whole grains, seem to be mucus-forming for many individuals. If this is the case, pay attention to what you eat and try to reduce or eliminate pastas, gravies, and breads if the elimination of dairy foods hasn't helped already.

Even if you work daily, you can still make your own bread every week. Determine how much your household actually consumes, obtain the ingredients, set aside 20 to 25 minutes for the actual work, and arrange the rising and baking times around your schedule. For example, if you work 9 to 5 Monday to Friday, perhaps Saturday morning you take care of household chores. To make unyeasted bread, prepare the dough Thursday night before you go to sleep; punch it down Friday morning when you get up; punch it down again Friday evening when you get home. Just before you go to sleep, around midnight or later, punch it down again, and if it has risen, put the dough in the pans. Saturday morning, some 6 to 7 hours later, either bake the bread, or put it in pans and allow it to rise until you are ready to bake it. With a little practice and pre-planning, you will never want for good, homemade bread again.

What's In It?

There are many books of bread recipes and countless varieties of breads, yet all the recipes contain three basic elements:

1) Flour   2) Water   3) Leavening

1) For a western style bread, at least 50–60% of the flour should be whole wheat. When kneaded, whole wheat develops gluten, which provides the elasticity that allows the bread to be sliced thin with little crumbling. The remainder can be any variety of flour or cooked grain, such as rye, corn, barley, rice, buckwheat, or soy (the last two should be no more than 10% of the total flour, otherwise the bread will be too heavy). Wheat flours vary in the rate in which they absorb water, therefore, flour measurements will vary. Use 2½ to 3½ cups of flour per cup of water for a firm dough.

2) The water should be as uncontaminated as possible. Bread made with good quality spring or well water has a definite advantage both in taste as well as nutritional quality. Also, natural starters or rising techniques do not work well with chemically treated water. To decide on the quantity of bread to be made, I find it easier to measure the water first rather than the flour; thus, 2 cups of water makes one good-sized, 1½-pound loaf.

3) The leavening can be yeast, a starter, or even air-borne micro-organisms. Very different tastes are obtained from the same ingredients with different leavening agents.

Salt is added to all breads except dietetic ones; it adds flavor, checks excessive rising, and helps retard the growth of undesirable bacteria. Sea salt is preferred in a proportion of ½ teaspoon for each cup of water used.

Many breads also contain sweeteners to aid the development of the yeast or to provide flavor. I find sweeteners unnecessary. The development of the yeast can be helped with a sprinkling of flour over the water in which it is dissolved or with a teaspoonful of apple juice added to the water. Bread for healthy adults should be solid, chewy, aromatic, and definitely unsweet.

For a good consistency, thorough kneading by hand is essential for developing the gluten which makes the dough hold together. Machine kneading, as well as unkneaded and batter doughs, often produce crumbly bread that does not slice well. To knead properly without exhausting yourself, find a surface of a comfortable height—about the level of your hip joint. This allows you to lean forward into the dough, and find a rhythm and body movement that is not only non-tiring, but actually invigorating. Practice and attention will help as will the experience of watching someone doing it.

Following are some basic recipes to help you get started that are more than recipes; they are techniques as well. Feel free to experiment with both the ingredients and the techniques until you create *your* bread, one that you and your family will not tire of eating week after week. All recipes will make two standard loaves.

Easy Unyeasted Bread

4 cups spring or deep well water
2 teaspoons sea salt
2 tablespoons corn oil
1 cup soy flour
12 to 15 cups whole wheat flour (buy a 5-pound bag)

1) In a large bowl or pot, mix the water, salt, and oil; add the soy flour, then add approximately 8 cups of the whole wheat. Mix and beat with a wooden spoon for 5 minutes.

2) Add the rest of the flour cup by cup, mixing after each addition, until it becomes too thick to stir.

3) Add some more flour; scrape the dough from the spoon and turn the mixture onto a board or kneading surface, scooping everything out of the bowl. Gently work all the dough pieces toward the center, up from the periphery and down into the middle, together with the flour. If the dough gets sticky, flour the kneading surface lightly and knead the dough over it; the flour will be incorporated without lumps. Continue kneading until the dough is not sticky any more, but feels cool and smooth, about the consistency of your earlobe.

Now the real kneading begins. Lean into the dough with both hands and straight elbows; sliding your left hand under the dough, flip it a quarter turn towards you, clockwise, then fold the dough over and lean into it again, thus squeeze-rolling the dough between the heels of your hands and the table. In four kneads, then, the ball of dough has had a complete turn-around.

Keep in mind that 1) all parts of the dough should eventually come to the top; 2) it's easiest to work from the *waist*, not the wrists; 3) the ball of dough always should stay in roughly the same place through the kneading process; 4) it helps to develop a rhythm. Try kneading to music, for instance.

Continue kneading for approximately 300 strokes, or for 15 to 20 minutes. With practice, you'll soon think nothing of it.

4) Form the dough into a ball, then oil your hands lightly, and run them over the ball. Now place the ball in a large bowl or pot, cover with a cloth *and* a cover (to avoid formation of a dry crust), and allow to rest.

5) Plan on a fermentation or rising time of 30 to 36 hours. Every 6 to 8 hours, punch the dough around and turn it over. The first two or three times, it will look as though very little is happening; but after 28 to 32 hours, when you go to punch down the dough, you will find it has risen and has a totally different texture and aroma.

6) When the dough has risen, take it out of the bowl, knead a few times on the table, and form it into 2 loaves. Place in 2 lightly oiled bread pans or side by side in 1 shallow baking pan, turning over once so the tops get oiled. Cut two or three deep slits into the top surfaces, cover with a wet cloth, and place in a warm area for 3 to 6 hours until the loaves rise half again their height.

7) Place the loaves in a cold oven, then turn the heat to 300°F. and bake for 1½ hours or until the loaves sound hollow when tapped and dislodge easily from the pans. Cool before slicing.

Store the loaf you're using in a paper bag or breadbox at room temperature; store the loaves you're not using in a plastic bag in the refrigerator. The breads in this section do not mold or spoil unless they are kept in a plastic bag at room temperature for at least two days.

Easy Yeasted Bread

3 cups spring or deep well water
1½ teaspoons sea salt
1½ tablespoons corn oil
2/3 cup soy flour
10 to 12 cups whole wheat flour
1 teaspoon active dry yeast

In a small pan, warm ½ cup water to body temperature (test with a finger: it will feel neither warm nor cold). Sprinkle ¼ teaspoon flour over the surface of the water or add 1 tablespoon apple juice; sprinkle the yeast over it as well. Allow to ferment while you follow step no. 1 of the preceding recipe: *Easy Unyeasted Bread.* When the yeast is frothy and smells like beer, stir well, and add to the batter, mixing thoroughly with a wooden spoon. Continue with step nos. 2 through 4 in the preceding recipe; then allow the dough to stand for 3 to 4 hours until it doubles in size.

5) Punch down the dough, cover again, and allow to rise for another 1½ hours.

6) Punch down the dough again; turn onto a kneading surface and knead a few times; then shape into 2 loaves and place in 2 lightly oiled bread pans or side by side in a shallow baking pan. Cut a deep slit in the surface of each loaf; cover with a wet cloth, and allow to rise in a warm place for 1½ hours or until almost doubled in size (check often; rising times vary).

7) Preheat the oven to 350°F. at least 30 minutes before baking the loaves (if the breads are rising on top of the stove, they will benefit from the warmth). Bake at 350°F. for 20 minutes, then reduce heat to 300°F.; continue baking for 45 to 50 minutes until the bread sounds hollow when tapped and easily dislodges from the pan. Cool before slicing so the bread will not crumble.

If you encounter a problem with the bread, perhaps you will find the remedy in one of the following suggestions.

1) *If the dough doesn't rise:* a) *Unyeasted bread:* Wait up to 46 hours, then bake. The bread will be dense but delicious. Slice very thin and chew thoroughly. b) *Yeasted bread:* The water for the yeast was either too hot or too cold, or the yeast was too old. If the dough is made, proceed as for unyeasted bread.

2) *If you forgot the salt:* You will have a bland bread. Spread some salted sesame butter or miso spread on it.

3) *If you forgot the oil:* You will hardly notice (oil simply makes the crust a bit crustier).

4) *If you forgot to oil the pan:* The bread will stick to the pan. You will have to settle for chunks instead of slices (the chunks taste good with thick lentil soup).

5) *If you can't obtain the soy flour, or you simply don't have it on hand:* Replace it with any other flour or cooked grain. Remember, whole wheat can be as low as 60% or as high as 100% of the total.

6) *If the crust is too hard:* Wrap the bread in a cloth as soon as you take it from the pans, or store in a bread box and the crust will soften overnight. Storing the bread in a plastic bag in the refrigerator will soften the crust also. Next time, lower the heat or reduce the baking time.

7) *If the bread is not crusty enough:* Return to the oven for 15 minutes at 350°F.

8) *If the crust is hard but the inside is underdone:* Lower the heat and lengthen the baking time.

9) *If the bread sticks to the pan:* Return it to the oven for another 10 minutes. If the bread persists in sticking, see #4 above.

Breadcrumbs

Soften stale leftover crusts by dipping in water and placing them in a 350°F. oven for 10 minutes. Grind into breadcrumbs in the blender, and store in a glass jar in the refrigerator. The crumbs can be used for topping casseroles and as a base for stuffings or bread pudding.

Appendix

SUPERMARKETS: Kasha, beans, dried legumes of all kinds, fresh vegetables and fruits. Supermarket "health food" section: brown rice, nuts and seeds, whole wheat flour, unrefined oils, dried fruits, imported dried mushrooms.

DELICATESSEN: Half-sour or sour dill pickles (ingredients: cucumbers, water, salt, some spices), loose Greek olives.

JAPANESE AND ORIENTAL FOOD MARKETS: Tofu, shiitake mushrooms, sea vegetables (nori, wakame, hiziki, kanten, kombu), varieties of miso (ingredients: soybeans, rice or barley, water, salt), umeboshi plums (ingredients: plums, water, salt, beefsteak leaves), aduki beans, bancha tea.

MIDDLE EASTERN STORES: Tahini, couscous, red lentils, green (regular) lentils.

HEALTH FOOD STORES: Whole grains and flours, beans, unrefined oils, sea salt, natural shoyu, misos, sea vegetables, kuzu, unsweetened whole grain breads, rice cakes, tahini and other nut butters, dried fruits, nuts, apple butter, tofu, apple juice, maple syrup, barley malt, *yinnie* syrup, sesame salt, bancha or kukicha tea, other herb teas, grain coffees, et cetera.

Bibliography

Cookbooks

Abehsera, Michel. *Cooking with Care and Purpose*. New York: Swan House, 1978.

———— *Cooking for Life*. New York: Swan House, 1970 (cloth); New York: Avon, 1971 (paper).

———— *Zen Macrobiotic Cooking*. New York: University Books, 1964 (cloth); Avon, 1968 (paper).

Aihara, Cornellia. *The Chico-San Cookbook*. Chico, Calif.: Chico-San Inc., 1972.

———— The Dō of Cooking. Vol. I: *Spring Cooking*; Vol. II: *Summer Cooking*; Vol. III: *Fall Cooking*; Vol. IV: *Winter Cooking*. San Francisco: The George Ohsawa Macrobiotic Foundation, 1972–73.

Aihara, Herman and Cornellia. *The Soybean Diet*. San Francisco: The George Ohsawa Macrobiotic Foundation, 1974.

Bellichi, K., Colbin, A., and Kushi, A. *East-West Holiday Cooklet*. Brookline, Mass.: East-West Journal, 1977.

Day, Harvey. *About Bread*. London: Thorson's Publishers, Ltd., 1966.

Esko, Wendy. *An Introduction to Macrobiotic Cooking*. Boston: East-West Publications, 1978.

Farmilant, Eunice. *Macrobiotic Cooking*. New York: Signet/New American Library, 1972.

———— *The Natural Foods Sweet-Tooth Cookbook*. New York: Doubleday and Co., 1973.

Hewitt, Jean, ed. *The New York Times Natural Foods Cookbook*. New York/Chicago: Quadrangle Books, 1971.

Holt, Calvin, and Carradine, Patch. *Zen Hash* (gift edition title, *Brown Rice and Love*). New York: Pyramid Books, 1971.

Kushi, Aveline. *How to Cook with Miso*. Japan: Japan Publications, 1978.

Ohsawa, Lima with Nahum Stiskin. *The Art of Just Cooking*. Brookline, Mass.: Autumn Press, 1974.

Oles, Shayne. *The New Zen Cookery: Practical Macrobiotics*. Woodland Hills, Calif.: Shayver Corp.

Rhoads, Sharon Ann. *Cooking With Sea Vegetables*. Brookline, Mass.: Autumn Press, 1979.

Rossi, Barbara, and Biber, Tom. *The Everyday Macrobiotic Cookery Book*. London: Tandem, 1971.

Shurtleff, William, and Aoyagi, Akiko. *The Book of Tofu*. Brookline, Mass.: Autumn Press, 1975.

———— *The Book of Miso*. Brookline, Mass.: Autumn Press, 1976.

———— *The Book of Kudzu*. Brookline, Mass.: Autumn Press, 1977.

Teeguarden, Iona. *Freedom Through Cooking*. Boston: Order of the Universe Publications, 1971.

Wiener, Joan, and Thralls, Barbara. *Victory Through Vegetables*. New York: Holt, Rinehart and Winston, 1970.

Zurbel, Victor and Runa. *The Vegetarian Family*. Englewood Cliffs, N.J.: Prentice Hall, 1978.

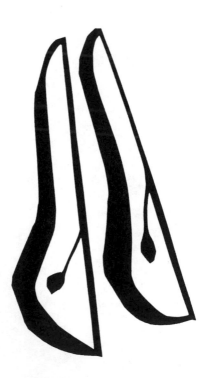

Reference Books

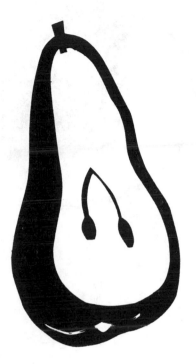

Abrahamson, E.M., M.D., and Pezet, A.W. *Body, Mind and Sugar*. New York: H. Holt & Co., 1951.

Aihara, Herman. *Acid and Alkaline*. San Francisco: The George Ohsawa Macrobiotic Foundation, 1971.

_____ *Seven Macrobiotic Principles*. San Francisco: The George Ohsawa Macrobiotic Foundation, 1973.

Barkas, Janet. *The Vegetable Passion: A History Of The Vegetarian State Of Mind*. New York: Charles Scribner's Sons, 1975.

Bieler, Henry. *Food is Your Best Medicine*. New York: Random House, 1965.

Burr, Harold Saxton, Ph.D. *Blueprint for Immortality: The Electric Patterns of Life*. London: Neville Spearman, 1972.

Day, Harvey. *About Rice and Lentils: Foods For Strength And Stamina*. London: Thorsons Publishers Ltd., 1970.

De Vries, Arnold. *Primitive Man and his Food*. Chicago: Chandler Book Co., 1962.

Dufty, William. *Sugar Blues*. Radnor, Penn.: Chilton Book Co., 1975 (cloth); New York: Warner Books, 1976 (paper).

Gerrard, Don. *One Bowl*. New York: Random House/Bookworks, 1974.

Goldbeck, Nikki and David. *The Supermarket Handbook: Access To Whole Foods*. New York: Harper & Row, 1973.

Hauschka, Rudolph. *Nutrition*. London: Stuart & Watkins, 1967.

_____ *The Nature of Substance*. London: Vincent Stuart Ltd., 1966.

Hunter, Beatrice Trum. *Fermented Foods and Beverages: An Old Tradition*. New Canaan, Conn.: Keats Publishing, 1973.

Inglis, Brian. *The Case for Unorthodox Medicine*. New York: G.P. Putnam's Sons, 1964.

Kervran, Louis. *Biological Transmutations* (English version by Michel Abehsera). Binghamton, N.Y.: Swan House, 1972.

Kushi, Michio. *Oriental Diagnosis*. Edited by William Tara. London: Red Moon, 1976.

_____ *The Book of Macrobiotics*. Tokyo: Japan Publications, 1977.

_____ *The Macrobiotic Way of Natural Healing*. Boston: East-West Publications, 1978.

_____ *The Teachings of Michio Kushi*, Vols. I, II, III. Boston: Order of the Universe Publications/The East-West Foundation, 1971–72.

_____ *Macrobiotic Seminars of Michio Kushi*: 1) *Disease, Origin, Causes, and Cures*; 2) *Ancient and Future Worlds* (Transcribed by Joan Mansolilli). Boston: The East-West Foundation, 1972–73.

Levy, Phil. *Talking Food Pamphlets. Salt; Vegetable Oil; Water*. Charlestown, Mass.: Talking Food Company, 1976–77.

Longgood, William. *The Poisons in Your Food*. New York: Grove Press, 1962.

Moon, J. Yogamundi. *A Macrobiotic Explanation of Pathological Calcification*. San Francisco: The George Ohsawa Macrobiotic Foundation, 1974.

Moore Lappé, Frances. *Diet for a Small Planet*. New York: Friends of the Earth/Ballantine, 1971.

Muramoto, Naboru. *Healing Ourselves* (edited and supplemented by Michel Abehsera). New York: Swan House/Avon, 1973.

Null, Gary and Steve. *Protein for Vegetarians*. New York: Pyramid Books, 1975.

—————— *The Complete Handbook of Nutrition*. New York: Dell, 1972.

Nutrition Almanac. Nutrition Search, Inc., John D. Kirschman, director. New York: McGraw Hill, 1975.

Nyoiti, Sakurazawa. *You Are All Sanpaku* (English translation by William Dufty). New Hyde Park, N.Y.: University Books, 1965 (cloth); New York: Award Books, 1969.

Ohsawa, George. *Zen Macrobiotics* (revised, edited, and annotated by Lou Oles). Los Angeles: The Ohsawa Foundation, 1965.

—————— *The Book of Judgement* (revised and edited by Lou Oles). Los Angeles: The Ohsawa Foundation, 1966.

—————— *The Macrobiotic Guidebook for Living* (revised and edited by Lou Oles). Los Angeles: The Ohsawa Foundation, 1967.

—————— *The Unique Principle: The Philosophy of Macrobiotics*. Edited by Herman Aihara. San Francisco: The George Ohsawa Macrobiotic Foundation, 1973.

—————— *Cancer and the Philosophy of the Far East*. Edited by Herman Aihara. Binghamton, N.Y: Swan House, 1971.

—————— *Macrobiotics: An Invitation to Health and Happiness*. Edited by Herman Aihara. San Francisco: The Ohsawa Foundation, 1971.

—————— *Practical Guide to Far Eastern Macrobiotic Medicine*. Edited by Herman Aihara. San Francisco: The Ohsawa Foundation, 1973.

Oski, Frank A., M.D., with John D. Bell. *Don't Drink Your Milk*. New York: Wyden Books, 1977.

Ott, John N. *Health and Light: The Effects of Natural and Artificial Light on Man and Other Living Things*. Old Greenwich, Conn.: The Devin-Adair Co., 1973.

Page, Melvin, D.D.S., and H. Leon Abrams, Jr. *Your Body is Your Best Doctor*. New Canaan, Conn.: Keats Publishing, 1972.

Price, Weston A., D.D.S. *Nutrition and Physical Degeneration*. Los Angeles: The American Academy of Applied Nutrition, 1939–45.

Rodale, J.I. *Natural Health, Sugar, and the Criminal Mind*. New York: Pyramid Books, 1968.

Rosenberg, Max H. *Encyclopedia of Medical Self-Help*. New York: Books Inc., 1962.

Sams, Craig. *Everything You Want to Know About Macrobiotics*. New York: Pyramid Books, 1973.

Sanford, David, editor. *Hot War on the Consumer*. New York: Pitman Publishing Corp., 1969.

Schroeder, Henry A., M.D. *The Trace Elements and Man*. Old Greenwich, Conn.: The Devin-Adair Co., 1973.

Schul, Bill. *The Psychic Frontiers of Medicine*. Greenwich, Conn.: Fawcett, 1977.

Schulman, Max. *Anyone Got a Match?* New York: Harper & Row, 1964.

Schwab, Gunther. *Dance with the Devil*. London: Geoffrey Bles, 1963.

Steiner, Rudolph. *Spiritual Science and Medicine*. London: Rudolph Steiner Press, 1975.

Stiskin, Nahum. *The Looking Glass God: Shinto, Yin-Yang, and a Cosmology for Today*. Brookline, Mass.: Autumn Press, 1972.

Turner, James. *The Chemical Feast*. Ralph Nader Study Group Report on the Food and Drug Administration. New York: Grossman Publishers, 1970.

Verrett, Jacqueline, Ph.D., and Carper, Jean. *Eating May Be Hazardous to Your Health*. New York: Simon and Schuster, 1974.

Watson, George. *Nutrition and Your Mind: The Psychochemical Response*. New York: Harper & Row, 1972.

Williams, Roger J. *Biochemical Individuality*. Austin: University of Texas Press, 1977.

Winter, Ruth. *Poisons in Your Food*. New York: Crown Publishers, 1969.

Yudkin, John, M.D. *Sweet and Dangerous*. New York: Peter H. Wyden, 1972.

Government Publications

Select Committee on Nutrition and Human Needs. *Dietary Goals for the United States*. Hon. George McGovern, Chairman. Washington: U.S. Government Printing Office, February, 1977.

U.S. Department of Agriculture. *Composition of Foods*. USDA Handbook #8. Washington: U.S. Government Printing Office, 1963.

Magazines and other publications

Alternatives (Monthly). P.O. Box 330139, Miami, FL 33133.

Brain-Mind Bulletin. (Bi-weekly). P.O. Box 42211, Los Angeles, CA 90042.

East-West Journal (Monthly). 233 Harvard Street, Brookline, MA 02146.

Macrobiotic Review (Bi-monthly). 6209 Park Heights Avenue, Baltimore, MD. 21215.

New Age (Monthly). 32 Station Street, Brookline, MA 02146.

New Realities (Bi-monthly). 680 Beach Street, San Francisco, CA 94109.

Index

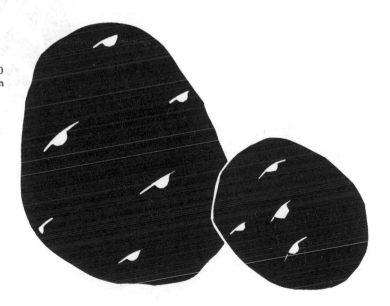

About The Author

Annemarie Colbin, the daughter of a Dutch mother and a Hungarian father, was brought up in Argentina on an international vegetarian diet. Her professional interest—she has been teaching natural foods cooking classes for eleven years—began, she says, simply out of curiosity to find out more about herself and other people: "I was intrigued by the idea of being able to control the way you feel by what you eat."

Colbin founded the Natural Gourmet Cookery School in 1977, where she conducts regular weekly classes. She lives in New York City with her two daughters.